CHILDREN'S
KNOWLEDGE
BANK

Volume-IV

Acknowledgement

This project of **Children's Knowledge Bank** is not the result of an individual effort but is the product of collective wisdom and experience of specialists in different fields. We have tried to make it as authentic and interesting as possible and for this, help has been taken of well known works of international standards and of national importance. It is not feasible to list all of them but we express our gratitude to the following publications for the help in preparing these volumes.

References

ENGLISH

1. The Giant Book of What Do You Know, The Hamlyn Publishing, London.
2. 365 Things to Know, The Hamlyn Publishing, London.
3. Knowledge, in 10 volumes, G. Britain.
4. The World Atlas of Mysteries, by Francis Hitching Collins, London.
5. Natural Wonders of the World. P.J. Banyard.
6. Collins Children's Encyclopaedia, Nature, by Kenneth Bailey.
7. Junior Science Encyclopaedia, The Hamlyn Publishing, London.
8. A New Answer Book, 2 Volumes, by Marg Elting and Rose Wyler.
9. Questions and Answers, World International Publishing Ltd., Manchester.
10. Tell Me the Answer, by Andrea Bonanni.
11. Charlie Browns Cyclopaedia, 20 volumes, Funk and Wognalls Inc. New York.
12. The Children's Book of Questions and Answers, by Anthony Addison.
13. The Answer Book About You, by Marg Elting and Rose Wyler.
14. The Science Library, 6 volumes, by Robert Scharff.
15. The Illustrated Reference Book of Modern Technology, by James Mitchell.
16. Encyclopaedia Britannica (Micropaedia), 10 volumes Encyclopaedia Britannica Inc. London.
17. Encyclopaedia Britannica (Macropaedia), 20 volumes.
18. The Raintree Illustrated Science Encyclopaedia, 20 volumes.
19. The Marshall Cavendish Illustrated Encyclopaedia of Knowledge, Marshall Cavendish Books, London.
20. Tell Me Why, 6 volumes, by Arkady Leokum, The Hamlyn Publishing, London.
21. How and Why in Science, 5 volumes, by R.G. Lagu, Homi Bhabha Centre, Bombay.
22. Reader's Digest Library of Modern Knowledge, in 3 Volumes.
23. Science Reporter, A CSIR Publication, Rafi Marg, New Delhi.
24. The New Illustrated Encyclopaedia of World History, 2 volumes, William L. Langer.
25. The New Junior World Encyclopaedia, 20 volumes.
26. The University Desk Encyclopaedia, Dutton, Elsevier.
27. The Penguin Encyclopaedia of Places, W.G. Moore.
28. You and Your Health, 3 volumes, Shryock, Swartout.
29. Joy of Knowledge, in 14 volumes, James Mitchell.
30. 'Finding Out' Magazine, Purnell & Sons Ltd., London.
31. Understanding Science Magazine, UK Publication.
32. McGraw Hall Encyclopaedia of Science and Technology, 15 volumes, McGraw-Hall Co., USA.
33. Von Nostrands Scientific Encyclopaedia.
34. The Family Encyclopaedia of Science, Windward.
35. Asimov's Biographical Encyclopaedia of Science and Technology, by Isaac Asimov.
36. Scientific American Magazines.
37. Guinness Book of World Records.
38. Guinness Facts & Feats Series.

हिन्दी

1. भारत के पक्षी : सालिम अली
2. भारतीय पक्षी : कुवंर सुरेश सिंह
3. भारत का वन्य जीव : ई.पी.जी., अनु. विराज. एम. ए.

Apart from the above reference books, help has been taken from many English and Hindi Books, Dictionaries and Government approved technical glossaries.

CHILDREN'S KNOWLEDGE BANK (Volume IV)

BY

Dr Sunita Gupta, Ph.D. (Phy. Chemistry)
Dr Neena Agrawal, M.B.B.S.

Advisory Board

Dr C.L. Garg, M.Sc., Ph.D.
Scientist, Defence Science Centre,
Ministry of Defence, Government of India
(Chief Advisor)

Dr Padam Gupta, M.B.B.S.
R.K. Gupta, M.Sc. (Mathematics)

PUSTAK MAHAL®
DELHI • MUMBAI • PATNA • BANGALORE • HYDERABAD

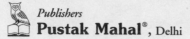

Publishers
Pustak Mahal®, Delhi

J-3/16, Daryaganj, New Delhi-110002
☎ 23276539, 23272783, 23272784 ▪ *Fax:* 011 23260518
E-mail: info@pustakmahal.com • *Website:* www.pustakmahal.com

Sales Centres
10-B, Netaji Subhash Marg, Daryaganj, New Delhi-110002
☎ 23268292, 23268293, 23279900 • *Fax:* 011-23280567
E-mail: rapidexdelhi@indiatimes.com

Branch Offices
Bangalore: ☎ 22234025
E-mail: pmblr@sancharnet.in • pustak@sancharnet.in
Mumbai: ☎ 22010941
E-mail: rapidex@bom5.vsnl.net.in
Patna: ☎ 3294193 • *Telefax:* 0612-2302719
E-mail: rapidexptn@rediffmail.com
Hyderabad: *Telefax:* 040-24737290
E-mail: pustakmahalhyd@yahoo.co.in

Printed at : Param Offsetters, Okhla, New Delhi-110020

Publishers' Note _____

We are pleased to present this new and thoroughly revised edition of **Children's Knowledge Bank**. The overwhelming response to our earlier edition is what set us about the task of improving and updating the volume in your hand. The edition is a little behind schedule but it is essentially owing to our constant endeavour to bring the reader absolutely the latest and authentic information. In overall presentation too the edition has undergone major changes. It has also been made more exhaustive and contains six sections, viz. *General Knowledge, Science & Technology, Plants & Animals, Human Body, Scientists & Inventions* and *Sports & Entertainment*.

In fact the present project had been conceived and created with the specific purpose of satisfying the inherent curiosity of a child by providing answers to his basic queries – the **'hows', 'whys'** and **'whats'** that arise in his mind from time to time. For this purpose the language has been deliberately kept simple and lucid, and the contents are backed by lively illustrations. All this, of course, could not have been possible but for the painstaking and sincere efforts of our editorial and art department for which we are thankful to them.

Initially the work was conceived as an encyclopaedic series with four volumes. But as we embarked upon the project we found it difficult to limit its scope. Because after all, is there any end to a child's queries? And if we wished to make it truly a treasure house for children we had to include more and more. As a result the series was stretched to six volumes. Our basic objective, however, is not to just supply information, but to kindle the curiosity, to provide the spark to illuminate a child's mind.

We sincerely hope that the revised edition would prove even more useful and satisfactory to the reader, because our greatest reward lies only in your satisfaction.

— *Publishers*

Contents

A Glimpse of Questions Answered in
CHILDREN'S KNOWLEDGE BANK Vol. I
Divided into seven sections it deals with 157 questions

Section I—General Knowledge
- Why does ice float on water?
- How is dust useful to us?
- What is hypnotism?
- How is the rainbow formed?
- Why is gold so costly?
- Are the molecules of all substances in motion?
- Why do watches have jewels?
- How did America get its name?
- What is Red Cross and how was it born?
- Why was the Great Wall of China built?
- What is Nobel Prize?
- How is dew formed?
- Why do hot things burn us?
- How is Silicon useful to us?
- How is liquid converted into vapour?
- How is oxygen useful to us?
- Why is the Census taken?
- What is helium?
- How is copper useful to us?
- How do we get wool from sheep?
- How are the pearls formed?
- When did the Postal System start?
- Why does the rising and setting Sun appear red?
- What is rubber?
- How was the Calendar started?
- How did arithmetic originate?
- Where have the Seven Wonders of the World gone?
- What is echo?
- How did the various religions originate?
- Why and when was the Police system started?
- How were the weekdays named?
- Which is the smallest country of the world?
- How did banks start?
- Why are fireworks colourful?
- What are the Olympic Games?
- What are antibiotics?
- What is marble?
- How do we get petrol?
- When did national anthems originate?
- How is silk produced?
- When did motor races start?
- What is uranium?
- What is Interpol?
- What is water?
- What are the constituents of milk?
- Where is Mona Lisa today?

Section II—Science & Technology
- How do we see clearly with spectacles?
- What is dry ice?
- What are the methods of time measurement?
- What is plastic?
- What are different types of telescopes?
- What is Plastic Surgery?
- How does a washing machine work?
- How does a dish washer work?
- How is food packed in cans?

- What is StarTelevision?
- What is a cellular phone?
- How are skyscrapers built?
- How is synthetic rubber made?
- What is an Alkaline Battery?
- What is automatic door operation?
- What is the remote control of a television set?
- How does a steam iron work?
- What is LPG?
- What is bar code?
- What is the principle of an autopilot?
- What is a Compact Disc?

Section III—Plants & Animals
- How can an owl see clearly at night?
- Do ants also have their kingdoms ?
- Why does the dog go mad?
- Why do the eyes of some animals shine in the dark?
- How far can a Kangaroo jump?
- What is a Virus?
- What is Fungus?
- What are bacteria?
- What is regeneration?
- Is bamboo a tree or grass?
- How do some creatures make a shell on their body?
- How do animals and plants survive in deserts?
- How do migratory birds find their way?
- Can animals reason?
- How do plants take and make their food?
- How is bark formed?
- Why can't animals talk like us?

Section IV—Human Body
- How does our tongue tell us the taste?
- Why don't women have beard?
- How do we lose our memory?
- How long can man survive without food?
- What happens to our body in sleep?
- What causes people to faint?
- Why are people dwarf?
- How do we remember things?
- Why does man grow old?
- What causes baldness in people?
- Why are vitamins essential for us?
- Why do we get fever?
- How do bones mend?
- How does a wound heal?
- Which of the body parts can be replaced with artificial parts?

Section V —Earth Science
- How was the Earth formed?
- What is there inside the Earth?
- How do we measure the mass of the Earth?
- What is the Earth's force of gravity?
- Why don't we feel the Earth's motion?

- How many kinds of climate are there?
- How seasons change?
- What is atmosphere?
- What is air and how is it useful for us?
- Does air have weight?
- How is the wind velocity measured?
- How does it rain?
- What is monsoon?
- How are clouds formed?
- What are tornadoes, hurricanes and cyclones?
- How are hails formed?
- How is fog formed?
- What are lightning and thunder?
- How were mountains formed?
- How were rivers formed?
- How are caves formed?
- How are volcanoes formed?
- What causes an Earthquake?
- How are lakes formed?
- How are springs formed?
- How are waterfalls formed?
- What are glaciers?
- Why is the sea water salty?
- How were the oceans formed?
- What is Dead Sea?
- Are there mountains inside the sea?

Section VI —The Universe
- How did the universe come into existence?
- What is the Milky Way?
- How are stars formed?
- Why are some stars brighter than others?
- What is the Solar System?
- What is the Sun?
- What are the Sun spots?
- What is Solar Eclipse?
- What are Meteorites?
- What is the Moon's force of gravity?
- What are Comets?
- What are the rings of the Saturn?
- What is Moon—the only satellite of the Earth?
- How distant are stars from us?
- What is lunar eclipse?
- What is the Zodiac?
- Is there life on other planets?

Section VII —Scientists & Inventions
- Who invented transistor?
- How was the telephone invented?
- What is Superconductivity?
- How was the submarine invented?
- How was the rocket developed?
- What is an Atom Bomb?
- What is a radar and how does it work?
- How does an Aerosol spray work?
- How does an Electric Typewriter work?
- How does a Zip Fastener work?

Big size 176 Pages   Fully Illustrated

A Glimpse of Questions Answered in
CHILDREN'S KNOWLEDGE BANK Vol. II
Divided into six sections it deals with 157 questions

Section I — General Knowledge
- What is Multimedia?
- What is FM transmission?
- What is Darwin's theory of evolution?
- Who was Socrates?
- Who is called 'The Lady with the Lamp'?
- How are valleys formed?'
- What is a Hydrogen Bomb?
- When did people first use money?
- What is a Dragon?
- What is Internet?
- Why can't we fly like birds?
- How are submarines detected under the sea?
- Do some plants eat insects?
- Who created the Frankenstein's monster?
- What is Electronic Mail?
- What is Paging Service?
- How can we test the purity of milk?
- How is the distance of stars from the earth measured?
- Which animals resemble man?
- What is a space suit?
- What is a Silicon Chip?
- How fast can marine animals swim?
- What is a flying fish?
- Why do giraffes have a long neck?
- What are pain relievers?
- How does a currency counting machine work?
- Which planets have satellites?
- Why do objects appear coloured?
- Does a black cat bring bad luck?
- How is soil formed?
- How can we reach the bottom of the sea?
- Does any metal exist in a liquid state?
- How is aluminium obtained from the earth?
- What is diamond?
- How is iron obtained from the earth?
- Why does the leaning Tower of Pisa not fall?
- What is a mirage?
- What causes ocean currents?
- When was the construction of bridges started?
- What causes tides in the sea?
- Why does bread have pores?
- How does snowfall occur?
- How is the depth of the sea measured?
- What is fire?
- Who was Alexander the Great?
- What is smoke?
- How are icebergs formed?
- Why does the size of the moon appear to change?
- Why does wind blow?
- Why do we perspire?
- Why do we resemble our parents?
- Why do women have a sweet voice?

Section II — Science & Technology
- How does a microwave oven work?
- Why do stars twinkle?
- What are radio waves?
- How does a pressure cooker work?
- Which material does not burn in fire easily?
- How are millions of substances made from only a few elements?
- What are infra-red radiations?
- What is pasteurization?
- How is weather forecast made?
- How does sound travel?
- Why are all the heavenly bodies round?
- What are the different states of matter?
- How does a thermos flask work?
- What are asteroids?
- What are the wonders of X-Rays?
- Can matter be converted into energy?
- What is the structure of an atom?
- Why can't we see stars during the day?
- Why does thunder follow lightning?
- Why does iron get rusty?
- How does a microscope work?
- What is a nuclear reactor?
- What are nebulae?
- What is electromagnetism?
- Why does the sky appear blue?
- How do we find direction in the sea?
- How is light produced by an electric bulb?
- What are the different forms of energy?
- How is glass made?
- What are constellations?

Section III — Plants & Animals
- How did life begin on earth?
- What is the difference between fruits and vegetables?
- How does a chameleon change its colour?
- Which medicines are obtained from animals?
- How fast can animals run?
- How do bees make honey?
- Why do elephants have trunks?
- Why are some fruits sweet while others are sour?
- How do we estimate the age of a tree?
- Why do flowers have fragrance?
- Why do camels have humps?
- Why do trees shed their leaves?
- Why don't spiders get caught in their own webs?
- What are mammals?
- Why insect bites are dangerous?
- Why is the colour of leaves green?
- How do fish breathe inside water?
- How are bats different from birds?
- How does a wall lizard get rid of its tail?
- How does a firefly glow at night?
- Which are the warm and cold-blooded creatures?
- Can animals identify different colours?
- Why is lion called the king of the beasts?

Section IV — Human Body
- What determines the sex of a child?
- Why do we feel hungry?
- Why do we hiccup?
- Why do we get tired?
- How are we able to speak?
- How do the ears detect sound?
- How do female mammals produce milk?
- Why is the blood red?
- Why do tears come out while weeping?
- How is our body temperature maintained?
- What makes people sneeze?
- How is urine formed in our body?
- Why do some people snore during sleep?
- How do we breathe?
- Why does the human skin have different colours?
- What is roundworm infestation?
- Why does the blood group vary from person to person?
- Why is one of our feet bigger than the other?
- Why do some people become deaf?
- Why do we feel thirsty?
- How do intoxicants affect our body?
- What is pulmonary tuberculosis?
- How are twins born?
- How do we digest food?
- Why are some people left-handed?
- What causes pneumonia?
- Why does our body stop growing after a certain age?
- How does the nose detect smell?
- Why is cutting of nails and hairs painless?
- What causes headaches?
- What are the common eye disorders?
- How does the intake of salt help our body?
- How do muscles work?

Section V — Scientists & Inventions
- Why is Newton called the Father of Physics?
- How did Archimedes detect impurity in the golden crown?
- How was wheel invented?
- What was discovered by Enrico Fermi?
- Who discovered radium?
- Why is Einstein called the greatest scientist of the 20th century?
- Why is Galileo called a great scientist?
- Why is Edison called the Inventor of Inventors?

Section VI — Sports & Entertainment
- What is Sumo wrestling?
- Who is called the Black Pearl ?
- What is Figure Skating?
- When did people start playing cards?
- Where did the game of chess originate?
- Why was Dhyan Chand called the Hockey Wizard?
- What is Kabuki?
- Why is Dada Saheb Phalke award given?
- Who created Mickey Mouse?
- Who was Mozart?
- How do parrot and myna speak like us?

Big size 176 Pages   Fully Illustrated

A Glimpse of Questions Answered in
CHILDREN'S KNOWLEDGE BANK Vol. III
Divided into six sections it deals with 153 questions

Section I—General Knowledge
- Is there any hill that changes its colour ?
- Which are the great mountain ranges of the world?
- Where is Angkor Wat — the largest temple?
- How would you put out a fire ?
- Why shouldn't we watch television in a darkened room ?
- Who was Picasso ?
- How is the rainfall measured ?
- Where did Gypsies come from ?
- Where does wax go from a burning candle?
- What are Calories ?
- How was coal formed?
- How is milk turned into curds ?
- Why was the Eiffel Tower built ?
- What is China clay ?
- Why is Bermuda Triangle so mysterious ?
- Why is Netherlands called the Land of Windmills ?
- What are fossils ?
- What is acupuncture ?
- Why is the Ganges considered sacred ?
- What are the lightest and the heaviest metals ?
- Why do we cup our hands around ourmouth when we call someone ?
- Why doesn't frozen food get spoiled ?
- Why does the flame always rise upwards ?
- What is friction ?
- Where is the International Court of Justice ?
- What are the main classical dances of India ?
- What are the latitudes and longitudes?
- Why don't oil and water mix ?
- Why is electric shock dangerous ?
- Which language has the greatest number of words ?
- How is sulphur obtained ?
- Where is the Death Valley ?
- How is pollution harmful to us ?
- Why does a dead body float on water ?
- Where is World Bank ?
- Do hair really grow even after a person is dead?
- Why do we dream ?
- Does everyone have unique fingerprints ?
- Why don't all nations have one currency ?
- Why do we use fertilizers ?
- Why do we call 1st April a Fools' day ?
- Why was the Taj Mahal built ?
- What is a Light Year?
- How did the continents originate ?
- How is atmospheric pressure measured ?
- Why don't all planets have an atmosphere ?
- What is Disneyland ?
- What are the polar regions ?
- What are the different kinds of fuels ?
- What is inflation ?
- Why do we pay taxes ?

Section II—Plants & Animals
- How did animals get their names ?

- Why do some animals chew their cud ?
- Is there life on other planets ?
- Why do snakes shed their skins ?
- Do plants also breathe ?
- What is a flying fox ?
- What are the magical qualities of garlic ?
- Can a squirrel really fly ?
- Is there any animal which commits suicide ?
- Does the vampire bat feed on blood ?
- Why is a dog's sense of smell better than that of ours ?
- Why do rabbits have large ears ?
- What is a coral ?
- Which animal never drinks water in its entire life?
- How does an insect breathe ?
- When did plants appear on the earth ?
- How useful is the banana ?
- What is a sea-horse ?
- What were the dinosaurs?
- Can a snake swallow an animal whole?

Section III—Inventions & Discoveries
- Who invented the shoes?
- Who discovered Australia ?
- How did the circus begin ?
- When was the stethoscope invented ?
- Who developed the shorthand ?
- How was geometry invented ?
- How did weapons come into use ?
- When was the first light house built ?
- How were the explosives developed ?
- How did the English language originate?
- Where did democracy originate ?
- Who started the kindergarten ?
- When were the museums started ?

Section IV—Modern Science
- How are perfumes made ?
- How does a tape recorder work ?
- What are sulfa drugs ?
- What are alloys ?
- What are isotopes ?
- How does a transformer work ?
- How can we test the purity of pure ghee ?
- Who was the first man to land on the Moon ?
- How is cement made ?
- What are communications satellites ?
- What are cosmic rays ?
- What is a planetarium ?
- How is paper made ?
- How does a fluorescent light work ?
- What are holograms ?
- What is a lie detector ?
- What are laser beams ?
- Can air be converted into a liquid ?
- What is a test-tube baby ?
- How does a soap clean things ?
- How does an electron microscope work ?
- How does a photostat machine work ?

- What is solar energy ?
- How do we take a photograph with a camera ?
- What is a dry cell ?
- How does an airconditioner work ?
- How does a refrigerator work ?
- How does a vacuum cleaner work ?
- Can one element be changed into another ?
- What are video games ?

Section V—Human Body
- What is our body made of ?
- What causes a heart attack ?
- How do we get pimples ?
- How do we see different colours ?
- What causes common cold ?
- What makes the blood clot ?
- What is the function of tonsils ?
- What is saliva ?
- What are hormones ?
- Why does our hair turn grey ?
- Why does our skin wrinkle ?
- How do the blind read and write ?
- What are our teeth ?
- Why is skeleton necessary for us ?
- What elements constitute the human body ?
- Why are vaccinations necessary?
- What is a phobia ?
- Which language is used by deaf-mutes ?
- What is cancer ?
- How does our brain work ?
- Why do our eyes blink ?
- What is the function of the kidneys ?
- What is epilepsy ?
- What causes a peptic ulcer ?
- How is pus formed ?
- Why do we feel sleepy after a heavy meal ?
- What is food poisoning ?
- What is a pacemaker?
- What is Positron Emission Technology ?

Section VI—Sports & Entertainment
- Which is the oldest game in the world ?
- Where did the game of basketball originate ?
- What is marathon ?
- When did rowing begin ?
- Who have been some of India's great sportspersons ?
- What are the popular games of India ?
- When was swimming included as a sport ?
- When did mountaineering become a sport ?
- What is Ballet ?
- What is Jazz ?
- Did Sherlock Holmes really exist?
- What is show-jumping ?
- How did cinema commence ?

Big size 176 Pages   Fully Illustrated

A Glimpse of Questions Answered in
CHILDREN'S KNOWLEDGE BANK Vol. V
Divided into six sections it deals with 152 questions

Section I—General Knowledge
- What is a Computer Virus?
- What is Carbon Dating?
- How does a hovercraft work?
- How does an airplane stay up in the air?
- Can we measure intelligence?
- Who was Aristotle?
- Where do people live on boats?
- How do traffic lights work?
- What are the different types of calculators?
- What is Bonsai?
- What is Guerrilla Warfare?
- Where is the Big Ben?
- What is a Cosmic Year?
- What is the legend behind the Trojan Horse?
- When was the United Kingdom formed?
- What is a boomerang?
- What is the Food Chain?
- What is the International Date Line?
- How was the Grand Canyon formed?
- Who were the Incas?
- How does a steering wheel make a car turn?
- How can we locate the North Star?
- When did the scout movement begin?
- Who was Columbus?
- What are whispering galleries?
- What was the Stone Age?
- What are pesticides?
- Where is the highest railway line in the world?
- Where is the Alhambra?
- How did the use of Christmas trees begin?
- What is a semaphore?
- Why is Egypt called the Gift of the Nile?
- Who was Gautama Buddha?
- What is a rain forest?
- What is ozone gas?
- Why do forward moving wheels sometimes appear turning backwards?
- How is cheese made?
- What are the methods of sewage disposal?
- What is a poison?
- What is an avalanche?
- Where did ice-cream originate from?
- What was the French Revolution?
- What is Fool's Gold?
- What is a Theodolite?
- Which is the oldest city in the world?
- What is the black magic of witch doctors?
- Which is the largest river in the world?
- What is Palmistry?
- What is Opera?
- Why is Shakespeare regarded as the world's greatest poet and playwright?
- What are the different types of mirrors?
- What are solar flares?
- Which British Sovereign had the longest reign?
- What is the weight of our atmosphere?
- Where does all the garbage go?
- What is a Chemical Warfare?

Section II—Science & Technology
- What are Novae and Supernovae?
- How does a jet engine work?
- Why does a ship float on water?
- What is Doppler Effect?
- How do detergents perform the cleaning action?
- What is an ammeter?
- What is the science of ballistics?
- What is a welding torch?
- How do we measure the hardness of materials?
- What are the different abrasives?
- What is a clinometer?
- What is electroplating?
- How do satellites stay up in space?
- How is sulphuric acid manufactured?
- What is light?
- How does a siren produce sound?
- How are metals anodized?
- How does a turbine work?
- How does a battery torch work?
- How does a screw jack work?
- Why is 'pi' ( ) such a unique number?
- What are the contact lenses?
- How are different paints made?
- What is a shadow?
- What is a Range Finder?
- How does a siphon work?
- How fast do the objects fall?
- What is the refraction of light?
- How does a parachute work?
- What is a prime number?
- What is Electricity?
- What is a pyrometer?
- What Is solar wind?

Section III—Plants and Animals
- Do some plants also move?
- Can one tree produce the fruit of a different tree?
- Why do plants and animals become extinct?
- How do we study the internal structure of plants?
- How do some animals recognise their offspring?
- Why do cats purr?
- Which insects swim upside-down?
- Can the fishes hear?
- Which birds cannot fly?
- Why do birds sing?
- Does any bear wear 'glasses'?
- Which lizard squirts blood from its eyes?
- Can a scorpion kill a man?
- Which fish keeps its eggs in its mouth?
- Why are stripes a boon to the zebras?
- How did the first bird evolve?
- How do the plant seeds get dispersed?
- How do the fishes smell things?
- Which are the birds of prey?
- Who is called the king of fishes?
- How did different plants get their names?
- Which animal spends its life upside down?
- Which animals are extinct now?
- How do plants and animals defend themselves?
- How is Nightingale distinct from other birds?
- Why are crocodiles so dangerous?

Section IV—Human Body
- What is Extrasensory Perception?
- What is LSD?
- Why is it said: An apple a day keeps the doctor away?
- What are tranquillizers?
- What causes a reflex action?
- What are emotions?
- What is Electroencephalography (EEG)?
- Why do we shiver on a cold day?
- What are the different methods of birth control?
- Why do we get 'Pins and Needles'?
- What are the different mental illnesses?
- Why do we have a belly button?
- What is anaemia?
- How does our nervous system function?
- What is cirrhosis of the liver?
- What is the Rh factor?
- What is electroshock therapy?
- What is jaundice?
- How is sunlight beneficial for us?
- When did the first human heart transplant take place?
- How does a human baby grow inside its mother's womb?
- What are goose pimples?

Section V—Scientists and Inventions
- Who is called the Father of Modern Chemistry?
- When was Morse code first used?
- How is S.N. Bose associated with Einstein?
- What is gyroscope and who invented it?
- Who is called the Father of Indian Nuclear Science?
- Who is known as the Father of Indian Space Research ?
- What is Shanti Swarup Bhatnagar Award?
- What were Sir J. C. Bose's contributions to science?
- How was the ballpoint pen invented?

Section VI—Sports & Entertainment
- What is the sport of Fencing ?
- How is the game of Table Tennis played?
- What is Hang Gliding?
- When did the sport of Weightlifting begin?
- Who was Marlyn Monroe?
- Who were the Beatles?

Big size 176 Pages   Fully Illustrated

A Glimpse of Questions Answered in
CHILDREN'S KNOWLEDGE BANK Vol. VI
Divided into six sections it deals with 156 questions

Section I—General Knowledge
- What is Artificial Intelligence?
- Why was the Statue of Liberty built?
- Why does Mars appear red?
- Who was the founder of the United States of America?
- What is PIN Code System?
- Where is the world's oldest underground railway?
- Who's brighter: Girls or Boys?
- Can fresh water be obtained from the sea?
- Why were the pyramids of Egypt built?
- What is the Mafia?
- Why does the rising or setting sun appear bigger?
- What are different National Awards?
- Why is the cotton plant called Daughter of the Sun?
- Why are there only ten numbers with single figures?
- How was Suez Canal built?
- Why do we need a passport for going abroad?
- What are political parties and pressure groups?
- What are our National Emblem and National Flag?
- Why are some deserts getting bigger?
- How is flood caused?
- What is First Aid?
- Why does milk spill out when boiled?
- Why is it difficult to see things immediately when we enter a dark room?
- How does wool keep us warm?
- Why do people get married?
- What are Five Year Plans?
- How do we get common salt?
- How was the Giant's Causeway formed?
- What is Ikebana?
- Why was the First World War fought?
- Why are some people tattooed?
- What are the Stone Towers of Arizona?
- Who built the giant statues of Easter Island?
- How can you find out date with the help of stars?
- What are the seas of the moon?
- How do ice columns grow inside caves?
- What is the absolute zero?
- Why does sound change continuously when a vessel is filled up with tap water?
- What is Ceramics?
- How can we use the internal heat of Earth?
- What is a Black Box?
- What is Carbon Cycle?
- How heavy loads are lifted by pulleys?
- What are fuel gases?
- Why are there three pins in a plug?
- What is a CAT scanner?
- What are Antifreeze Compounds?
- What are Mercenaries?
- How did the practice of shaking hands begin?
- What were the main causes of the Second World War?
- What is the Metric System?
- What are our Fundamental Rights?
- What is UNESCO?
- What are precious stones?
- What are the functions of the Supreme Court of India?
- What are luminescent materials?
- How is vinegar made?
- How is the President of India elected?
- What are Kepler's laws of planetary motion?

Section II—Science & Technology
- What is Greenhouse Effect?
- How does a hair drier work?
- How does a video telephone work?
- How does a motorcycle engine work?
- What is a Bolometer?
- What is a space shuttle?
- Why does camphor change into gas without turning into a liquid first?
- How is sugar made?
- How does an escalator work?
- How does a wet battery work?
- What is interference of light?
- How is electricity transmitted over long distances?
- What is a lathe machine?
- How does a water pump function?
- What is Bernoulli's Effect?
- What is Quantum Theory?
- What are cathode rays?
- How are acoustically sound buildings designed?
- How does a colour television function?
- How does a sodium lamp work?
- What is a Hydrofoil?
- How does a camera's flashlight work?
- What is Liquid Crystal Display?
- What is an embossing machine?
- How do you distinguish between force, work, energy and power?
- What is ammonia gas?
- How do a mixer and grinder work?
- How is wax made?
- How does an electric fan function?
- How do electrically heated appliances work?
- Where would a ball fall when thrown inside a running train?
- What is Osmosis?
- How do trawlers fish?
- How does an Electric Bell function?

Section III—Plants and Animals
- Why do animals have a tail?
- Why do trees change colour in autumn?
- Do snakes love music?
- Which is the most beautiful reptile?
- Which are the largest and smallest flowers?
- Where is cocoa grown?
- Does any animal have three eyes?
- Why do flowers of Raat Ki Rani bloom only at night?
- Why do dogs pant in summer?
- Where do crabs climb trees?
- Which is the largest seabird?
- Which animal can see with its eyes closed?
- How do living beings adapt to their environment?
- How do animals release their tension?
- How do different animals move?
- How do plants protect themselves from frost?
- Which fish spits at insects?

Section IV—Human Body
- What is cholesterol?
- What is consciousness?
- Which substances work as fuel in our body?
- What is electroretinogram?
- Why do we see stars when hit on the head or eyes?
- Why do we belch?
- What is arthritis?
- Does our body have a built-in-clock?
- How are cells, tissues, organs and systems formed in the body?
- Why do we feel pain?
- What causes an itch?
- Does everybody have a different smell?
- What is appendicitis?
- Does our body generate electricity?
- What are the functions of the pancreas?
- What is Electromyogram?
- How is artificial insemination done?
- What causes ringworm?
- How is fluoride useful to our teeth?
- What are hereditary diseases?
- Why do our hands and lips get chapped in cold days?
- How is vision tested?
- What causes influenza?
- What is genetics?
- Who discovered vitamins?
- What is ecology?

Section V—Scientists and Inventions
- When were the guns first made?
- Who was Aryabhatta?
- What were Marconi's contributions to science?
- Who discovered neutrons?
- Who invented Seismograph?
- Who was Pythagorus?
- What were Ramanujan's contributions to mathematics?
- What are Dr. S. Chandrasekhar's contributions to astrophysics?
- When was the first balloon flight made?

Section VI—Sports & Entertainment
- What is Decathlon?
- What is the game of Golf?
- Who was Charlie Chaplin?
- What are Asian Games?
- What is the sport of karate?
- How is kho-kho played?
- Who were Laurel and Hardy?
- What are the seven notes of music?
- Why is Satyajit Ray called a legend in Indian Cinema?
- Who founded the city of Rome?
- Who was Beethoven?

Big size 176 Pages   Fully Illustrated

1
General Knowledge

• When did the first alphabet appear? • How do astronauts walk in space? • What is the Nitrogen Cycle? • When did the first Indian Empire arise? • When was the first artificial satellite launched? • What are Black Holes? • How many stars can we count at night? • When was the Sahara desert covered by Ice? • How do deep-sea divers operate? • Why is it harder to walk uphill than downhill? • Who was Plato? • What was the Ice Age? • What is weightlessness? • Why does the Mediterranean Sea appear blue and the Atlantic Ocean green? • What is the United Nations ? • What is the mystery of Sphinx? • Why do woollen clothes kept in boxes get holes? • Why are Ajanta and Ellora Caves famous? • Who was Napoleon Bonaparte? • How far can we see on the surface of earth? • What are Auroras ? • What are ultraviolet rays? • Who was Confucius? • Why is the Panama Canal so famous ? • What is a litmus paper? • What is a Kaleidoscope? • What is magnetism ? • Who was Kalidasa ? • Who was the founder of Din-i-Ilahi? • What are proteins ? • Why is Khajuraho famous ? • What are the two houses of our parliament ? • What is ionosphere ? • Which is the Land of Midnight Sun ? • What is a sextant ? • Why do soldiers salute? • How did different countries get their names ? • Why is a ship's speed measured in Knots? • When were the stupas of Sanchi built ? • How is the altitude of a flying airplane determined ? • What are the underground rivers ? • What is a catalyst ? • How did the Egyptians preserve mummies ? • What are the various artificial sweetening agents ? • What do A.M. and P.M. mean ? • How does water become cool in an earthen pitcher ? • How did different superstitions begin ? • What is an Electric Fuse ? • When did the Industrial Revolution begin ? • Which cities are built on canals?

1

When did the first alphabet appear?

The origin and development of any language can be traced back to the rudimentary symbols the primitive people used in their verbal interaction. These symbols when used over a long period take an established pattern thus giving rise to a new language. But the growth of a language does not stop at oral communication — a script for writing is developed on the way. But when did the first alphabet appear that enabled man to express himself in writing?

The earliest people used pictures for writing which we call pictograph. The stone age people used this form in their writing. In pictograph a particular sign represents an object such as a tree or a bird which in turn communicates a specific meaning or idea. Ideas could be communicated through picture writing in the sense that the picture of a bird might mean flying. The ancient Egyptians also used picture-writing. But this form had its limitations. It required thousands of pictures, which were also called characters, to symbolise a few things. This drawback of pictograph led to the discovery of signs that represented sounds used in verbal communication. These signs representing different sounds were grouped differently to form new words. But when did the sound-signs first appeared which we now call alphabets?

About 3,500 years ago, the Phoenicians in eastern Mediterranean, invented the first alphabet. Later the Greeks and Romans developed their own alphabets which were improvements of the Phoenician script. In fact the word 'alphabet' is derived from two words alpha(α) and beta(β) which were the first two letters in the Greek alphabet.

Phoenician	Ancient Greek	Modern English
	A	A
	B	B
	Γ	C G
	Δ	
	E F	D E F
	Z	Z
	H	H
	Θ I	I J
	K	K
	Λ M N	L M N
	Ξ O Π	X O P
	Ρ	Q
	Σ	R S
	T	T
	Υ Φ	U V W
	X Ψ	Y
	Ω	

The 26 letters in the English alphabet came from the Roman alphabet of 2500 years ago

The appearance of alphabets made it easier to create thousands of words using a few alphabets. For example, there are only 26 letters in English alphabet but just imagine how many words we make out of these 26 letters! Pictograph lacked this advantage since one picture represented only one meaning or idea.

Now most of the languages in the civilised world have their own alphabets but the number of letters in the alphabets and their pronunciation differ from language to language.

○○○

2

How do astronauts walk in space?

An astronaut could perform several tasks while walking in the space like repairing of a damaged artificial satellite in the orbit

It appears strange but true that astronauts can walk in the space. This is so because in ordinary walking we rest our feet on the surface of the earth and the force of earth's gravity pulls us towards it. But when there is nothing in the empty space — neither any surface to walk on nor any gravitational force to pull the feet down onto the ground — how does an astronaut walk in the space?

Space walking by astronauts is quite different from the normal walking. To walk in the space the astronauts take the help of hand rockets which provide them the force to move. The hand rockets follow the principle of rocket propulsion. In rockets, the ejection of gas with a great force from the backside pushes the rocket forward with an equal thrust. This working principle is based on Newton's third law of motion which states, 'To every action there is always an equal and opposite reaction'. Similarly in hand rockets when the engine is powered the exhaust thrust pushes the rocket in the opposite direction and the astronaut walks alongwith this force as he carries the hand rocket with him. In fact, it is not 'walking' in the strict sense as there is no surface in the space to rest the feet but rather 'floating' — to express more accurately.

But why do the astronauts walk in the space? Apart from experimental reasons, sometimes they are required to shift from one spacecraft to another or need to carry out a repairing work on the outer surface of the craft. During such operations they use the specially designed hand rockets and the direction of the exhaust outlet is pointed opposite to the desired direction of walking.

The first spacewalk was made in March 1965 by a Soviet astronaut, A. Leonov, who stayed outside the aircraft for 24 minutes. Another important walk was made in 1973 when the American satellite *Skylab* was to be repaired for a damage in the heat shield that made the craft dangerously hot.

○○○

3

What is the Nitrogen Cycle?

Our atmosphere contains about 78% of nitrogen. A certain amount of this nitrogen is constantly being removed, and an approximately equal amount is being returned. This continuous circulation of nitrogen among the soil, water, air and living organisms is known as the Nitrogen cycle. Let us see how the percentage of nitrogen in the air remains constant.

All living things need nitrogen. It is part of proteins and nucleic acids, both of which are vital for life. How nitrogen is removed from atmosphere and again returned to the atmosphere is given below.

A part of the atmospheric nitrogen is removed from the air by lightning. The sudden discharge of electricity causes some of the nitrogen and oxygen components in the air to combine, forming the oxides of nitrogen. When these nitrogen oxides are dissolved in water, they combine with other elements to form nitrogenous compounds.

Some nitrogen is removed, from the air by certain bacteria and algae in a process called nitrogen fixation. Symbiotic bacteria present in the nodules of roots of some plants, such as peas, beans, gram etc. take up atmospheric nitrogen directly, and pass it on to the plants. Plants take up nitrogen compounds and convert them into proteins. These proteins are assimilated by animals. Some other plants, like rice, have symbiotic blue-green algae which fix atmospheric nitrogen.

As a result of death, decay and excretion by plants and animals, the organic matter is converted into ammonium salts in the soil. Special nitrifying bacteria convert ammonia into nitrogenous compounds that are used up by plants. Animals get their nitrogenous compounds by eating plants, or other animals that eat plants.

Thus an approximately equal amount of nitrogen is also being constantly returned to the atmosphere. Denitrifying bacteria change some of the nitrogenous compounds in the soil, back into gaseous form of nitrogen. These gases then return to the air.

Thus nitrogen from the atmosphere passes into the soil, plants and animals and finally returns to the air. It may take thousands or millions of years, but every molecule of nitrogen eventually returns to the air.

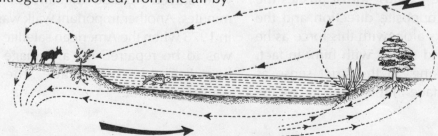

Plants and animals consume nitrogen, mostly from the soil, and return it to the soil in various ways ○○○

16

4

When did the first Indian Empire arise?

Empires rise and fall but the nation survives. India has survived as a great nation because unity in diversity has become an inherent feature of our country built over thousands of years. One of the most important pillars of this unity is the political unification, the present one being a gift of the British rule though the pre-independence British empire was much larger. But long before the British empire, India had witnessed great empires at different phases of its history; for example during the reigns of Ashoka, Samudragupta, Harshavardhana, Akbar, Aurengzeb etc. But when did the first great Indian Empire arise?

During the pre-christian era some great civilizations had flourished in India but they had their geographical and political limitations. Thereafter arose some well-organized and better governed states but they were very small independent kingdoms. It was only after Alexander's invasion that India saw the growth of its first ever large empire, under the adventurous leadership of Chandragupta Maurya. Initially Chandragupta was the Commander-in-Chief of the army of Nanda dynasty who were then ruling South Bihar in Eastern India. For some reason or other, Chandragupta attempted a revolt but was unsuccessful. He fled away and met Alexander the Great seeking his co-operation. When Alexander left India putting behind one of his generals in charge, Chandragupta again approached and got the help of this general. He became the ruler of Punjab and Bihar. A great political thinker of those times, Chanakya, also helped Chandragupta in his mission since he had also to settle scores with the Nanda dynasty. Thus the seeds of the first great Indian Empire were sown in around 321 B.C. and the rule of the great Maurya dynasty began. Later he extended his empire from the mouth of river Ganges in the east to the mountains of Hindukush between modern Pakistan and Afghanistan. This was the first really large and powerful centralised state in India.

After empire building Chandragupta concentrated on defence and public administration. He maintained an elaborate spy network and an efficient bureaucracy. Though there was autocratic government at the top yet democracy prevailed at the village level.

Later, Ashoka the Great became the third ruler of this great empire under whose reign the empire was further extended to the whole of India except the deep south and south-east. The state progressed and flourished in all fields.

ooo

5

When was the first artificial satellite launched?

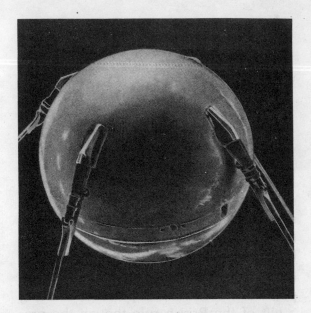

The first artificial satellite was Sputnik-1 launched by the erstwhile Soviet Union on October 4, 1957

A satellite is a body that orbits around another but the term is usually applied to small bodies which orbit around the planets. Most of the planets have satellites revolving around them. For example, moon is the only satellite of earth. But apart from the natural satellites of the planets, several man-made or artificial satellites have been launched which now orbit the earth and some of the other planets in the solar system. But when did man send the first artificial satellite into the space?

The first artificial satellite was launched into the space by the former USSR on 4 October 1957 which was called *Sputnik I*. *Sputnik* is the Russian word for a travelling companion. It was spherical in shape with a diameter of 58 cms and weighed 83 kilograms. It orbited the earth every 96 minutes. A month later the launching of *Sputnik 2*, which weighed 500 kg, created another landmark in the space history as it carried the first ever space traveller, a dog named Laika. This established the fact that a warm-blooded animal could live in space thus paving the way for man's venture into the space which finally succeeded in 1961 when Yuri Gagarin of USSR orbited the earth in his spacecraft *Vostok I*.

The first American satellite was *Explorer I* which was launched on 31st January 1958 and weighed only 14 kilograms. The first American astronaut to be in space was John Glenn in 1962. The first woman space traveller was Valentina Tereshkova of USSR.

But what functions do these artificial satellites perform in the space? They are used for radio and TV communications, weather forecasting, geological surveys, telecommunications, defence and spying purposes, scientific studies like space and astronomical observations, crop patterns and oceanography. Depending on their function they are called communication satellites, weather satellites, scientific satellites, earth resources satellites etc. Some satellites perform a number of functions and are called multipurpose satellites.

OOO

6

What are Black Holes?

Twentieth century astronomers have predicted dark areas in space. The gravitational attraction of these areas is so high that anything which goes into it cannot come out. Even light cannot escape their gravitational pull. Hence they do not emit light. These areas are called Black Holes or collapsars.

A German astronomer, Karl Schwarzschild predicted the existence of black holes in 1907. He theoretically proved that black holes are the end results of all stars whose mass is much greater than that of the sun. The existence of black holes was first theoretically proved in 1939 by J. Robert Oppenheimer and Hartland S. Synder as a consequence of General Theory of Relativity.

Let us consider a star whose mass is greater than that of the sun. Its size remains normal due to the balance between the two forces — one being the expansion force caused by the enormously high temperature which tends to expand the star's material, and the other being the enormous gravitational pull which tends to contract the star's substance.

At some stage in the star's life, after thousands of millions of years, its nuclear fuel decreases causing a fall in it's core temperature. As a result, the gravitational pull becomes stronger than the expansion force. Gradually, the star begins to collapse.

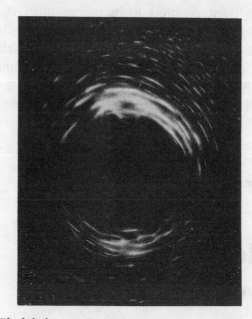

Black holes are thought to be the final stage in a star's life. There are millions of black holes in the Milky Way as suggested by scientists

In this process, the atoms present in the star break into electrons, protons and neutrons. The mutual repulsion between the electrons prevents further contraction. The star, at this stage, is known as 'White Dwarf'. In this process, the star is reduced to one-hundredth of its original size, thereby the gravitational pull in the White Dwarf becomes about 10,000 times more than the original value.

Under certain conditions the gravitational pull becomes strong enough to overcome the electron repulsion. The star begins to contract further and in this process of contraction, electrons and protons combine to form neutrons. The star at this stage is called "Neutron Star". It's size is now reduced to five hundredth part of the dwarf star and the gravitational attraction becomes about 100,000,000,00 times that of the original star.

The light emitted from the neutron star reduces its energy and as a result its size further decreases. At some stage, no radiations come out from this star. It is then called a Black Hole which is the smallest and most dense object in the universe.

Scientists are still looking for evidence of the actual existence of black holes in the universe. They have detected Cygnus X-1 as a black hole in 1974. In 1983, US astronomers detected another X-ray source in the large Magellanic cloud.

OOO

7

How many stars can we count at night?

On a clear night, if we look up at the sky, we will see innumerable stars — small and big, bright and dim. Have you ever tried counting them? You'll be surprised to find that out of these innumerable stars about 6000 can be seen without the help of a telescope!

That does not mean that a person can just look up and count 6000 stars. From any one place on earth, only one-half are visible at one time as the rest of them are on the other side of it. Many of the stars near the horizon cannot be seen on account of haze. Hence if someone starts counting the stars, he would probably not be able to count more than 1000 of them.

By using a very powerful telescope we can see even very dim and distant stars. This way it would be possible to photograph more than 1,000,000,000 stars. Today astronomers have succeeded in identifying more than 4,57,000 stars.

We can count more stars on a photograph taken by attaching a camera with a telescope

Now the question arises - why can't we count more stars?

Stars vary considerably in size, temperature, brightness and distance from the earth. We can count only those stars which are bigger in size, nearer to the earth, and bright enough to be seen by naked eyes. We can't see the faint, smaller and distant stars without a telescope. However if we take a photograph from the same place by attaching a camera with the telescope, we can count more stars on the photograph, than we would with the naked eye.

OOO

8

When was the Sahara desert covered by Ice?

Sahara is the world's largest desert covering an area of 9 million sq km. in northern Africa. It extends from the coast of Atlantic ocean in the west to the Red sea and Iraq. It includes parts of Algeria, Chad, Egypt, Libya, Mali, Mauritania, Morocco, Sudan and Tunisia. One third of the desert is covered by sand dunes and the rest consists of rocky uplands and stony plains. Crude oil and natural gas have been discovered beneath the Sahara and now being extracted. But there was a time when this great desert was covered by ice. Do you know when?

The first clue of ice was discovered when geologists found evidence of glaciation in the bedrock of the Algerian desert. The approximate time of the ice covering was calculated to be about 450 million years ago. The location of the desert at that time, as research studies have found out was near the South Pole. The size, shape and position of the continents or landmasses of the earth have been constantly changing over the years. This happens due to the movement of plates in the earth's crust. When these giant plates move they carry the continents along with them. As per the available evidences, 200 million years ago there was a supercontinent called Pangaea. It was formed when separate continental plates drifted together but later Pangaea also broke apart. But geologists are not sure about the continental locations before the formation of Pangaea. But rock studies provide some clue to the then location of Sahara. They suggest that Sahara was situated near the South Pole which eventually leads us to believe that it was covered by ice during that period of history. This period, according to geological classifications, is called the Ordovician period when North Africa was at South pole ice-cap and the equator ran diagonally across today's North America.

The rock studies reveal that million years ago Sahara was situated near the South Pole. This leads us to believe that it was then covered by ice

○○○

9

How do deep-sea divers operate?

Since ancient times, man's curiosity has led him to explore the dark, mysterious world of the deep seas. Diving has therefore developed to be an important sport over the years. But how do men stay under water for long periods of time?

The first practical diving apparatus was devised by a German scientist, named Augustus Siebe in 1819. It comprised a metal helmet with a shoulder plate attached to a waterproof leather jacket. A tube running from the helmet was attached to an air pump. This was the first of many major experiments he carried out in trying to perfect a safe method of staying and working under-water. In 1830 he designed and developed a complete suit and helmet with air valves. Although many improvements have since been made, Siebe's principles remain in universal use.

Deep sea divers, such as those who search shipwrecks for treasure, are divided into groups. They are skin divers who wear rubber suits that fit tightly like the skin, and divers known as 'hard hats' who wear heavy diving dress.

A deep sea diver should use seven essentials : (a) An air pump for pushing air downwards to him. (b) A helmet, usually of steel, with glass windows to see. (c) A flexible waterproof suit fitting closely at

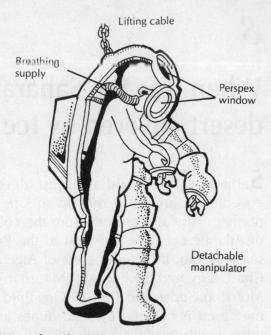

A modern deep-sea diving suit. The diver can breathe air at atmospheric pressure 400 metres below water

wrists and ankles. (d) A length of air tubing that must be flexible, but must not collapse under the pressure of water. (e) A pair of heavy boots to keep the feet on the bottom. (f) Lead weights, hooked to chest and back, to prevent floating up to the surface. (g) A life-line to communicate with the surface by a system of jerks. One jerk may mean danger, and so on!

Some divers also have a telephone so that they can talk to the ship. The wires for these telephones are built into the lifelines.

Water pressure is a big problem for deep sea divers. The deeper a diver goes, more becomes the pressure of water around him. So the air pumped down must enable him to breathe properly and also balance the water pressure outside.

In the past, deep sea divers used to breathe ordinary air, which contained nitrogen.

This was very dangerous because when the pressure was very high, nitrogen would dissolve in the blood. When the diver surfaced, the pressure quickly returned to normal, which caused the nitrogen to bubble out of the blood. This led to a very painful illness which could even kill the diver, called as 'Bends' or 'Caisson disease'. To avoid this, divers now breathe a mixture of oxygen and helium. Helium does not dissolve in the blood, so it is safer to use. But breathing helium makes divers speak with a high, squeaky voice because sound travels three times as fast as it does in air!

In recent years, diving has not only become a popular sport, but is also useful in performing important jobs. Divers are needed for the construction and repair of bridges. They study plant and animal life beneath the surface of water. They aid in finding drowned people, and they also help in the search for buried treasure!

ooo

10

Why is it harder to walk uphill than downhill?

Generally while climbing up the stairs of a building, a person gets more easily exhausted, than while coming down. To lift heavy articles, greater effort is required. It is harder to walk uphill than downhill. Have you ever wondered why?

We know that our earth attracts everything towards its centre. This is known as the force of gravity of the earth. It is the force of gravity that holds us on the surface of earth. When we move away from the earth's surface, we have to do work to overcome the force of gravity.

So while going uphill, our muscles have to do more work to lift the weight of our body against the gravity of the earth. For this the heart has to pump more blood to the cells. As a result, our lungs have to do more work to pump out the carbon dioxide from the heart, and to replace it with oxygen. Hence for a steep climb we breathe more quickly.

If we climb a mountain by two different paths — one more steep, and the other less — we would feel greater fatigue in the case of the steeper one.

In comparison to the energy required for walking on a horizontal plane, the total value of the extra energy needed for climbing is the weight of the body multiplied by the total height to be climbed.

When we walk down a hill, very little energy is required because the body is carried down the slope due to the earth's gravitational pull. This is why our muscles do less work, and we do not feel tired while walking down a hill.

ooo

11

Who was Plato?

Plato was a great philosopher of ancient Greece whose writings and teachings still carry great importance. The works of this great thinker are read all over the world even now. He was a student of Socrates and teacher of Aristotle. Infact the ideas of Socrates were translated into writing by his great disciple Plato. He is also credited with implanting the seeds of Aristotle's thought and intellect.

Plato's philosophy is still widely read all over the world

Plato was born in 427 BC in Athens. He belonged to a wealthy aristocratic family and joined Socrates as his pupil at the age of 20. When Socrates was poisoned to death in 399 B.C. Plato left Athens in disgust and spent a few years in travelling. But he returned soon to establish his famous *Academy* in Athens in 388 B.C. which is considered as the first university in the world.

Plato's teaching covered a wide range of subjects. But his views and thoughts on education, justice, ideal state and ideal rulers are still hotly debated and discussed among the intellectuals. For him, 'philosophy' was the supreme thing and no learning is complete without it. He advocated the rule of philosophers, he said, "either Philosophers should be Kings or Kings should be Philosophers". Justice for him was the performance of one's duties. His model code for ideal rulers suggested that rulers should neither get married nor own property. He said that there is an ideal world beyond the real world which can be experienced only in one's mind and man should always strive to bring the real world closer to the ideal one.

There was another interesting aspect of Plato's method of teaching. He didn't permit his lectures at the *Academy* to be circulated in written form as he was afraid that readers outside the *Academy* might not understand his ideas correctly. His logic was that a man gets the opportunity to defend himself in a debate but can not do so in his writings. So when he started writing his ideas he did so in the form of dialogues that provided the mention of different viewpoints alongwith his own.

Among his books, the most famous is *The Republic* which is a political dialogue providing the requirements for an ideal state. This great philosopher died in Athens at the age of 80.

○○○

12

What was the Ice Age?

Ice Age was those early periods of the earth's history when most of the northern part of the earth was covered by a vast sheet of ice.

During the earth's long history, there have been several ice ages. The earliest was in, what is called the late Pre-cambrian times, some 700 million years ago. Another ice age occurred during the late Carboniferous and early Permian periods, about 280 million years ago. Finally about 2 million years ago, an ice age began which lasted nearly until our own times. This is known as the Pleistocene Ice Age. Here we shall discuss about the Pleistocene Ice Age only because information about the first two Ice Ages is not available.

The Pleistocene Ice Age consisted of four periods. During each period, the ice formed and advanced southward, then melted back towards the North Pole. This happened four times. The 'cold periods' are called 'glacial ages' and the warm ones (when the ice melted) are known as 'interglacial' periods.

The first period of ice came about two million years ago, and is known as Nebraskan. The second period came about 12,50,000 years ago and is called the Kansan. The third one came about 500,000 years ago. It is called the Illinoian period. The fourth period, known as Wisconsin period, came about 100,000 years ago.

In between these glacial periods, there have been three interglacial periods. These interglacial ages are called the Aftonian, the Yarmouth and the Sangamon Ages. A typical glacial age lasts about 40,000 to 60,000 years, and interglacial age lasts about 40,000 years. Ice of Wisconsin period began to melt about 40,000 years ago and ended some 10,000 years ago. According to geologists, the earth at present may be in an interglacial age.

Geologists have learnt a lot about ice ages by studying fossils. Whole of Canada and one-third of northern United States, as far as New York city and the Missouri River valley, were covered by ice. In places the thickness of ice was from 2400 to 3000 m (8000 to 10,000 ft). In Europe ice covered whole of northern Europe, the British Isles and much of northern Russia. During the Pleistocene epoch, more than 30% of the earth's surface was covered with ice.

Plants and animals, too, were much affected by the advance and retreat of ice. A number of new animals such as camels, cattle and modern horses appeared during this Ice Age. Many lakes, such as the Great Lake of North America, were also formed during this period.

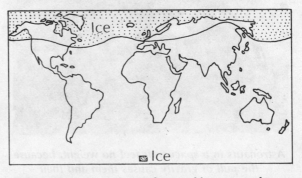

During the ice ages, vast sheets of ice covered parts of America, Asia and Europe

○○○

13

What is weightlessness?

Man experiences weightlessness in a spacecraft. Anything that is not fixed or tied down just floats. Astronauts have to use special devices to eat and drink. The crew members have to learn to adjust the vigour of their actions to keep from crashing into the walls and equipments. During sleep also astronauts feel unstable and that is why they use belts during sleep. Let us understand more about this phenomenon.

The mass of a body is the amount of matter contained in it. In fact, it is the measure of inertia of the body. The weight of a body is the force with which the body is attracted towards the centre of the earth. Weightlessness occurs when there is no gravitational pull on the body such as in a spacecraft or when a satellite orbits the earth. If the force of gravity is balanced by the centrifugal force, the man in the spacecraft experiences a state of weightlessness. A body falling freely under gravity also experiences weightlessness.

Sometimes, weightlessness causes nausea and giddiness because the working of the balancing organs in the inner ear gets upset. Particles floating in the spacecraft do not settle down easily and may be harmful for health. Astronauts are able to adapt to weightlessness through training.

To make up for lack of gravity, regular exercise is essential in a spacecraft to keep the muscles in a good condition. It has been observed that in space, astronauts tend to 'grow' taller. This is because the pads of cartilage between the bones of the spine are no longer under pressure from gravity, and they expand. This increase in height can be as much as 5 cm. However, the astronaut returns to his original height when he returns to earth.

Under the conditions of weightlessness it is possible to conduct certain scientific experiments that are impossible on earth. Absolutely perfect crystals can be grown and alloys of very high homogeneity can be made under the conditions of weightlessness which are very difficult to make under the pull of gravity.

Scientists have been conducting experiments to find out whether a woman may become pregnant in weightlessness condition — and if so, what could be the effect of zero gravity on such children. In recent years, it has been discovered that prolonged periods of weightlessness can cause depletion of calcium in astronauts.

Astronauts in a spacecraft feel no weight, because the pull of gravity causes them and their spacecraft to accelerate together towards the centre of the earth

14

Why does the Mediterranean Sea appear blue and the Atlantic Ocean green?

Do you know that about 3/4 of the earth's surface is covered with water? There are three main oceans : The Atlantic, the Pacific and the Indian Ocean. The Arctic Ocean is taken to be a part of the Atlantic Ocean, and the Antarctic Ocean is made up of the southern parts of other oceans.

The Atlantic Ocean is a great mass of water that separates Europe and Africa, from the American continent. It is shaped like an hour glass, with a 'waist' where Africa and South America bulge out towards each other. Although in area it is less than half of the Pacific Ocean, it has many 'Secondary' water bodies, such as the Arctic Ocean and the Mediterranean sea.

The Mediterranean Sea lies between Southern Europe, Africa and South-West Asia. It is linked to the Atlantic Ocean through the narrow strait of Gibraltar in the west and to the Black sea in the north-east by the sea of Marmara.

One of the surprising facts about the Mediterranean Sea and the Atlantic Ocean is that while the water of the former appears blue, that of the latter appears green! Can you guess why this happens?

The varying colours of the Mediterranean Sea and the Atlantic Ocean depend mainly on the amount of sunlight scattered from their surface. The colour of the scattered sunlight depends upon the substances dissolved in sea water. Generally, of the seven colours of the sunlight blue is scattered most. That is why most oceans appear blue. However, in the case of the Atlantic Ocean, the green effect is produced by the decaying plants in the ocean bed. When these plants decay, yellow pigments are released which get dissolved in the water. The water now scatters both blue and yellow light, and the resulting mixture produces the characteristic green shade.

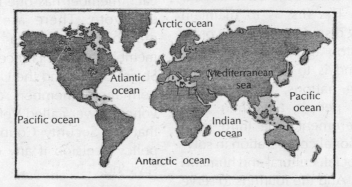

The decaying plants in Atlantic release yellow pigments the effect of which when combined with the effect of blue produces a green shade ○○○

15

What is the United Nations ?

The UN flag represents the world surrounded by two olive branches — the traditional symbol of peace

After the World War II, an international body called the United Nations was set up to keep peace and prevent war, and to build a better world by dealing with problems which can only be solved through international cooperation. Today it has 184 member countries.

The Charter of United Nations was signed at San Francisco Conference on June 26, 1945 by representatives of 51 nations. The Charter came into force on October 24, 1945 when the governments of India, France, the United Kingdom, the Soviet Union and the United States and a majority of other states had ratified it. The name, United Nations, was adopted at the suggestion of President Roosevelt of U.S.A. and the preamble to the Charter was largely the work of Field Marshal Smuts.

According to the Charter the U.N. has four chief purposes. The first is to maintain peace by settling disputes peacefully or by taking steps to stop aggression (armed attack). The second is to develop friendly relations among nations, based on the equal rights of people and their own choices of government. The third is to achieve international co-operation in solving economic, social, cultural and humanitarian problems. And the fourth is to serve as a centre where the actions of nations can be combined to attain these aims.

The U.N. is divided into six main groups: The first is the General Assembly (GA). It is the policy making body of the UN. All UN members are represented in the General Assembly each with one vote. It meets once a year. It fixes the budget. It also elects members on the recommendation of the Security Council, elects the judges of the International Court of Justice, appoints the Secretary General on the recommendations of the Security Council.

The second is the Security Council (SC) which is responsible for the maintenance of peace. It consists of 15 members and each member has one representative and one vote. There are five permanent members and ten non-permanent members. China, France, Great Britain, the Soviet Union and the United States are its permanent members and have special voting power called Veto Power. It means that the Security Council cannot take a policy decision if any of these countries says 'no'.

The non-permanent members are elected for a two year term by a two-thirds majority of the General Assembly. Retiring members are not eligible for immediate re-election.

The third is the Economic and Social Council (ECOSOC) with 27 members. Its job is to promote the welfare of people and to further human rights and fundamental freedoms.

The fourth is the Trusteeship Council (TC). It supervises the welfare of administered territories and helps them to achieve self government.

The fifth is the International Court of Justice (ICJ) which settles international legal issues or legal disputes between nations. It is the principal judicial organ of the United Nations. The Court sits at The Hague (Netherlands).

The sixth is the Secretariat, the administrative office of the UN. Its chief executive is the Secretary-General. He is appointed for a five year term by the General Assembly on the recommendations of the Security Council. He may be re-appointed.

The United Nations headquarters are in New York. It has its own flag. The official languages of the UNO are English, French, Chinese, Russian, Arabic and Spanish. The working languages are English and French only. The UN has a large number of specialised agencies like International Labour Organization (ILO), Food and Agriculture Organization (FAO), United Nations Educational, Scientific and Cultural Organization (UNESCO), World Health Organization (WHO), International Atomic Energy Agency (IAEA) etc. The Head-

The UN Headquarters are in New York.
The Headquarters of various UN organs and
agencies are in different cities all over the world

quarters of ILO, FAO, UNESCO, WHO, IAEA are in Geneva, Rome, Paris, Geneva, Vienna respectively. Other prominent UN agencies are United Nation's International Children's Emergency Fund (UNICEF), World Meteorological Organisation (WMO), International Monetary Fund (IMF), World Bank or International Bank for Reconstruction and Development (IBRD). Their Headquarters are at Paris, Geneva, Washington, Washington respectively.

It is an organisation which not only provides peace and security to the world but is also meant to look into various welfare and cultural aspects of life.

OOO

16

What is the mystery of Sphinx?

If you visit the three pyramids of Giza, you will be surprised to see a colossal statue of a beast with a man's head and a lion's body! This is the great Sphinx that sits in the desert of Egypt, about 12 km from Cairo. The statue has mysterious eyes and enigmatic expression. It gazes over the desert with a kind of mystical superiority. It is one of the most famous monuments in the world.

The Sphinx was carved out of the hill rock left over from the building of the Great Pyramid. It is about 20 m in height and 70 m in length. According to the popular belief, it was made some 5000 years ago to resemble the face of Chephren, a king of the fourth Egyptian dynasty. It was built during the reign of the Egyptian king Khafre.

Now the question arises - why was the Sphinx built? The Sphinx was a mythical monster. The Greeks thought of it as having the head of a woman, and body of a lion with wings. The Egyptians thought of it as a wingless lion with the head and breast of a man. It was believed that the Sphinx would ward off all evils from the cemetery around the pyramids.

Apart from the great Sphinx of Giza, there are many other Sphinxes in Egypt. Their heads represent different kings. In ancient Egypt, kings were considered to be descendants of the Sun God called *Ra*. When a king died, he himself was supposed to become the Sun God. Kings were also believed to have the strength of various beasts. So the Egyptians, sculptured their Gods and Kings in the shape of half human and half beast.

There is another Sphinx with a female face. It is made after the Queen Hatsphepsut, who had seized the throne and ruled the country. This Sphinx has a beard which represents queen Hatsphepsut's masculine powers.

Legend says that the Greek Sphinx often punished passers-by if they could not answer her questions

OOO

17

Why do woollen clothes kept in boxes get holes?

Most people think that holes in woollen clothes are made by some species of moths. But this is not true. Moths do not eat wool. Then how is this damage caused?

There are some larvae (caterpillars) of certain moths which feed on wool and other fabrics. The life-cycle of a moth is completed in four stages : egg, larvae, pupa

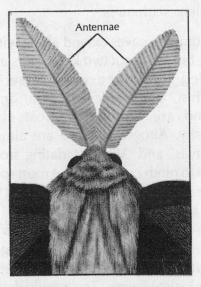

The caterpillar or larvae of certain moths feed on wool for their growth. They have strong and biting jaws

and adult. The female may lay more than 1000 eggs on wool, furs, rugs etc. In about a week, the eggs hatch into caterpillars. Caterpillar is the name given to the larvae of butterflies, moths and sawflies. During this stage, the caterpillar's main function is to eat and grow.

Examples of different kinds of moths are : the case-making moth, the webbing moth and the tapestry moth. Caterpillars have mouths with strong, biting jaws that can chew cloth and fur.

The case-making caterpillar makes a little tubular case out of the wool it eats and lines it with silk. The caterpillar of the webbing moth always leaves a cobwebby trail of its silk and spins a silk cocoon. The tapestry caterpillar eats into the wool, makes a series of tunnels and lines them with silk. When fully grown, it goes into one of the tunnels and stays there until it is ready to come out as a moth. This is how caterpillars make holes in our clothes.

Clothes can be protected against such damage by making sure that no eggs are laid by moth on the clothes. Before clothes are put away for the summer, they should be aired and brushed to ascertain that there are no eggs of moth on them. It is good to wrap clothes in heavy paper because moths cannot eat through paper. Moth balls keep the moths away, but do not kill the eggs or larvae which may already be present. The best way is to get the clothes dry cleaned before packing for the summer.

○○○

18

Why are Ajanta and Ellora Caves famous?

The Ajanta and Ellora caves attract many thousands of tourists every year. These caves are famous for their rock temples. The Ajanta caves are near Ajanta village, about 102 km north of Aurangabad (Maharashtra State). The Ellora caves are near Ellora village, about 29 km north-east of Aurangabad district.

The nearest rail head for those visiting Ajanta is the town of Jalgaon, though

Kailashnath Temple at Ellora built by the Rashtrakutas in the 8th century

Aurangabad is almost as close. There are also some provisions for accommodation around these caves.

At Ajanta, there are about 30 caves. All of them have Buddhist rock cut cave temples and monasteries. The temples are hollowed out of granite cliffs on the inner side of a 22 m (70 ft) high ravine in the Wagurna River Valley. These caves were excavated between the Ist century B.C. and the 7th century A.D. They are of two types : 'Chaityas' (sanctuaries) and 'Viharas' (monasteries). In the larger caves, the pillars reach upto the roof. Most of the interior walls are painted and depict the episodes of Buddha's life. The cave numbers 1, 2, 16, 17 and 19 possess some of the exquisite specimens of painting, while in the cave 1, 4, 17, 19, 24 and 26 one may find excellent sculptures.

At Ellora, the caves extend along with face of the hill for about two kilometers and are divided into three distinct series — Buddhist, Brahmanical (Hindu) and Jain — and are arranged almost chronologically. Altogether there are almost 34 'Chaityas' and 'Viharas' dating from the fourth to ninth centuries. The most splendid is the Kailashnath temple, 50 m (165 ft) long and 29 m (96 ft) high, cut from a single outcropping of rock. It is extensively carved with exceptionally vigorous sculptures of Hindu divinities and mythological figures. The temple dedicated to the Hindu God Shiva was built in the 8th century A.D. during the reign of the Rastrakutas. It has an open 'mandapan' in which colossal elephants and obelisks stand. It also has the sacred bull.

○○○

19

Who was Napoleon Bonaparte?

When Napoleon was a mere boy, he used to identify himself with the great heroes of ancient history he read about. Today he is remembered as one of the few men in history who have been immensely powerful and exercised much influence on others. He was a benevolent dictator, i.e. he used his power for the good of the people and not simply to meet his own ends.

Napoleon was born on August 15, 1769 in Ajaccio on the Island of Corsica. He was educated in France and when he was barely sixteen years old, he graduated from the military academy in Paris and became an army officer in 1785. When he was just twenty four years old, he fought during the French Revolution and was promoted to the rank of Brigadier General in 1793.

The threat of revolt brought him the command of the army of the interior in 1795. He, then, commanded the army of Italy in several victorious campaigns. His expeditions to Egypt and Syria in 1798-99 were unsuccessful, and he was defeated by the British. However, he finally returned to France. A coup in 1799 brought him to supreme power as the First Consul and he instituted a military dictatorship.

In the early 1800s, Napoleon made

Napoleon Bonaparte (1769–1821)

numerous reforms in the government and education. Under his rule industry expanded and universities flourished.

He defeated the Austrians in 1800, went to war against Great Britain in 1803 and had himself crowned the emperor in 1804. His greatest victory, the battle of Austerlitz against Austria and Russia came in 1805. Thereafter, except for temporary setbacks in Spain, he was successful until his disastrous invasion of Russia in 1812. In 1812 he invaded Russia with an army of more than six hundred thousand men. Even though he captured Moscow, his army didn't have enough supplies. So he had to retreat. Only about one hundred thousand men survived to march home.

After several other defeats, Napoleon abdicated and was sent into exile on the Island of Elba. He escaped from Elba and returned to France. He gathered a new army and regained power for the period known as 'the hundred days'. On July 15, 1815 he was defeated at Waterloo by the

British commander the Duke of Wellington. Napoleon surrendered to the British, and was exiled to the remote Island of St. Helena in South Atlantic Ocean, 1200 miles off the African Coast. He was to spend the last six years of his life on this Island. He frequently quarrelled with Sir Hudson Lowe, the Governor, who had repeatedly prevented Napoleon from escaping. However Napoleon never gave up these attempts to escape.

He also found time to write his memoirs.

He died on May 5, 1821. It was rumoured that he had been poisoned, but modern historians and doctors refute this misconception. Now it is believed that he probably died of stomach cancer.

Napoleon was a great soldier and a skilful diplomat, but he caused great sufferings to millions of people and ruined their lives.

OOO

20

How far can we see on the surface of earth?

When we look at the sky, we can see the sun, the moon and the stars which are millions of miles away from us. But if we stand on the sea shore, and look at the horizon, we may not be able to see beyond 4km. Why is it so?

We know that our earth is spherical in shape, i.e. it has a definite curvature. Though it is flat at the poles and bulges

out at the equator yet the curvature is everywhere.

If we stand on the sea shore, the higher we stand, the further we would be able to see. The horizon would appear further away with every increase in height above the sea level. At a height of 6m, we can see upto 10km. From the top of a 90m cliff we can see upto 34km, while at the summit of 1050m on a mountain, we would be able to see upto 130km. From an aircraft flying at a height of 4800m, we might see upto a distance of 265km.

So it is due to the curvature of the earth, that we cannot see beyond a certain distance.

The more the height above the sea level, the farther we can see on the surface of the earth

OOO

21

What are Auroras ?

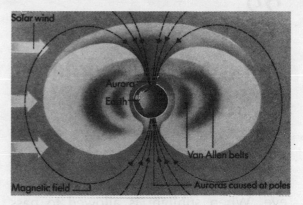

Auroras are usually restricted to the polar skies. They are also visible occasionally at lower latitudes due to fluctuation in the solar wind

An Aurora is a beautiful pattern of light that can sometimes be seen in the sky at night. The sky gets a glow with brilliant green, red, blue and yellow colours. An aurora near the north pole is called Aurora Borealis, or the Northern lights. An aurora near the south pole is called as Aurora Australis or the Southern lights. Sometimes both the phenomena are called "Aurora Polaris". But what exactly are auroras?

Systematic scientific studies in this field began in 1716, when a spectacular aurora appeared in Europe and was visible in the entire continent. The English astronomer Edmund Halley proved a relation between auroras and the earth's magnetic field. The most widely accepted theory about their origin is as follows.

We know that our sun is a hot ball of fire. It produces heat due to fusion reactions. As a result, charged particles like protons, electrons, etc. constantly flow out of the sun. The flow of these charged particles is called solar wind. These particles travel through space in all directions at a speed of 480km per second. As they enter the Earth's atmosphere, they are attracted by the Earth's magnetic field. The magnetic north and south poles change the direction and speed of these particles. These particles then collide with air molecules in the cold, thin upper atmosphere. This causes ionization, resulting in the production of coloured lights. These coloured lights are called Auroras.

Auroras are most pronounced, when the Earth's magnetic field is most disturbed or when there is an unusual increase in solar activity.

Aurora Borealis is most frequently seen around 70° north latitude, while Aurora Australis is seen around 70° south latitude. They are usually seen at heights of 80 km. Some may be as high as 1000 km. These phenomena have numerous forms. Some are like curtain arcs, while others are like rays and fan shaped coronas. They often produce crackling sound in the sky. They apparently move so fast that they are also called the 'Merry dancers'.

Some of the best displays of these natural lights can be seen around the Hudson Bay region in Canada, Northern Scotland, Southern Norway and Sweden. They are also seen in South Australia and Sri Lanka. At one time, the natives of Sri Lanka regarded them as messages from Lord Buddha! ○○○

22

What are ultraviolet rays?

Ultraviolet rays are electromagnetic waves that cannot be seen by the human eye. When sunlight is allowed to pass through a prism, it splits into seven colours. These colours are violet, indigo, blue, green, yellow, orange and red. Wavelength-wise distribution of the seven colours is known as spectrum. The ultraviolet rays form an invisible band, just outside the violet end of the visible spectrum. The band just beyond the red end is called infrared.

Light travels in the form of waves. These waves are produced by electrical oscillations. The frequency or wavelength of each colour in the spectrum is different. Frequency is measured by the unit 'hertz'. If a body vibrates once in a second, its frequency is said to be one hertz.

In the seven colours of the sun's spectrum, violet has the maximum frequency and red has the minimum frequency. In other words, wavelength of the violet colour is minimum, while that of red is maximum.

The observed wavelengths in the visible spectrum range from about 7.5×10^{-5} cm to 4×10^{-5} cm. Waves having wavelengths more than that of red light (7.5×10^{-5} cm) are called infrared waves. Infrared radiations comprise wavelengths ranging from 1 mm to about 7.5×10^{-5} cm. Waves having wavelengths more than infrared radiation are called microwaves. The range of microwaves lies between 1 mm to 30 cm. Waves with wavelengths more than those of microwaves are called radiowaves. On the other hand, radiations having wavelengths less than that of violet colour (4×10^{-5} cm) are called ultraviolet rays. Ultraviolet rays lie in the wavelength range of 4×10^{-5} to 10^{-6} cm. Beyond ultraviolet rays come X-Rays which roughly lie in the wavelength range of 10^{-6} to 10^{-8} cm. Beyond X-Rays come gamma rays. As we go from ultraviolet rays to gamma rays the wavelength decreases or the frequency increases. As the frequency increases, the amount of energy associated with the waves also increases. Thus X-Rays and gamma rays are very high energy radiations.

Energy associated with ultraviolet rays is also quite high. Overexposure to ultraviolet rays can cause skin burns, and may even lead to skin cancer. The sun produces a large amount of ultraviolet light most of which are absorbed by a gas called Ozone, in the upper atmosphere of the earth and as a result very small amount reaches the earth. If the entire amount of ultraviolet light were to reach us, life wouldn't have been possible on earth.

Ultraviolet rays are useful also but only in small amounts. They kill certain bacteria and help to change certain chemicals in the skin into Vitamin D. These rays are very harmful for the eyes as they cause eye-cataract. While working with ultraviolet light, one must wear coloured glasses. When these rays fall on certain substances, they produce fluorescence.

OOO

23

Who was Confucius?

Confucius was one of the greatest moral teachers and philosophers of China. He studied ancient Chinese writings with great devotion. These works taught him many new ideas about character development. In Chinese his name was 'Kung Fu-tzu'. This name was distorted by the catholic missionaries and became Confucius.

Confucius was born in the state of Lu, now part of Shantung in China. His family belonged to the lowest level of the aristocracy. His parents died when he was still young, and he grew up in poverty. Later, he became an official in the government of Lu, and was much respected.

China, during those days, was ruled by an Emperor who was a mere figurehead with very little powers. The provinces were controlled by corrupt and greedy feudal lords. The people were poor and neglected. Confucius felt disgusted at this state of affairs and left Lu in 484 B.C. He started preaching whatever he had learnt from the ancient Chinese writings. Human behaviour, morality and politics were the main elements of his teaching. At the age of 22, three years after his marriage, Confucius had started teaching how to lead a happy life. He said, 'Don't do to others, what you would not wish them to do to you.' He taught 'Thou shalt love thy neighbour as thyself'. He was a modest man who always said 'I teach nothing new.

Confucius (551-479 B.C) was a great moral teacher and thinker of ancient China

I only pass on the ancient wisdom.'

When he returned to Lu, he also held some important positions in the local government of his province. When he was made the governor of a city, he cleared the state of robbers, reduced taxes, improved people's living conditions and persuaded the ruling classes to lead charitable lives. According to one account, he was also made a minister. He tried his best to remove the evils ingrained in all branches of social life. But soon he realised that they were deep-rooted. So he resigned in disgust at the age of 54.

Confucius' own sayings were collected by his disciples and written down much later, in the book 'Lun Yu'. Confucius died in 479 B.C.

The religion founded by him is known as Confucianism. It includes ancestor worship, belief in the Supreme God and belief in nature spirits. Even today it influences millions of lives. ooo

24

Why is the Panama Canal so famous ?

The Panama Canal and the Suez Canal are the two most important man-made waterways of the world. The Panama Canal is an inter-oceanic waterway connecting the Atlantic and Pacific Oceans through the Isthmus of Panama. Ships sailing between the east and west coasts of the United States shorten their journey by about 8000 nautical miles by using this canal!

The history of the Panama Canal construction is very interesting. In the 16th

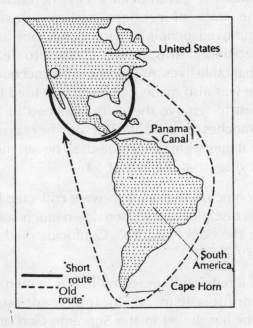

The Panama Canal has shortened the distance by 8,000 nautical miles from one coast of USA to the other coast

century, the Spanish conceived the idea of constructing a canal across the Isthmus. In 1846 the United States concluded a treaty with Columbia. In 1855, the United States extended financial help for the project. The Panama Canal company was formed which was headed by Ferdinande Lesseps — the builder of the Suez Canal. However, within ten years due to faulty planning, graft and the ravages of yellow fever, malaria and cholera, the company became bankrupt. In 1894, the new Panama Canal Company reorganised the work, but made little progress due to lack of money. Following Panama's declaration of Independence from Columbia in 1903, and the conclusion of the Hay-Bunau-Varilla Treaty between USA and Panama the canal building rights passed into U.S. hands. Work began in 1904 and finally the Canal was completed and first opened to traffic in August 1914. Since then many additions have been made. Its length is about 82 km. On 31st December 1999, Panama will take over full control of the canal from US.

The Canal consists of short sea-level sections at each end, three pairs of locks that lift ships to 26m above sea level, a 32 mile elevated section that includes Gatun Lake and a narrow eight-mile long excavated Channel, known as Gaillard Cut, running through the continental divide. The dimensions of its lock chambers (1000 ft in length, 110 ft in width and 41 ft in depth) permit most commercial ships as well as main navy ships to pass through the canal. Only very big ships cannot pass.

The canal locks operate by gravity flow of water from Gatun and Madden lakes. The locks are of uniform length, width and depth and permit simultaneous transit of ships in either direction. Each lock gate has two leaves 65 ft wide and 7 ft thick, set on hinges. The gates range in height from 47 to 82 ft. Their movements are controlled by motors. They are operated by a control tower.

The ships, including the waiting time, require 15 hours to negotiate the canal. Once a ship has been authorized to proceed, the average transit time through the canal, however, is seven to eight hours in deep water. The traffic through the Panama Canal has risen from 807 transits in 1916 to 15,523 transits in 1970. The cargo carried in 1970 amounted to 132,500,000 tons. Presently, average transits of ships carrying goods have been increased manifoldly.

The Canal has helped to reduce greatly the travelling distance for ships. Ships no longer need to go around Cape Horn to go from the east to the west coast of America. From one coast of North America to ports

Panama canal is a short-cut route between the Atlantic and Pacific oceans

on the other side of South America, the distance has been shortened by 3500 miles. Ships sailing between Europe and East Asia or Australia save about 2000 miles by using the canal.

In view of the increasing size of bulk carriers and container ships and the inability of the present canal to accommodate the large aircraft carriers of the U.S., there have been proposals to expand the present waterway.   OOO

25

What is a litmus paper?

Litmus is used in chemistry to detect the presence of alkalis and acids. Litmus is a dye made from small plants called lichens. It is either red or blue in colour and is used

in the form of a solution which is sometimes on a test paper.

When a lichen called *Rocella Tincotoria* is allowed to react with ammonia, potassium carbonate or lime, it gives a blue colour material. The paper is dipped into it and dried. This is known as a blue litmus paper, and is used to test acids. Acids turn blue litmus red.

Orchil or cudbear is a red dye obtained from another species of lichens. This is used to make red litmus paper. Alkannet or alkanna is another dye obtained from the root of the plant *Alkanna Tinotoria*. The colouring ingredient, alkannin, is soluble in alcohol, benzene and others. When white paper is impregnated with an alcoholic solution of alkannet, it becomes red. This red paper is turned blue or deep violet by alkalis.

Neutral solutions (neither acid nor base) do not change the colour of litmus.

When a chemist wishes to neutralize an acid solution, he first adds litmus solution. This changes its colour to red. The base is then added, until its colour changes to violet. The solution then becomes neutral, i.e. neither base nor acid and one more drop of base turns the solution blue.

When acids and bases react, they produce salts by neutralization. For instance, the common salt that we use in our food, is produced by the reaction of caustic soda and hydrochloric acid.

Nowadays, litmus paper is made from several substances such as azolitmin, crysthrolitmin, spaniolitmin etc. These are apparently mixtures of closely-related compounds that were identified in 1961 as derivatives of the heterocyclic compound phenoxazine. ooo

26

What is a Kaleidoscope?

A kaleidoscope is an optical instrument used to produce symmetrical geometric patterns on carpets, sarees, wallpapers etc. It is also an entertaining toy for the children.

Kaleidoscope was invented by a Scottish physicist, Sir David Brewster in 1816. It illustrates the image forming properties of combined inclined mirrors by successive reflections. If one object is placed between two plane mirrors, at right angles to each other, three images are produced by successive reflections. Similarly, if the mirrors are inclined at 60°, five symmetrical images are formed.

A kaleidoscope consists of three strips of mirrors inclined at an angle of 60° to one another. They are enclosed in a cylindrical tube. One end of this tube is closed by means of a piece of ground glass, while the other is closed by a piece of cardboard with a hole at its centre. Several multi - coloured glass pieces and beads are loosely enclosed between the three inclined mirrors with the help of a disc made of plane glass. Now when viewed through the hole of the cardboard, along the axis of the tube, a symmetrical pattern of images of the coloured glass pieces are seen.

When a person turns the kaleidoscope, the coloured glass pieces and beads change positions, thereby new patterns are produced. And so in this manner, an infinite number of combinations and patterns can be formed. The tubes used in most of the kaleidoscope are usually 25cm in length and 5-8cm in diameter. It is a very useful instrument for the designers. ooo

27

What is magnetism ?

Magnetism owes its name to the fact that the early Greeks found the natural magnetic material called Lodestone, in an area called Magnesia, a province of Asia Minor in 800 B.C. This stone was of black colour and an ore of iron called magnetite. This stone has several interesting properties.

Firstly, it has a strong attraction for iron. On experimenting, it was found that if a piece of lodestone was dipped in iron fillings and then lifted out, the fillings mainly get attached to certain parts, the other parts remaining bare. These regions of greatest attraction were called the poles and the place where there was little attraction was called a neutral region.

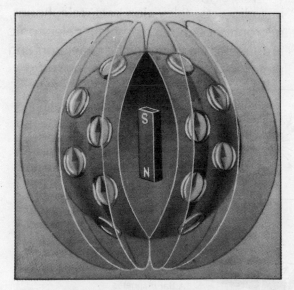

The earth acts as a great magnet, producing a magnetic field over the entire globe

It was also discovered that if a piece of lodestone was suspended by a thread or floated on a piece of wood, it came to rest in a definite direction — pointing towards north and south. The part pointing towards the north, was called the north pole, and the one pointing towards the south was called the south pole. This property was used by the Chinese in the 13th century to make use of magnets as compasses for finding the direction in sea voyages.

Experiments in this field further revealed that if two lodestones were brought together, the north and south poles attracted each other while the north-north and south-south poles repelled each other. This established the fact that dissimilar poles attract each other and similar poles repelled each other.

If a bar of iron or steel is rubbed from one end to the other end with a piece of lodestone, it also acquires magnetic properties and becomes a magnet. Such a magnet is known as an artificial magnet.

Gradually scientists working in this field also discovered that a magnet could be made by winding an insulated wire around a piece of iron and passing an electric current through it. This is called an electromagnet. Such magnets are used in electric motors.

The next important discovery in the field of magnetism came in 1600. The English scientist, Sir William Gilbert, suggested that the earth was a giant magnet. Thus he explained why a freely suspended magnet points to the north and south of the Earth.

During the next few hundred years, more

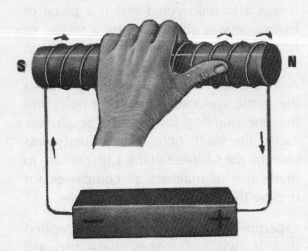

When electric current is passed through a wire wound around a piece of iron, it becomes an electromagnet

discoveries were made in the field of magnetism. However the phenomenon of magnetism was not properly understood, until the 19th century.

Now scientists know that magnetism is caused by moving electrons. All matter is made up of atoms, and atoms have a central core called nucleus, around which electrons revolve in different orbits. These electrons carry negative charge. Whenever an electric charge moves, it produces a

magnetic effect. So the moving electrons make a substance magnetic. Sometimes the magnetism of different electrons make a substance magnetic. Sometimes the magnetism of different electrons in each atom gets neutralized. That is why some materials are non-magnetic in nature. In fact the magnetic materials have magnetic domains which on magnetisation get lined up and the substance becomes a strong magnet. When a magnet is cut or broken each piece is still magnetic because its domains are still lined up.

Magnetism occurs most strongly in three metals: iron, cobalt and nickel. These metals can be used to make strong magnets. Iron is most commonly used because it is the cheapest and easily available of the three metals. Usually magnets are made of steel — an alloy of iron.

Magnets are very useful in our daily life. They are used in making the Mariner's compass to guide ships. They are also used in radio sets, television sets, telephones, microphones and in many other electronic instruments, such as electric generators and motors.

Magnetic fields of force are created around a magnet. When iron filings are sprinkled on a card resting on a bar magnet, the filings are found to be arranged in a series of curved lines, called the lines of force

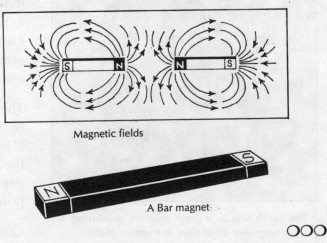

Magnetic fields

A Bar magnet

28

Who was Kalidasa ?

Kalidasa was a famous Indian poet and dramatist. He was a master of Sanskrit language and perhaps the greatest writer of any Indian epoch. He is usually compared with Shakespeare, the great English dramatist.

Kalidasa was known to be a Brahmin who was orphaned in childhood and brought up by a cowherd. He did not receive any formal education for eighteen years. Then, as luck would have it, he came to marry a princess — the marriage being brought about by a minister of the princess's father, with a view to teach her a lesson ! The boy was introduced as a learned Pandit. When the princess came to know of the truth, she was highly distressed. She insisted on Kalidasa acquiring higher education by pleasing goddess Kali. The goddess took pity on him and blessed him. Soon Kalidasa became a very learned man and a great poet. He called his wife as his 'guru'.

As legend goes, Kalidasa was one of the nine distinguished courtiers of King Vikramaditya of Ujjain. He lived some time between 170 B.C. when the Sunga King Agnimitra ruled and 634 A.D. to which Aihole inscription dates. Many scholars opine that Kalidasa was present during the reign of Chandragupta II (380 A.D. - 415 A.D.). According to a Sinhalese account, he died in Ceylon during the reign of Kumaradasa in the 6th century A.D.

Kalidasa was probably a very cultured man, full of humour and buoyancy. He had high esteem for women.

There are seven famous works of Kalidasa — three plays and four long poems. All of them are in Sanskrit.

Abhijnana Shakuntalam ('Shakuntala recognised") is regarded as his greatest play, and usually judged as the best Indian literary effort of any period. Taken from an Indian legend, it tells of the love between the nymph Shakuntala and King Dushyanta, his rejection of the girl and his child and their subsequent reunion in heaven. The work is important because of the child, Bharata, after whom Bharatvarsha came to be named.

The second play *Vikramorvasi* ('Urvasi won by valour') tells of a legend as old as the Vedas. Its theme is the love of mortal for a divine damsel.

The third play is *Malvikagnimitra*. Three famous long poems of Kalidasa are *Raghuvansa* (Dynasty of Raghu), *Kumar-Sambhava* (Birth of the War God) and *Meghaduta* (Cloud Messenger). The first recounts the legends of Rama's forebears and descendants. The second tells the story of Siva and Parvati. The third deals with the message of a lover for his absent beloved. The fourth one is the *Ritusamhara* (The Garland of the Seasons) — perhaps an early work.

Kalidasa's works reflect on the aristocratic society, sure of its dignity and power. To him goes the credit of exploiting Sanskrit to the full. Till today he is regarded as unrivalled by any other Indian writer.

OOO

29

Who was the founder of Din-i-Ilahi?

Jalal-ud-Din Mohammed Akbar, the greatest of the Mughal Emperors of India, founded in 1582, a new religion called Din-i-Ilahi (or Divine Religion). This religion tried to bring together the Hindus and Muslims by combining the good points of Hinduism and Islam. Akbar wanted Hindus and Muslims to worship God at the same shrine in a common ritual.

Din-i-Ilahi was essentially an ethical system, prohibiting such sins as lust, sensuality, slander and pride and laying emphasis on virtues of piety, prudence, abstinence and kindness. The soul was encouraged to purify itself, through yearning for God, celibacy was condoned and the slaughter of animals was forbidden. There were no sacred scriptures or a priestly hierarchy in this newly-founded religion.

But this religion did not attract many followers and practically died with Akbar.

Akbar (1542-1605) was the son of Humayun and the grandson of Babur. He was born on October 15, 1542 at Umarkot, Sind which is now in Pakistan. Akbar became the governor of Punjab at the age of 13, and succeeded his father, Humayun, to the Mughal throne in 1556. With able

Akbar was one of the most secular rulers of medieval India

generalship, he overthrew his rivals and embarked upon a career of conquest, which by 1562, gave him domain over Punjab and Multan, the basin of the Ganges and Jamuna rivers, Gwalior to the south and Kabul in Afghanistan. Subsequently he crossed the Narmada river into the Deccan, and intended his dominion southward. By 1605 his empire contained 15 provinces, or *subahs* and stretched from the Hindu Kush mountains to the Godavari river and from Bengal to Gujarat.

In order to preserve the unity of his empire, Akbar maintained good relations with the non-muslim population. He won the loyalty of the Hindus as well as other communities also. He reformed and strengthened his central administration, centralised his financial system and reorganized tax collection procedure. Akbar was loved by everyone.

ooo

30

What are proteins ?

Proteins are very important chemical compounds contained by all plants and animals. Probably life would not exist without proteins.

The word 'protein' originated from a Greek word which means 'first', because proteins are considered to be the most essential part of the living matter. These chemical compounds are made up of chains of amino acids. There are more than 21 amino acids. Each amino acid has carbon, nitrogen, oxygen and hydrogen as its constituents. The different amino acids combine in different ways to form thousands of proteins.

Proteins work in many different ways in the body. An important group of proteins, called enzymes act as catalysts in many biochemical reactions. Enzymes are essential for metabolic activity of the body. Some hormones, such as insulin, are also proteins. They are called regulatory

proteins because they regulate blood pressure and blood glucose level. Immune proteins protect the body against infection. Transport proteins such as haemoglobin carry vital substances to different parts of the body. Movement of the muscles is helped by proteins called contractive proteins. Thus proteins are vital for the body.

Proteins are made of amino acids. Each amino acid has carbon, nitrogen, oxygen and hydrogen in it, some also have small amounts of other elements. Plants make their own amino acids, and can therefore make their own proteins. Animals make some amino acids, but not all that are necessary for life. These amino acids which animals cannot make themselves are called essential amino acids. Animals get them from their food. When an animal eats protein-rich food, the proteins are broken down into individual amino acids. These amino acids are then used by the body to make different proteins, through a process known as protein synthesis.

Protein-rich food is necessary for the well-being of an organism. Foods such as milk, eggs, fish, meat and cheese have sufficient proteins, as well as the essential amino acids. Some substances such as rice and potato, do not have certain essential amino acids, and are not considered as good protein sources.

A deficiency of proteins makes a person slow, listless and highly susceptible to infectious diseases. Protein deficiency may also cause brain damage and mental retardation. Hence one is advised to take a balanced diet, rich in proteins. ooo

Foods rich in protein are meat, fish, cheese, eggs, peas, beans, and nuts

31

Why is Khajuraho famous ?

The figures in the temples of Khajuraho are the finest examples of art, architecture and sculpture

The village of Khajuraho is in the Chattarpur district of Madhya Pradesh. This place was the capital of Chandela kings from 9th to 13th century. These kings built 85 temples between 950 A.D and 1050 A.D. Out of these only 20 temples survive today. These temples were dedicated to Siva, Vishnu, Brahma and the Tirthankaras.

During this age India was called the Asian El dorado. The people were prosperous and happy and the fertile land yielded plenty of crops, fruits and flowers. This climate was most conducive to creative efforts and temple-building emerged as its chief form.

The Khajuraho temples are of the Indo-Aryan type. Each temple stands on a high platform and the customary enclosure is absent. The temples are in three groups and occupy an area of about eight square miles. The western group, the largest and most important, is situated at the axis of the Lalguan-Rajnagar road. The eastern group comprises Brahmin and Jain shrines close to the present Khajuraho village. The southern group is almost one mile away from the south of the village.

The western group comprises the oldest Chaunsath Yogini, the Kendriya Mahadeva, the Devi Jagadambe, Chitragupta temple, Vishwanatha and Nandi temples. The other temples of this group are Parvati temple, Lakshmana temple, Matangesvara and Varah temples.

The Eastern group consists of Vamana temple, Javari temple, Brahma temple, Adinatha temple, Parsvnatha temple and several other Jain temples.

The Southern group has only two temples — Duladeo temple and Chaturbhuj temple.

The temples of Khajuraho present a unique art and sculpture. They have engraved figures of gods and goddesses, celestial nymphs and hand-maidens ('apsaras' and 'surasundaris'), bold serpents and leonine beasts and myriads of women. 'Mithuna' couples (rioting figures of love and lust) have accorded Khajuraho a distinctive status. At the centre of each temple there is the statue of an honoured god.

In addition to these temples there is a small Archaeological Museum at Khajuraho, showing mainly sculptures collected on temple sites. The temples are visited by thousands of visitors every year.

○○○

46

32

What are the two houses of our parliament ?

The parliament or the Central Legislature of India consists of the President and the two Houses: The Rajya Sabha (the Upper House) and The Lok Sabha (the Lower House).

The President is an integral part of our parliamentary democracy, but it is still in many ways above the parliament. All bills passed by the parliament must have his assent before they become law. The parliament has to meet atleast twice a year and at an interval of not more than six months.

The maximum strength of the Lok Sabha is 545 (525 from the States and 20 from the Union Territories), and of the Rajya Sabha 250 (12 nominated).

The Lok Sabha, whose life is five years after every general elections, is the lower house of the parliament and comprises members directly elected by the people. Every citizen of India who is 18 years of age or above has been given the right to vote. To qualify as a candidate for election to the Lok Sabha, one must be a citizen of India and should not be less than 25 years of age. He should also possess qualifications prescribed by the parliament. The Lok Sabha elects two of its members as Speaker and Deputy Speaker for a term in consistent with the life of the Lok Sabha. The Speaker is the presiding officer of the Lok Sabha. He does not vote but can use his vote in case of a tie. He presides over the joint sitting of the Lok Sabha and the Rajya Sabha. The Speaker or the Deputy

The Parliament House of India

Speaker does not preside when a resolution for his removal is discussed in the House. The Lok Sabha can be dissolved before the stipulated or due time.

The Rajya Sabha is the upper house of the parliament, and is made up of representatives from the states or the constituent units of the Indian Union. It is a permanent body, one-third of its members retiring every two years. Thus every member enjoys a six - year term. The Rajya Sabha can not be dissolved since it is a permanent body. To qualify for election to the Rajya Sabha, the candidate should be a citizen of India, and not less than 30 years of age. He should possess such other qualifications as may be prescribed, under any law made by the parliament. The Vice-President is the ex-officio Chairman of the Rajya Sabha. The Deputy Chairman is elected from amongst the members of the Rajya Sabha.

The Lok Sabha is more powerful than the Rajya Sabha. No bill can become a law, until it has been passed by it. The Lok Sabha shares with the Rajya Sabha the power of amending the constitution. It can also initiate a charge of impeachment against the President. The elected members of this house form a part of the electoral college for the election of the President. The Vice-President is also elected by members of this house jointly with the members of the Rajya Sabha.

No bill can become a law unless it has been passed by the Rajya Sabha. It shares the power with the Lok Sabha to amend the constitution. It can also introduce any bill except a money bill. No money bill can originate in the Rajya Sabha. All money bills passed by the Lok Sabha are sent to the Rajya Sabha for its recommendations. Such bills should be returned within 14 days, otherwise, they are deemed to have been passed. The members of the Rajya Sabha take part in the election of the President and the Vice-President. OOO

33

What is Ionosphere ?

The story of the discovery of the Ionosphere is very interesting. On December 12, 1901, G. Marconi demonstrated with his newly discovered wireless equipment that radio waves could travel across the Atlantic Ocean. This demonstration could not be explained with radio waves travelling in straight lines over the spherical shaped earth for such a long distance. So the scientists came to believe in the existence of some layer in the upper atmosphere, which acts like a mirror for radio waves and reflects them.

In 1902, O Heaviside of England and A.E. Kennelly of the United States confirmed the existence of such a layer. This was called Heaviside-Kennelly layer. Watson Watt, the inventor of radar, coined the name ionosphere to this layer. Later in 1925, E.V. Appleton and M.A.F. Barnett of England experimentally proved the existence of the ionosphere.

How did the ionosphere come into existence ?

The ionosphere owes its origin mainly to the ultra-violet radiations coming from the sun and the cosmic rays. We know that our upper atmosphere contains a thin layer of air and ozone gas in the atomic state. So when the ultra-violet rays and cosmic rays hit the atoms of these gases, electrons and positive ions are produced and the gases get ionized. This ionized region of upper atmosphere is called ionosphere. The ionosphere is electrically neutral because the number of negatively charged electrons and positive ions is equal. This state is known as the plasma state. The ionosphere extends from about 50 km to 500 km above the earth's surface.

When a radiowave below a certain frequency (30 MHz) is incident on the ionosphere, it is reflected back to the earth, just as a beam of light is reflected by a mirror and can be received by radio receivers. In fact, the ionosphere is mainly responsible for short-wave global communications. Without it radiowaves would not have been reflected back to the earth, and consequently reception would have been impossible.

There are three distinct ionized layers in the ionosphere — D, E and F. Usually D layer exists between 50 to 90 km above the earth, E layer 100 to 120 km and F layers at 130 to 450 km. It does not end at F layer, but extends many thousand kilometres beyond F layer. The F layer is made up of two layers F^1 and F^2.

The ionosphere is thought to be produced by absorption of Sun's ultra-violet radiation

When a signal from a transmitting station passes through the different layers of the ionosphere, the electric field of the electromagnetic waves interacts with the electrons present in the ionosphere. As a result of this interaction, the signal gets reflected in a similar way, as light gets reflected from a mirror. There is a critical frequency beyond which the signals are not reflected by the ionosphere, but get transmitted through it. Television frequencies are high enough not to get reflected from the ionosphere. That is why, ionosphere is not used for TV transmission.

The ionosphere is thus nature's boon which is highly useful for global communications.

ooo

Which is the Land of Midnight Sun ?

The land of the midnight sun is the popular name of the Scandinavian country of Norway, where from mid-May till the end of July, the sun doesn't set completely. As a result, there is a long twilight, instead of night during this period. On its northernmost tip, the sun never sets completely for about two months in the summer, but at the same time there is no sun for two months in the winter.

The midnight sun is seen in the polar regions when the sun appears above the horizon at midnight. Due to the tilt of the earth's axis to the plane of its orbit by 23.5 degrees, each hemisphere is inclined towards the sun during the summer and away from it during winter. Due to this, the Arctic and Antarctic regions see the midnight sun for some time each year. When there is winter in the Antarctic region, day is indistinguishable from night. The sun does not rise and there is total darkness in the Antarctic circle.

At this time (April to July) the Arctic circle enjoys summer with the sun visible for 24 hours a day. The sun rises in the sky and moves very slowly. Towards evening, it begins to set, until it reaches the horizon. Then it begins to climb again. At the Arctic circle, this continues for about two months, but the actual midnight occurs on June 21.

After six months, the Arctic region plunges into darkness and the Antarctic circle is bathed in sunlight. Midnight Sun occurs in Antarctic from mid-November to the end of January.

Extreme northern latitudes are sometimes called the 'Lands of the Midnight Sun'. The Midnight Sun can also be seen near Bylot, an island of northern Canada. Every year thousands of tourists flock here to see one of the most impressive and extraordinary sights — the midnight sun.

Midnight sun appears due to the constant appearance of the sun within the Arctic and Antarctic circles above the horizon during summer

OOO

35

What is a sextant ?

The word sextant comes from the Latin word "sextus" which means one-sixth. The sextant is an instrument used for measuring angles, primarily altitudes of celestial bodies like the sun or a star. It is also used in navigating ships and planes to determine the latitude. The height of the tall buildings and pillars can also be measured with the help of a sextant.

Sextant was invented by an Englishman, John Hadley in 1731. The device consists of an arc of a circle, which is usually one-sixth of a circle or 60 degrees, and a movable radial arm pivoted at the centre. A movable mirror is fixed at the end of the arm. The other end extends to the scale. A telescope is mounted on the sextant, and a glass mirror is mounted in front of the telescope.

To operate the sextant, the operator looks through the telescope straight at the horizon. Moving the mirror, the sun or any particular star is made to appear exactly on the horizon. The arm which moves the mirrors gives the required measurement of the angle. From this angle and the exact time of the day, the latitude is determined by means of published tables.

The invention of sextant has laid the foundation of modern navigation.

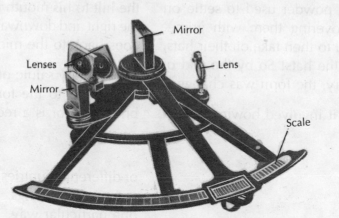

The navigational sextant is an invaluable instrument for sailors wishing to pinpoint their position at sea

36

Why do soldiers salute?

The custom of saluting has always existed in all cultures. A salute is a gesture of respect to a person of superior rank.

Until the 18th century, junior officers saluted by doffing their hats. In fact civilians still salute in this manner. This custom probably goes back to the middle ages when a knight would raise his helmet visor or uncover his head before a lord.

After the 18th century, there came a change in the method of saluting, for a very practical reason ! When soldiers fired their muskets, black powder used to settle on their hands, covering them with grime. And if they had to then take off their hats, it would spoil the hats! So by the end of the 18th century, the form was changed.

In some cases it involved bowing and in

A salute is a sign of expression of greeting or respect often by raising the right hand to the forehead in a certain way

others kneeling or laying on the ground or gesturing with hand and arm in a special manner. An officer or soldier carrying a sword at the shoulder salutes by bringing the hilt to his mouth and then the point to the right and downward. This form of salute goes back to the middle ages.

The military salute of today — raising the right hand to the forehead or to the hat brim or visor is a recent innovation.

ooo

37

How did different countries get their names ?

We do not know, how the naming of places started in the beginning. The names of different countries, like the names of so many other things, did not originate in one particular way. They have originated in a variety of ways from different sources.

For instance, the name India began with a Sanskrit word 'Sindhu' meaning a river, which originally applied to the great stream on the western edge of the peninsula. The Greeks called it Indus, and the country near it, India. The other name 'Bharatvarsha' originated from 'Bharat'- the brave son of Shakuntala.

Some countries owe their names to their discoverers, some others to their tribals or even to their conquerors. For example, America is named after Amerigo Vespucci, the explorer ; France after the Frankish invaders and England after the Angles.

The Greeks and Romans called England 'Albion' which is probably derived from the latin word 'Albus'. It means white, referring to her white natives — the first thing the Romans would have seen on their arrival.

There is an interesting story about the origin of Quebec's name. The French sailors who first saw the rocky promontory cried 'Quel bec' ! This means 'What a beak'?

The official name of Holland is the Netherlands. Finland is called Suomi by its inhabitants. Tasmania has been named after its dark-skinned natives called Tasmanoids. Similarly Australoids were the ancestors of the present inhabitants of Australia.

Similarly origin of the names of all other countries can also be traced one way or the other. ooo

38

Why is a ship's speed measured in Knots?

Sailors in olden times developed a very interesting method of measuring the speed of a ship. They used a log of wood for the purpose. The log had a weight tied to one end and a long rope attaching the other end to the stern or back of the ship. The log floated behind the ship and the rope was released slowly as the ship sailed on.

The speed of the ship could be calculated by measuring how much rope had been let out in a given time. Later, knots were tied at equal distances along the rope. A sailor counted the number of knots passed through his hands in a certain time. This gave the speed of the ship. Hence 'knot' became the unit of measuring speed!

The knot is the abbreviated term for one nautical mile (6076.12 ft) per hour. It is slightly longer than the statute mile (5280 ft). It is equal to 1852 m.

Logs are still used to gauge the speed of the ship. But today there are special metal rods with flat blades around them. As the ship sails through water, the metal rod rotates and twists the rope. The spinning rope works as a device back on the ship, that shows the actual speed.

The world's fastest ship is a 112-ton U.S. Navy test warship, the SES - 100 B, which in 1976, reached a speed of 88.88 knots or 102.35 mph. However, in 1980 a US 100-ton Navy hovercraft achieved a speed of 91 knot or 170 km. per hour.

ooo

39

When were the stupas of Sanchi built ?

Sanchi is famous for its stupas. This historic site is located to the west of Betwa river in Raisen district, Bhopal (Madhya Pradesh). It is about 90 m above its surroundings, and is the site of many famous Buddhist monuments. But how did the stupas come in to existence ?

Sanchi is the site of three stupas. Stupa No. 1, also called the Great Stupa, is one of the most magnificent monuments of its time. Its construction was probably started by the Emperor Ashoka in the mid-third century B.C. and later it was enlarged. It is enclosed by a massive stone railing pierced by four gateways. These gateways have elaborate carvings depicting the life of Buddha. Each gateway is made up of two square posts, topped by statues of animals and dwarfs. It consists of a base, bearing a hemispherical dome (*anda*) representing the dome of heaven enclosing the earth. It is surmounted by a square-rail unit (*harmika*) from which rises a mast (*yatsi*). It symbolizes the cosmic axis. The mast bears umbrellas (*chhatras*) that represent the various heavens (*devaloka*).

Stupa No. 2, with railing decorations, has carvings relating to late Sunga period (1st century B.C.). Stupa No. 3, with its single gateway (*torana*), was constructed in the late first century A.D. These stupas have become an important site for tourist attraction. Thousands of people visit them every year.

Certain other specimens of celebrated Indian sculpture are to be found at Sanchi. These include a commemorative pillar erected by Emperor Ashoka (265-238 B.C.) and the famous Gupta Temple built in the early 5th century.

Sanchi stupa is covered with designs craved in stone. It depicts incidents in the life of Buddha

OOO

40

How is the altitude of a flying airplane determined ?

While travelling in a plane, have you ever looked down and wondered why everything on the earth looked so small ? The reason is that planes fly at great heights. The greater the height, the smaller will be the appearance of the objects on the earth. The height of the plane is measured by an instrument called the altimeter.

There are five main types of altimeters. The first is the pressure altimeter. It basically measures the decrease in air pressure as the altitude increases. The second is the radio altimeter. This is used to measure the time required by a radio pulse to travel from the airplane to the ground and back, much like a radar. The third type is the sonic altimeter which makes use of sound waves. The fourth type measures the altitude by using the effect of atmospheric pressure on the boiling point of a liquid. The fifth type is the capacitance altimeter.

The pressure altimeter is basically an aneroid barometer. It contains an aneroid capsule made of metallic bellows from which air has been exhausted. The bellows expand or contract as the atmospheric pressure changes. As the atmospheric pressure decreases with altitude, it measures the change in pressure by means

of an arrangement of levers and gears. The expansion or contraction of the bellows changes the rotation of pointers relative to a dial. A pressure altimeter has to be adjusted to the air pressure on the ground before each flight. It is also adjusted for variations in atmospheric pressure caused by weather changes.

In a radio altimeter, the radio pulses are sent to the ground. They get reflected from the ground, and are picked up by a receiver in the aircraft. The time taken by the radio pulse to travel from the aircraft to the ground, and back is measured. Half of this time, when multiplied by the speed of the radio pulse, gives the altitude of the plane. These types of altimeters are very accurate and hence are called absolute altimeters. They are used in automatic navigation and in blind landing systems.

The third type of altimeter makes use of sound waves instead of radio pulses. This is called sonic altimeter. It sends sound waves from the aircraft to the ground, which bounce back. The time taken by the sound waves, multiplied with the velocity of sound in air, gives double the height of the airplane. Half of this distance is the real altitude of the plane.

The fourth type of altimeter makes use of the effect of atmospheric pressure on the boiling point of a liquid. The instrument, known as a hypsometer, consists of a cylindrical vessel in which water is boiled. This is surrounded by a jacket through which the water-vapour circulates around a thermometer. The higher the altitude, the lower the pressure, and consequently lower the temperature at which the liquid boils. The boiling temperature is thus inversely proportional to the altitude. Hence by measuring the boiling point of the liquid, one can measure the altitude of the airplane.

41

What are the underground rivers ?

We all know about the rivers which flow on the surface of the Earth. But can you imagine a river flowing under the surface of the Earth? Such rivers are called underground rivers. How are these formed?

An underground river is formed when the uppermost surface of the earth easily allows rain water to pass through, to a more solid soil structure. This water starts flowing due to the pressure of the upper water, and hence forms an underground river.

The flow of water within rocks depends upon two properties : the rock's porosity and permeability. A porous rock is one which has sufficient empty spaces to allow for the passage of water. In general elastic rocks are porous, and crystalline rocks have low porosity. Permeability refers to the property with which a fluid can flow through the empty passages. It depends upon the size of the pores. Underground water flows along the steepest slope.

A capacitance altimeter indicates altitude by measuring the difference between electrical changes of the earth and the plane. Altimeters are thus very useful instruments for guiding and controlling aircrafts.

○○○

Limestone rocks are honeycombed, with tunnels and caves. When the rain water containing acid, falls on them, an interesting process takes place. The water starts flowing through the tunnels and caves seeking a way out. As the water moves along, it wears away more and more of the surrounding rock, to produce long tunnels. Eventually an underground river is formed which finally reaches the sea by surfacing at a certain place.

There is another process through which an underground river is created. When a powerful spring can't sprout forth, owing to the solidity and compactness of the rocks, it starts flowing underground.

The distance travelled underground by such a river varies. In some cases it is more and in some others, less. The famous Rhine of France travels only a short distance underground. There is a famous underground river in Somerest (U.K.).

Speleogists ,i.e. those who explore caves, have tried to follow the course of some underground rivers but many passages are too narrow to get through. In this regard a process has been devised by some researchers. It involves mixing of certain dye in a river's water to recognise it when it surfaces again.

○○○

42

What is a catalyst ?

A catalyst is a substance which changes the rate of a chemical reaction, merely by its presence and without undergoing any change itself. With the help of a catalyst, the reaction may become faster or slower. The process is known as catalysis.

Now the question arises— how does a chemical substance increases the rate of reaction simply by its presence ?

Catalysts may work in two ways. Surface or contact catalysts work by adsorption. The reacting chemicals are adsorbed to form a concentrated layer at the surface of the catalyst. Due to this, the chemicals react more quickly. For example, hydrogen and oxygen combine at the surface of powdered platinum to make water.

According to another theory, a catalyst forms an unstable intermediate compound with one of the reactants. This compound reacts with other reactants more quickly forming the final product. At the end, the catalyst is recovered in the original state by different chemical methods.

It has been observed from different experiments that only small quantities are enough to alter the rate of the chemical reaction. Enzymes in plants and animals are catalysts that speed up chemical reactions in them.

Catalysts are of several types but are mainly classified in two categories. Positive and negative. Positive catalysts are those substances which increase the rate of a chemical reaction, while negative catalysts retard it. For example, when potassium chlorate is heated to about 400°C, oxygen is liberated but when manganese dioxide is added to it, oxygen is formed only at 200°C. Manganese dioxide acts as a positive catalyst in this reaction. On the other hand gypsum which is added to portland cement to slow down the hardening process, acts as a negative catalyst. In some chemical reactions, the product itself acts as a catalyst. This is called autocatalysis. For example, the decolourisation of the potassium permanganate solution by oxalic acid is very slow in the beginning, but once it starts, it becomes very fast. This is due to the fact that manganese ions act as an autocatalyst.

If the reactants and the catalyst are in the same phase, the catalysis is called homogenous catalysis. But if the reactants and the catalyst are in different phases then it is known as heterogeneous catalysis.

Catalysis is very important for the production of plastics, rubber, gasoline, oils, fats, sulphuric acid and ammonia. Catalytic reactions also occur in our body. Enzymes act as catalysts to speed up the digestive process. Enzymes also speed up processes in the cells of plants and animals. In making Vanaspati ghee, nickel is used as a catalyst in the process of hydrogenation.

○○○

43

How did the Egyptians preserve mummies ?

A mummy is a dead body embalmed or treated for burial with preservatives. The Egyptians believed in life after death. They thought of the soul as a bird with a human face that could fly around by day, but must return to the dead body at night for fear of evil spirits ! The body was therefore preserved after death in the form of a 'mummy'.

The word 'mummy' comes from the Arabic word 'mummiyah' which means a body preserved by wax or tar. Before about 3000 B.C., the Egyptians used to bury their dead in a curled-up position in the hot sand of the desert. The sand preserved their bodies.

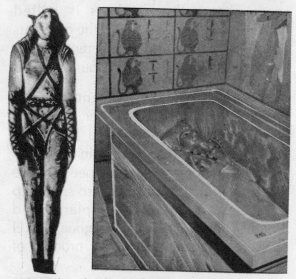

Mummies of rich people were preserved by using chemicals and wrapping them in linen cloths

Later, important persons were buried in tombs cut from the rocks. But the pyramids and rock tombs were not so dry as the desert sand, and moisture could have spoiled the body. So they had to develop some way for preserving the bodies in the tombs. This is why they developed the art of mummification.

The process of mummy preservation varied from age to age. When a person died, some of the internal organs like brain, digestive system and lungs were removed. These were preserved separately and placed in four vases called 'Canopic Jars'. Later they were replaced in the body. Then the body was treated with salts. The salts acted with the dry desert air to remove moisture from the body. Once dried, the body was bathed, rubbed with resin from pine trees, and wrapped in hundreds of meters of linen. This whole process took about 70 days.

In the meantime the special case for the mummy was made by carpenters. If the man was rich and important, a number of mummy cases were made—each one fitting closely in the other. Artists decorated the cases with many bright colours. The walls of the tomb were decorated with tents and pictures which told the story of the man's life. Then all the things that had made the man comfortable in his lifetime were collected and placed in the tomb. In this way, the Egyptians believed that they had prepared the man for his next life.

The Egyptians also believed that certain animals, like the cat, were sacred. These animals were also mummified and buried in animal cemeteries.

○○○

44

What are the various artificial sweetening agents ?

A large number of beverages and drinks make use of artificial sweeteners. People suffering from diabetes do not take sugar in their diet. Instead they depend on an artificial sweetening agent, Saccharin. Let us see what are the different artificial sweeteners.

Sugar or sucrose is a natural sweetening agent. Man obtains it from plants like sugarcane, sugarbeet, palm or maple juice. Fructose is another natural sweetening agent which is one and a half times sweeter than sugar. It occurs in various fruits and honey. Glucose, maltose, lactose etc are other natural sugars, but are less sweet than sucrose or fructose. All these sweetening agents possess food value and provide energy to the body.

Scientists have now developed artificial sweetening agents which surpass the sweetening power of natural sugars. These are the derivatives of various classes of organic compounds such as amides, imides, nitriles, oximes, ureas, nitroanilines etc and possess no nutritive value.

Saccharin was the first artificial sweetening agent. It was discovered by Ira Remsen and C. Fahlberg of John Hopkins University, U.S.A. in 1879. Its chemical name is O-sulphobenzimide and is prepared from toluene. It is an odourless white crystalline solid. It is 500 to 700 times sweeter than sugar. It is used as a sweetening agent in the form of sodium and ammonium salts.

The other common artificial sweetening agents are dulcine, perillartine, sucaryl, stevioside, P - 4000, beta-imino, beta-phenyl propionitrile etc. Dulcine is a urea derivative which is 300 times sweeter than sucrose. Perillartine is an oxime derivative. Sucaryl is a sulphamate derivative and is nearly 100 times sweeter than sucrose. Stevioside is a glycoside derivative and is 300 times sweeter than sugar. P-4000 is known as 2-amino-4-nitro-n-propoxy benzene and is a nitroaniline derivative. It is 4000 times sweeter than sucrose. Betaimino-beta phenyl propionitrilo is a nitrile derivative and is 330 times sweeter than sugar. The sweetest substance is called *Talin* — discovered in West Africa from certain plants' seed-covers. This substance is 6,150 times as sweet as a one percent sucrose solution.

Many artificial sweeteners have a poisonous effect on the human body. For example, P-4000 and Dulcine cause liver tumours. Therefore, almost all except saccharin and sucaryl have been prohibited as food additives.

○○○

45

What do A.M. and P.M. mean ?

What do we mean when we say the time is 6 a.m. or 6 p.m.? How did the expressions 'a.m.' and 'p.m.' originate ?

We know that the rotation of the earth about its axis causes day and night. The part of the earth which faces the sun has day, and the remaining part, night. From the time the sun rises in the east and till the time it sets in the west, there is daylight. When the sun is high in the sky, directly overhead, we call it noon or midday.

Ancient man could tell the time during day from the position of the sun in the sky. When the sun is overhead, we can draw an imaginary line across the sky, from the north to the south. This is called the meridian. It is derived from the Latin word *Meridies* meaning mid-day. While the sun is still to the east of this line or meridian, it is morning. So a.m. is an abbreviation for ante-meridian or before mid-day. After the sun has crossed the meridian, it is afternoon. So 'p.m.' is the abbreviation for 'post-meridian' or after mid day.

Hence to express the time from 12 noon to 12 O' clock at night, we use the term p.m., and from 12 O'clock at night to 12 O' clock noon we use a.m. ⭘⭘⭘

46

How does water become cool in an earthen pitcher ?

Water contained in an earthen pitcher becomes cool in a few hours. Do you know why this happens ?

According to a well-known principle of physics evaporation causes cooling. When a liquid evaporates its temperature falls because the heat required for vaporisation is supplied by the liquid itself. Due to the loss of heat, the temperature of the liquid goes down.

An earthen pitcher has a large number of pores. When water is placed in the vessel, it oozes out of the pores and evaporates. This evaporation causes cooling of water. If the same water is placed in a glass or metal container, no evaporation takes place as they don't have any pores. Since no evaporation takes place, the liquid does not become cool.

Similarly the cooling effect of a fan is due to the evaporation of the sweat coming out of the pores of our skin. Dogs hang out their tounges in order to expose them to the air for evaporation, so that they may enjoy the cooling effect. The watering of the streets in summer also produces a cooling effect by evaporation. ⭘⭘⭘

47

How did different superstitions begin ?

Superstitions have played a unique role in the human life right from the beginning of civilization. Even today we may find many people who are superstitious about different things. Do you know how different superstitions began?

Ancient man could not explain various natural phenomena like thunder, lightning and climatic changes. He knew little about the sun, moon, comets and meteors. So he formulated his own theories about these phenomena, thus leading to the first kind of superstitious beliefs.

A superstition is usually born out of fear, which is contrary to reason and cannot be proved by experience. For instance, a comet was a mysterious phenomenon, and was considered unlucky — a sign of imminent plague or war. People also believed that if one looked at the moon for a long time, he would get 'moonstruck'. In fact the word 'lunatic' has been derived from the Latin word *Luna* which means moon. Similarly, farmers used to think that a growing moon encouraged the growth of crops!

Superstitions were also built up around animals. In Egypt, cats were worshipped as sacred animals. In Europe, it is thought very lucky to have a black cat walk across one's path. In North America, the reverse is true. In India a black cat crossing your path is considered as a sign of bad luck. The howl of an owl is a sign of approaching death, and so on.

Over the centuries, superstitions about 'lucky' and 'unlucky' numbers were also developed. For example, 13 is considered to be an unlucky number throughout the world.

Ancient people in Scandinavian countries believed that thunder and lightning were caused when their God Thor threw his hammer at his enemies.

Sneezing is considered a bad omen. When someone sneezes, people often say 'God bless you'.

With the advance in science, man has come to understand more about the world around him. But somehow the old beliefs continue to have their hold on people.

Howling of an owl or crossing one's path by a cat are superstitiously considered as signs of death or a bad omen

○○○

What is an Electric Fuse ?

An electric fuse is a device that breaks an electric circuit when the current becomes excess because of a short or overload. It is essentially a small piece of wire having low melting point. It is usually made of a tin-lead alloy. The fuse wire has a carrier called the fuse holder. The fuseholder is made of porcelain or ebonite or some other insulating material. How does a fuse work and why is it needed?

A fuse is used as a safety device in an electrical circuit. When current flowing through the circuit becomes excessive due to a 'short' or 'overload' the fuse melts breaking the circuit. Hence it prevents the damage of domestic electrical appliances.

A 'short' occurs when two live wires touch each other. Due to this a large surge of current flows through the wires. This can even start a fire. An 'overload' occurs when too many electrical appliances are plugged into a single circuit. Here also, more current starts flowing through the wires.

There are two kinds of fuses: plug fuses and cartridge fuses. Plug fuses screw into sockets and carry light loads. They are mainly used in domestic circuits. Cartridge fuses are narrow cylinders that slide into spring loaded brackets.

The maximum safe current that can flow

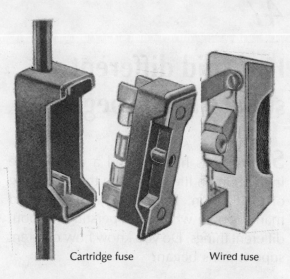

Cartridge fuse   Wired fuse

Fuse in electricity is a wire or strip of metal designed to melt when excessive current passes through it

through a fuse, without exploding it, is called fuse rating. This rating ranges from a few milliamperes to 50 amperes or even more. Fuses of lower ratings are thin wires, while those of higher ratings are thicker wires or strips. The rating of a fuse does not depend upon its length, it depends only on the thickness of the wire. If a low rated fuse is placed in a higher-rated circuit it would burn out immediately. A higher rated fuse, in a lower-rated circuit is dangerous. It allows too much current to flow into the circuit. The excess current may burn out or damage the appliance and cause overheating of wires.

But how does a fuse work ? A fuse is connected to the live wire of the connecting cord of an appliance. It allows a current to flow if it is less than its ratings. But if the current gets higher it becomes hot and melts. The circuit is then broken. This protects the appliance from damage.

○○○

49

When did the Industrial Revolution begin ?

The biggest change in man's daily life came about two hundred years ago. That was when a largely agrarian community changed to one in which industry, and particularly the use of machines, gained significance. This exciting period of human history is called the Industrial Revolution.

The Industrial Revolution began in England in about 1750 A.D. Machines began to take over some of the work of men and animals in the production of food and commodities. Before the machine age started, man could make use of machines like the plough, air-pump, printing press and spinning wheel, etc. But now, to operate new

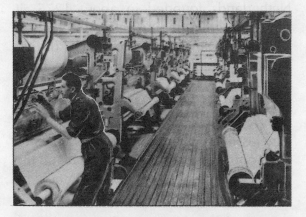

Industrial revolution not only brought about great changes in the field of science and technology but also in all other fields. Those changes created major social problems and evils too

machines, steam was invented as a source of power. This enabled man to build factories. These factories were built close to the source of raw materials, and markets.

Soon, with the increasing use of machines, the need for iron and steam increased tremendously. This gave impetus to new methods of mining coal. It also created a transport revolution. As a result, improvement of roads, building of canals, development of railroads and large ships followed in due course.

As man began to trade with markets all over the world, better communication also became important. This gave birth to telegraph and telephone systems. People began to work in factories and mills. This brought in division of labour and workers began to specialise in particular jobs.

The Industrial Revolution made it possible to produce plentiful and cheap goods which everybody could afford.

During the period of 50 years after the start of the Industrial Revolution, England became the world's leading industrial nation. After 1815, machines were introduced in France, Belgium, Switzerland and Germany. Russia was the last one to go in for industrialization on a big scale. The United States, after gaining independence from England took to industry around 1800. Japan was the first country in Asia to industrialize.

The Industrial Revolution led to cities becoming the centre of industries. Hence it created problems of housing, health and sanitation. No doubt, the Industrial Revolution has brought people together.

ooo

Which cities are built on canals?

The Bridge of Sighs in Venice. It links the Doge's palace with the old Venetian prisons

Since ancient times man has used rivers as a means of transportation of goods and passengers. But rivers could provide a limited destination points only through the areas where it flowed. Man could not go wherever he wanted to as the river didn't flow there. So he built artificial waterways or canals by creating subways of a river or connecting one river with another or with a lake or with the sea. There are also other important reasons for which canals are built, e.g. for irrigation, draining the land, fishing and pleasure boating, flood control and power generation, etc. We find canals everywhere in the world for their multipurpose utility. But do you know there exist some cities which are almost built on canals?

Venice in Italy, Amsterdam in Netherlands are the most prominent canal cities. In Asia, Bangkok in Thailand is also known as a canal city.

Venice is built on islands separated by canals. It lies in north-east Italy in the Adriatic sea. When the barbarians invaded the mainland Italy, some people escaped and founded the city of Venice in the year 452 A.D. It went on to become a rich trading city. Since the city was built on a number of small islands, canals were built to connect these islands as well as places within the islands. There are more than 1500 canals crossed by over 400 bridges. Many houses stand on wooden posts sunk in the mud of the canals. The islands are now sinking and many buildings have been damaged by rising water. A variety of boats called *gondolas* are found in the canals.

Amsterdam is the capital city of Netherlands founded in about 1275, it became a great trading centre in the 14th century. It stands on low-lying land, that is, below sea-level and is drained by a network of canals shaped rather like a spider's web. The city is situated close to the mouth of River Amstel. A 24 km long canal called North Sea canal connects its large port with the sea. River Waal and the Rhine are also connected with the city through another canal.

Bangkok, the capital of Thailand, is also another canal city and is called the 'Venice of East'. It is situated on river Chao Phraya.

ooo

2
Science & Technology

• What is a Robot ? • What are quarks ? • How does a film projector work ? • What is an Atomic Clock ? • What is Heavy Water? • What is stereophonic sound ? • How is talcum powder made ? • Can light travel through wires ? • How does a polaroid camera take instant photographs ? • How can we extinguish fires ? • What are Quasars ? • What is a Mass Spectrograph ? • How does a microphone work ? • What is dry cleaning? • How are different dyes made ? • Why do some acids cause burn ? • What are the different types of thermometers ? • How can the temperature of stars be measured ? • How are matches made ? • How does a video-tape recorder work ? • How are hard drinks made ? • What is a periscope ? • What is quartz? • How does an automobile engine work ? • How is electricity conducted through wires? • How is an automobile's speed measured ? • How does a crane work ? • How is nylon made ? • What is the Theory of Relativity ? • How do we see distant objects with binoculars ? • When was petrol first produced?

1

What is a Robot ?

A robot is an automatic machine which can work like a human being. It can replace man in various branches of scientific and industrial tasks because it does not suffer from human limitations. It may or may not resemble a human being but definitely can work like a human being. The robots which resemble humans are called androids.

The word 'robot' was first used in the play 'Rossum's Universal Robots' by the Czechoslovak dramatist, Karel Capek, who had derived it from a Czech word 'Robota' which means a forced or bonded labourer.

The industrial revolution and automations stimulated the invention of robotic devices to perform certain human tasks. A human worker, however superb a craftsman he may be, has certain limitations. He cannot work continuously in a hostile environment. He cannot work for long periods because he gets tired. He may be in short supply and may be expensive to hire. Modern industrial robotic devices aim to substitute a machine for man in hostile environments, cut costs by replacing expensive hand labour with cheap dependable machines, and provide versatile, all purpose robots or mechanical devices at predictable costs. Robot is such a machine which does not get tired, does not go on strike and does not demand increase in salary.

Robots can perform a variety of jobs such

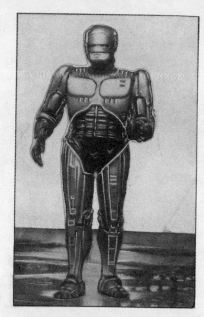

An industrial robot is a man-like machine and all instructions or programs are stored in the robot's computer brain

as welding and painting a car, house cleaning, cutting the grass of a lawn, working in nuclear plants or travelling to space. They can also play chess, work as a watchman, cut the wool of a sheep and pluck fruits from trees.

Robots of higher level are capable of adapting to changes in environment. They are also capable of making decisions with the help of computers. A more complex robotive device in modern transportation is the automatic aircraft pilot which can control routine flights. An android robot named Shaky Robot was developed at Stanford Research Institute in California to do a variety of research jobs.

Japan has the largest number of robots in the world. The United States of America, Britain, Germany, Sweden, Italy, Poland, France, India, etc are also using robotic devices for different purposes. All robotic devices are controlled by computers.

2

What are quarks ?

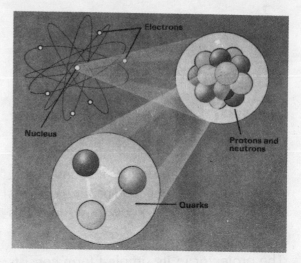

All matter is made up of small particles called atoms. These atoms are very tiny particles and cannot be seen with the naked eye. Atoms are made up of still smaller particles called electrons, protons and neutrons, which are known as subatomic or elementary particles. Physicists have discovered hundreds of other elementary particles such as mesons, muons, neutrino and positrons. Can you imagine a particle even smaller than these elementary particles ?

A few years ago, scientists discovered that elementary particles are made up of extremely small particles called quarks. So far quarks are only hypothetical particles and have not been observed in experiments. With the exception of protons, electrons, muons and neutrino, all elementary particles are made up of different quarks. This idea was suggested in 1964, by two American physicists, Murray Gell Mann and George Zweig.

There are probably four different kinds of quarks, carrying a fractional charge. Each has an anti-particle called anti-quark. Until 1974, only three types of quarks were known; two of very nearly equal mass, of which the proton, neutron and pi-mesons are composed, and a third, bigger quark

Quarks are extremely small particle of elements, even smaller than subatomic particles like mesons and positrons

which is a constituent of K-mesons and hyperons. These quarks are called the up quark (u), the down quark (d) and the strange quark (s). In 1974, one more quark, named charm quark (c) was also predicted. The existence of two other types, top quark and bottom quark, is also predicted.

The charges of the four quarks u, d, s and c are +2/3, −1/3, −1/3, +2/3 that of the electron charge.

Antiquarks have opposite charges. All quarks and antiquarks have equal spin which is 1/2.

These quarks combine to form different elementary particles. For example, protons are composed of three quarks (uud) and neutrons also of three quarks (udd). Each meson can be conceived as the union of a quark and an antiquark.

○○○

3

How does a film projector work ?

A projector is an optical instrument that shows on screen, enlarged pictures of slides or movies. Do you know how does this instrument work?

The projector in its simplest form consists of (i) a light source (ii) a concave reflector that focuses light (iii) a condenser lens and (iv) a projector lens. A powerful light source is needed to project images on to a screen. Most projectors use an incandescent ribbon lamp of 1000 watts. A highly polished concave reflector is placed at the back of the light source so that practically, the entire light is reflected towards the slide. The light so reflected is allowed to fall on a condenser or focusing lens. This lens is a combination of two planoconvex lenses, placed in such a position that their convex surfaces face each other. The condenser lens converges the divergent beam of the light, and throws it on the slide. The condenser lens helps to strongly illuminate the image. The concentrated rays then pass through the photographic slide or film that is placed upside down in a frame. The final or projector lens is a convex lens and is kept near the slide. It reverses and enlarges the picture of the slide and throws it on to the white opaque screen. The slide shown is systematically removed by the touch of a button and replaced by a new one. Slide projectors are also used by

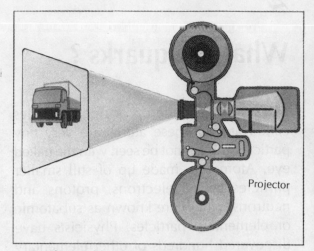

Projector

Continuous images appear on the screen due to the projection of a series of pictures in rapid succession — thirty-two films in a second

teachers and business people to illustrate subjects under discussion.

Movie projectors have electrically powered reels that move the film between the bulb and projecting lens at a speed of 32 films per second, so that images appear continuous to the eyes. Sprockets in the projector pull the film into the film gate. The film then stops for a moment and light from the lamp passes through the frame. The lens projects the picture on the screen. The sprockets then turn and advance the film. As the film moves, the blade of a rotating shutter passes between the lamp and the film so that the movement of the film does not show on the screen.

In sound film, light from the lamp passes through the sound track and strikes a light sensitive cell which produces an electric signal. It goes to an amplifier and loud speaker which provides the sound. In some cases, the sound is recorded on a magnetic strip along the film as in a video recording.

OOO

4

What is an Atomic Clock ?

Since long, man has used clocks and watches to measure time. But those were crude watches and didn't measure time accurately. A few years ago, scientists were able to develop a very sophisticated clock known as 'Atomic Clock'. With its development a new era has been ushered in the field of time measurement. It is a wonder clock, that remains accurate to one second for 1,700,000 years.

Today we have mainly three types of clocks and watches : mechanical, electrical and electronic. Mechanical clocks and watches are spring driven ; electric clocks are battery powered and the electronic ones are quartz based. All these clocks and watches show time quite accurately. But if they run continuously for long periods, they can get slow or fast.

Now the smallest internationally accepted unit of time is the atomic second. It is based on atomic clock, and defined as the time interval during which exactly 9192631770 cycles of the hyperfine resonance frequency of the ground state of the caesium atom occur. Prior to this the second was the standard of time which was measured as a portion of earth's rotation as 1/86400th of a day.

An atomic clock uses the frequencies produced by atoms or molecules. The time is measured by counting the number of vibrations. Most of the atomic clocks make use of frequencies in the microwave range from about 1400 to 40,000 MHz.

In 1947, an oscillator controlled by frequencies of ammonia molecule was constructed. An ammonia controlled clock was built in 1949 at the National Bureau of Standards, Washington D.C.

In 1955, a caesium-beam atomic clock of high precision was first put in operation at the National Physics Laboratory, Teddington, England. After that a number of laboratories started producing commercial models of caesium-beam atomic clocks.

In the caesium clock, the caesium is heated in a small oven. The caesium produces a beam which is directed through an electromagnetic field. The 5 MHz output from a quartz clock is multiplied to give 9192631770 Hz that controls the electromagnetic field. Part of the 5 MHz output is used to derive a clock display unit which indicates time.

During recent years, some other atomic clocks have also been developed which make use of ammonia maser, hydrogen maser and rubidium gas cells. Atomic clocks of 1960s were very large in size but by 1978 their sizes have been sufficiently reduced to fit in a small box.

Atomic clocks are being used as standard of time. They are also being used in some sophisticated navigation systems and deep space communications.

○○○

5

What is Heavy Water?

We know that ordinary water is a compound of hydrogen and oxygen. It has two atoms of hydrogen and one atom of oxygen and is represented by the chemical formula H_2O. Heavy water is a compound of deuterium (an isotope of hydrogen) and oxygen and is represented by the chemical formula D_2O.

In fact, hydrogen has three isotopes : protium (ordinary hydrogen), deuterium (heavy hydrogen) and tritium. Protium nucleus contains only one proton, while deuterium nucleus contains one proton and one neutron and the tritium nucleus contains one proton and two neutrons. Naturally occurring hydrogen contains 99.985% of protium, about .015% deuterium and about 1 part in 10^{17} tritium. Tritium is radioactive in nature. When deuterium combines with oxygen, it gives heavy water or deuterium oxide.

Ordinary water as obtained from most natural sources, contains about one part of heavy water for every 6760 parts of H_2O. Ordinary water has a molecular weight of about 18 while heavy water has a molecular weight of 20. Density, freezing point and boiling point of heavy water are higher than that of ordinary water.

Heavy water was discovered by Harold Clayton Urey, an American chemist in 1931. He was awarded the Nobel Prize in 1934 for this discovery. In 1933, Lewis and Donald were able to prepare a few millilitres of pure heavy water by long continued electrolysis of water.

Heavy water is prepared by electrolysis of water. If water is electrolysed the gas produced at cathode is mostly hydrogen and thus the residual water is enriched in deuterium oxide. Continued electrolysis of hundreds of litres of water yields pure heavy water. The operation of electrolysis is carried out on industrial scale. Bhabha Atomic Research Centre (BARC), Trombay has a big plant for the production of heavy water. It is also produced at Nangal, Vadodara, Kota, Talcher, Hazira etc.

Heavy water is used as a moderator for slowing down the fast neutrons in nuclear reactors. In laboratories, it is used as an isotopic tracer in the studies of chemical and biological processes. It is also used in the preparation of deuterium and its other compounds. It is also used as the coolant in nuclear reactors.

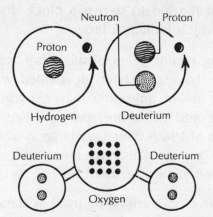

Heavy water (D_2O) contains deuterium in place of hydrogen. Deuterium is an isotope of hydrogen

○○○

6

What is stereophonic sound ?

The sounds we hear with our two ears are known as stereophonic sound because they give the exact idea of angular and lateral position of the sound source.

The sound signals reaching one ear are generally slightly different from those reaching the other. Their arrival times and intensities are also slightly different. Our brain is able to distinguish the differences in intensity and arrival time of sound waves at each ear. In fact, it can discriminate arrival time differences even as small as less than 1 milli second. If a pair of microphones is placed in front of a sound source, it will receive sounds with differing intensities and arrival times depending upon the position of the source relative to each microphone. When these separate, sounds are reproduced by a pair of loudspeakers, the listener's brain is able to use the reproduced time and intensity differences to locate the original sound. Such sounds localised in space by the brain are called phantom images. The ability of the listener to perceive phantom images is called stereophonic sound. Thus with our two ears, we are able to locate exactly both the angular and lateral positions of sound. The listener feels that he is actually present at the place of performance.

Stereophonic sound recording and reproduction requires two or more independent channels of information. It has been observed experimentally that a minimum of two sets of microphones and loudspeakers give satisfactory auditory perspective. Separate microphones are used in recording, and separate speakers in reproduction.

At the time of a stereo-recording two microphones are used, one of which receives more sound from the left, and the other from the right. The sounds detected by each are kept entirely separate and are encoded in two completely independent channels of the programmes. Stereo-production needs two separate loudspeakers.

The pick-up of a stereo record player produces two signals corresponding to right and left sound channels. These signals are amplified separately and fed into two loudspeakers

There are three basic techniques for stereophonic sound pick-up ; coincident, 'spaced apart' and 'individual instrument' or close miking. The concident technique employs two microphones located very close together. In 'spaced apart' technique, microphones are placed several feet apart, 'close miking' technique involves use of several microphones, each located close to one instrument. The outputs are recorded on tape. The reproduction loudspeakers should be identical and capable of broad-frequency response without distortion.

The effectiveness of stereophonic reproduction was demonstrated as early as 1933. Two track stereophonic tapes for domestic use became popular in the 1950s and single- groove two channel stereo-discs in 1958. In the early 1970s quadraphonic system, employing four independent channels of information, became commercially available.

OOO

7

How is talcum powder made ?

Perfumed talcum powder is used by a large number of people throughout the world to protect the skin from heat during the hot summer months. It gives a soothing effect to the skin. Do you know what this talcum powder is?

It is a fine perfumed powder made from a mineral called talc. Talc is the softest mineral known to man. When it is in solid form, it is called soapstone and is usually grayish or greenish in colour, and very soft and greasy to touch. Often it has brown spots. To make talcum, white-coloured soapstone is first ground to a very fine powder. Then this powder is sieved to remove the coarse grains. Desired scents are added to this sieved powder. Finally it is packed in tin or plastic containers for sale.

One of the remarkable features of talc is its simple, almost constant composition. It is basically magnesium silicate. Soapstone is often used in the making of household articles because it resists heat and can easily be shaped. Cooking utensils and parts of stoves are sometimes made from it. It is also used in the making of laundry tubs. As soapstone hardens at high temperatures, it is also used for lining furnaces. As it cannot easily be eaten away, slabs of this material are used for acid tanks in the laboratories. It is a poor conductor of electricity and for this reason, is used as a base for switch boards and electrical insulation.

The best quality talc comes from Italy. Its deposits are found in England, Canada, Germany and Rhodesia. The Atlantic Coast has more talc than all the other countries of the world. About three quarters of the talc processed in the West goes into the manufacture of paints, glazed tiles, ceramic products, paper and rubber.

OOO

8

Can light travel through wires ?

We all know that electricity travels from one place to another through metallic wires. Can light travel through wires too?

Light can also travel through wires, but these wires are not made of metals. They are made of glass or plastics. Light carrying wires are extremely thin and are called optical fibres. The branch of science dealing with the conduction and study of light through fibres is called Fibre Optics.

In 1870, a British physicist John Tyndal showed that light can travel along a curved rod of glass or transparent plastic. Light travels through transparent rods by the process of total internal reflection. The sides of the fibre reflect the light and keep it inside as the fibre bends and turns.

The narrow fibres have a thin core of glass of high refractive index surrounded by a thin cladding of another glass of lower refractive index. The core carries light and the covering helps bend the light back to the core.

Fibre are drawn from thick glass rods in a special furnace. The glass rod of higher refractive index is inserted in a tubing of glass of lower refractive index. Then the two are lowered carefully and slowly through a vertical furnace and the fibre drawn from the lower end is wound on a revolving drum. With this method, fibres of about .025 mm in diameter can be drawn.

Fibres so prepared have to be aligned properly in the form of a bundle. They should not cross each other, otherwise the image transported by it will be scrambled. They are kept in straight lines. Once the aligned bundle is made, it can be bent or turned in any desired direction.

There are many uses of fibre bundles. Physicians use instruments with fibre bundles to examine body cavities and the inner part of hollow organs by sending light from an external lamp. These instruments are known as fibre-scope. By introducing the bundle into the stomach or bladder, photographs can be taken of the internal organs.

Fibre optic devices can transmit television programmes and telephone conversations. In future, using laser beams and single bundle of optical fibres, scientists would be able to send throusands of telephone conversation simultaneously. Many developed countries have installed telephone exchanges using fibre optic cables. The use of optical fibres in video text, videophones and computer networks is increasing day by day.

ooo

9

How does a polaroid camera take instant photographs ?

The polaroid camera is also known as the 'instant camera' because it takes pictures and develops them in a matter of minutes. It was invented by Edwin H. Land of the United States and the first polaroid camera was sold in 1948. At that stage, it took only black and white photographs. Later, another camera was built that could take pictures and develop colour photographs.

Polaroid cameras are loaded with a double picture roll. One part is a negative roll of the film, and the other a positive roll of a special printing paper. Small pods (containers) of chemicals are joined to the positive roll. After exposure to light through the camera's lens, the negative and positive rolls are made to pass through a pair of rollers that break the chemical pods. The chemicals flow over the exposed portion of the negative roll and develop a negative image on the roll—the parts of the picture that should be black are white, and the parts that should be white are black. More chemical reactions take place between the pod chemicals and the chemicals coated on the positive roll, and a positive photograph is made — the white areas in the photograph are printed white and the black areas black. This process takes about 10 seconds for a black and white photograph and upto a minute for a colour one.

When the film is exposed to light, during the photograph, particles of a silver salt in the film are reduced by light to metallic silver. After the photo has been taken, a chemical is released which dissolves dyes in the film. These dyes diffuse upwards. When the dyes reach parts of layers

Polaroid cameras present instant printed photographs as they contain both the negative as well as positive rolls

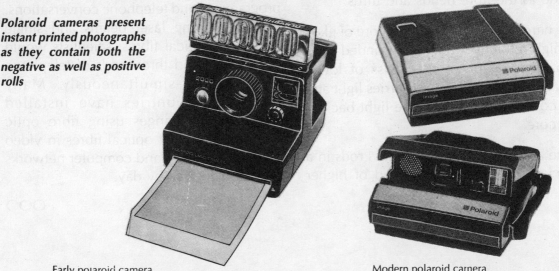

Early polaroid camera

Modern polaroid camera

containing metallic silver particles, they get oxidised and are fixed. But the dyes continue to diffuse upward, through parts of layers where the silver salt has not been reduced to metallic silver, until they reach the image-receiving layer. White light from the photographed subject stops all the dyes diffusing. Areas exposed to coloured light from the subject stops some dyes, but not other, and so it appears coloured in the photograph. Areas which receive no light stop none of the dyes, but the dyes combine to become black. The polaroid photograph is a true positive image of the photographed subject.

In 1972 Land introduced an improved 'pocket model' of his camera. In this camera, the photographic process is automatically controlled by tiny electronic circuits. About a second after pressing the shutter button, which opens and closes the aperture of the camera, a dry plastic square comes out of the camera. It develops quickly into a colour print.

In 1978 Land introduced an instant home movie system, called polar vision. In this system, movie films can be shown on the special projector just a few minutes after they are exposed.

Polaroid camera is a wonderful camera and is being used by mature photographers all over the world. During the recent years, the use of polaroid cameras has gone into scientific world for taking the oscilloscopic, microscopic and interferometric pictures. Now a days commercial world is also using these cameras for making instant prints.   OOO

10

How can we extinguish fires ?

We are all aware of the damage and disaster a fire can cause in certain situations. Now let us see how to control a fire and prevent it from spreading.

A fire is basically a chemical reaction during which heat and light are produced. Three factors are necessary for a fire to start — fuel, oxygen or air, and heat to raise the temperature of the fuel to its ignition temperature.

A fire can be extinguished when one or more of these agents is removed, i.e. fuel, supply of air and lowering the temperature of the combustible substance. All fire extinguishing methods make use of these principles.

The original fire extinguisher, a bucket of water, is still useful in controlling many types of fires. The principal effect of water on a fire is to cool the burning material, thus removing the heat — one of the factors without which combustion cannot continue. It can be applied in a variety of ways such as by flooding the fire with water. Jets of water are used to knock down the flames of fire, and sprays are used to absorb heat and drive back smoke and gases.

Another common extinguisher is the soda-acid type. It sprays a mixture of water and carbon dioxide on the fire. This is based upon the principle of cooling the burning material and cutting the supply of air by non-combustible carbon-dioxide.

In this extinguisher a solution of sodium bicarbonate is placed in a cylindrical vessel of steel. Sulphuric acid is kept in a bottle in a small compartment made within the cylinder, near the top. When required, the knob is hit against the floor. This brings the sodium bicarbonate and sulphuric acid in contact with each other. Immediately carbon dioxide is formed and it comes out of the fire nozzle which is directed towards the fire. These extinguishers are useful only for small and localized fires. They are not effective against gasoline, oil and electrical fires.

Foam extinguishers are based upon the principle of cutting off the supply of air by forming a fire-proof coating of foam around the burning material. In this, a mixture of sodium bicarbonate and aluminium sulphate containing licorice extract is sprayed. It produces foam and extinguishes the fire.

The other types of extinguishers that are used on oil and electrical fires are : Carbon dioxide extinguishers, dry-chemical extinguishers and vaporising liquid extinguishers.

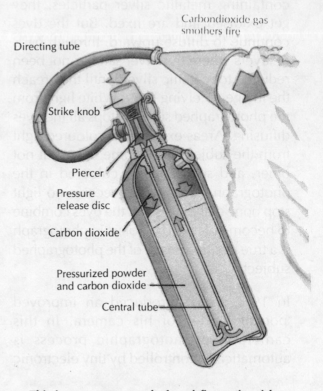

Carbondioxide gas smothers fire

Directing tube

Strike knob

Piercer

Pressure release disc

Carbon dioxide

Pressurized powder and carbon dioxide

Central tube

This is a very commonly found fire extinguisher which is used for small and localized fires

Water should never be used for extinguishing electrical or oil fires. In case of electrical fires, it can cause electrocution. If water is used on burning oil, the oil simply floats on top of water and continues to burn. As the water flows away, it can carry the oil with it and so spread the fire.

Fire extinguishers are provided by law in all public buildings, factories and schools. Most of the big cities have fire brigades for fire prevention and control. ○○○

11

What are Quasars ?

In 1960, very strong radio emissions were observed by an American astronomer, Allan R. Sandage to be coming from certain localized direction in the sky. When viewed on the photographic plate, they appeared like stars. But they were not stars, as proved by their other characteristics including a large red shift. The accurate position measurement of these starlike objects on optical photographs, led to the discovery of a new class of objects in the the universe, the quasars (quasi-stellar sources).

They appear starlike on the photograph because their angular diameters are less than about 1 second of an arc, which is the resolution limit of ground-based optical telescopes. Since stars also have angular diameters much less than this, they too appear unresolved or point-like on a photograph.

In 1962 a much brighter star like object

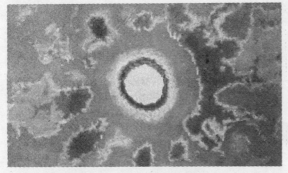

Quasars are super-bright galaxies much farther away than any normal galaxy

3C273 was identified by Maarten Schimdt with the help of a radio telescope in Australia. Its red shift was found to be 0.158. This red shift turned out to be far larger than any other that had been detected for ordinary galaxies. These observations established the existence of quasars beyond doubt.

Quasars are generally much bluer than most of the stars, except white dwarf stars. The blueness of quasars, as an identifying characteristic, led to the discovery that many blue star like objects have a large red shift, and are therefore quasars. Till today scientists have studied more than 1000 quasars but their nature and distance from earth remain a puzzle.

Quasars consist of a massive nucleus with a total size of less than a light year, which is surrounded by an extended halo of gas excited by the energy radiated by the central object. The central object emits radiation over a wide spectral range. Some quasars emit significant amount of energy at radio frequencies ranging from about 30 MHz to 100 GHz. It is believed that the energy emitted by quasars is gravitational and not thermonuclear in origin. More than 10^{60} ergs of energy is released in quasars over their 10^6 years life-time.

Till to day scientists have not been able to measure the exact distance of quasars from the earth. Various similarities of quasars with radio galaxies strongly suggest that quasars are also active nuclei of galaxies might be associated with the birth of some galaxies. Studies have shown that quasars must have been much more common in the universe about 10^{10} years ago. ○○○

12

What is a Mass Spectrograph ?

A mass spectrograph is an instrument used to analyse the constituents of substances. It not only detects different kinds of atoms and molecules present in the substance, but also finds out their relative amounts. By the use of electric and magnetic fields, it separates ions of different masses. Do you know how this instrument works ?

The working of the mass spectrograph first involves the change of the substance into a gas, which is passed into a vacuum chamber. A beam of electrons is bombarded to change the gas atoms and molecules into ions. The ions are then accelerated, by passing them through an electric field. Then the ions are passed through a magnetic field, where they get deflected. The positive ions are deflected one way, and the negative ions in the opposite direction. The amount of deflection is inversely proportional to the masses of the ions. The heavier the mass, the lesser the deflection. This separates ions of different masses. Ions of the same mass and charge stay together. The ions are then allowed to fall on a photographic plate. Different ions hit the plate at different places and as a result, this photographic plate records the amounts of various atoms and molecules. Photographic plate is used to identify different ions which have hit it. From the intensity variations on the plate, we can know the relative amounts of atoms or molecules present in the substance.

The mass spectrograph was developed by a British scientist, William Francis Aston. He was awarded the Nobel Prize in 1922 for this invention. After this, several other mass spectrographs were developed by many leading scientists like Dempster, Bainbridge, Nier, etc but all were just modifications of Aston's mass spectrograph.

The mass spectrograph is widely used in geology, chemistry, biology and nuclear physics. It is a very useful instrument for isotopic studies. Aston himself discovered 212 of the 287 naturally occurring isotopes. Mass spectrographs are also used as vacuum leak detectors.

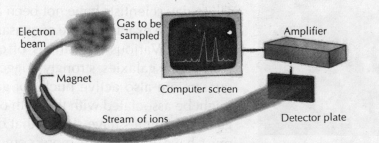

Mass spectrograph is an apparatus for analysing chemical composition of substances

13

How does a microphone work ?

Radio and television stations make use of microphones. They are also used in public address systems and in motion pictures and phonograph records. The mouth piece of a telephone is a simple type of microphone. Let us see what exactly is a microphone.

A microphone is a device which converts sound waves into electrical signals. These signals can then be broadcast through the air or sent over to distant points, where they can again be converted back into sound.

Microphones can be divided into two groups depending upon how they respond to sound waves. These are: the pressure type and the velocity type.

The pressure type microphones contain a thin metal plate called a diaphragm. This is stretched like a drumhead inside a rigid frame. The diaphragm is a part of the electrical circuit. When the sound waves strike the diaphragm, it starts vibrations at the same rate as the sound waves. These vibrations produce corresponding electric signals by changing the electric current that flows through the circuit.

The pressure microphones are of several types, such as condenser microphone, moving coil or dynamic microphone, the crystal microphone and the carbon microphone.

In the condenser microphone, the vibrating diaphragm changes the capacitance of a condenser. A moving coil microphone consists of a coil of wire attached to a diaphragm. As the diaphragm vibrates in response to the sound, the coil slides up and down the centrepiece of an M - shaped permanent magnet. The coil thus cuts through the magnetic lines of force which induce a fluctuating voltage in it. This fluctuating voltage represents the variations in sound pressure.

Crystal microphones make use of piezoelectric effect. Whenever certain crystals such as quartz are bent or twisted, they generate an electric voltage. Such crystals are called piezoelectric crystals. In a crystal microphone, a piezoelectric crystal is firmly clamped at one end and attached at the other to a flexible diaphragm. When someone speaks before it, the sound waves make the diaphragm vibrate. Due to this, a pressure acts on the crystal, and as a result, an oscillating voltage is produced. This is picked up by

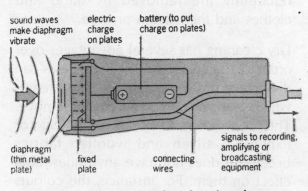

sound waves make diaphragm vibrate

electric charge on plates

battery (to put charge on plates)

diaphragm (thin metal plate)

fixed plate

connecting wires

signals to recording, amplifying or broadcasting equipment

The working principles of a microphone

79

the heads attached to the crystal surface. This is how sound waves are converted into electric signals and transmitted.

A carbon microphone works like a telephone transmitter. In this, carbon granules varies the current to create a signal. Ribbon microphones have a metal ribbon instead of coils.

The velocity microphone has a light ribbon of aluminium foil loosely held in a strong magnetic field. The sound waves vibrate the ribbon. The movement of the ribbon in the magnetic field induces a current along its length which is picked up by the connecting leads.

Several people including the American inventor Thomas Alva Edison have been credited with the invention of the microphone. The first practical microphone however was invented in 1878 by David Edward Hughes of United States. Other inventors who have contributed to the invention of the microphone are Emile Berliner, Philip Reis, Franus Blake and Henry Hunnings. OOO

14

What is dry cleaning ?

Man has been using soap and water as cleaning agents for thousands of years. The first soap was made in the middle east about 5000 years ago. The discovery of soapless detergents is not very old. The first synthetic detergent was not invented until 1916, but since then the manufacture of non - soap detergents became a major development of the petrochemical industry. New methods of fabric cleaning came into use, such as dry cleaning.

Dry cleaning is a method of cleaning fabrics with chemical solvents instead of soap and water. Many of these solvents are derivatives of crude oil. Petrol is the most important of them. Benzene is also used in dry cleaning. Their fumes can be dangerous if inhaled and they catch fire

easily. Some safer synthetic chemicals such as polychloroalkanes and alkanes have also been developed. The most common dry cleaning chemicals are carbon tetrachloride and trichloro ethylene.

In a dry cleaning establishment, clothes are usually treated first for stains. Then they are placed in the dry-cleaning machine with the cleaning fluid or solvent and tumbled slowly for up to half an hour. After a rinse in clean fluid, the clothes are spun around rapidly to extract the liquid, and are finally fluffed in hot air. Any stains remaining are removed by hand and clothes and then steam pressed.

Dry cleaning has several advantages over ordinary soap cleaning. Cleaning fluids can dissolve stains (especially oil and grease) which soap and detergents cannot remove. The process is most useful for delicate or expensive silken and woollen fabrics because it does not have any undesirable effect on them. For instance, the colours do not fade, as they might in water.
OOO

15

How are different dyes made ?

Dyes are colour substances which impart their colour to the fabrics on which they are applied and for which they have a chemical affinity.

Until the middle of the last century, the only dyes available were natural products obtained mostly from plants and flowers. Their range was limited. These natural dyes included : woad, a blue dye obtained from the plant woad; indigo, another blue dye from a plant. Some other dyes such as madder (red) safflower and turmeric (yellow) were extracted from certain kinds of sea-snails.

The most important breakthrough in this field was made in 1856 with the discovery

The Chinese practiced dying as early as 3000 B.C, using natural dyes obtained from plants and shellfish

of the first synthetic dye by William Henry Perkin. This was mauveine, a bluish-purple dye discovered accidentally by William Perkin during experiments aimed at synthesizing the drug quinine. After this discovery, efforts were made to develop dyes from coal tar. As a result of these efforts, several thousand dyes were synthesized subsequently.

These synthetic dyes were satisfactory when used with animal fibres such as wool, but they were easily washed off from vegetable fibres like cotton. This difficulty was overcome by treating the fibres with metal salts or with solutions of these salts in tannic acid before dyeing.

After these dyes a large number of azo dyes were developed. Azo dyes are two component dyes used for cellulose fibres. The material is first treated with one component, and then put in the solution of the other component. The two components react to produce a dye within the fibres themselves. These dyes are highly resistant to washing.

Another group of very stable dyes used for cellulose fibres is known as Vat dyes. These dyes, which include synthetic indigo used for dyeing blue denim, are mixed with chemicals to make them soluble for the dyeing process. After the material has been dyed, it is treated with other chemicals to make it more stable.

Today we have a large number of synthetic dyes obtained from coal tar or petroleum products which are not only used to colour textiles, but also plastics, paper, leather, fur, oil, rubber, soap, food, cosmetics, ink and metal surfaces. ○○○

16

Why do some acids cause burn ?

An acid is a chemical, which when dissolved in water, gives a solution containing hydrogen ions. Acids turn blue litmus red, they react with certain metals to release hydrogen, they react with bases to form salts and they promote certain chemical reactions.

All acids taste sour. Fruits such as lemons taste sour because they contain citric acid. Vinegar is sour because it contains acetic acid.

There are two main chemical groups of acids. They are organic and inorganic acids. Organic acids contain carbon while inorganic acids don't. Some examples of inorganic acids are hydrochloric acid, nitric acid and sulphuric acid. They are also called mineral acids and they are very strong. Formic acid, acetic acid, etc are organic acids. They are weaker acids.

Most of the organic acids are harmless. But inorganic acids can be dangerous as they can burn the skin. How do acids burn the body ?

Inorganic acids have a strong tendency to absorb water and release a lot of heat in the process. Since most of the living cells contain water, strong acids like hydrochloric, sulphuric and nitric acid react with them and kill the cells, causing severe burns.

Acids are also essential for the body. Our stomachs contain hydrochloric acid to digest food. The stomach lining protects us from the acid, if the lining breaks, the acid can burn and cause an ulcer. Amino acids are essential for all kinds of life. Eight special amino acids are needed to stay alive.

Acids also have tremendous industrial importance. Millions of tons of sulphuric acid is made every year and used for many industrial purposes. It dissolves rust and scale deposited on iron. Acids are also used in making fertilizers, pigments, dyes, plastics and synthetics. Aquaregia, which is a mixture of nitric and hydrochloric acid, is used to dissolve gold and platinum.

Certain precautions are taken by people handling acids. They wear special clothes to protect their bodies from burns. Acids must always be poured slowly into water and never the other way round. If you are burnt by an acid, you should wash your skin with a lot of water, followed by a weak ammonia solution. If your eyes are affected, wash them immediately with water and then with sodium bicarbonate solution, which neutralizes any acid left.

OOO

17

What are the different types of thermometers ?

A thermometer is an instrument used for measuring the temperature of our body or atmosphere. The first thermometer was produced by the Italian scientist, Galileo Galilei. Thermometers help in regulating chemical reactions by controlling temperatures of the solutions. They are used to measure the melting points of different solids, and boiling points of liquids.

The main types of thermometers are: I. Liquid-in-glass thermometers. II. Bimetallic strip thermometers. III. Electrical thermometers. IV. Gas thermometers.

Liquid-in-glass thermometers : The most common liquid-in-glass thermometer makes use of mercury or alcohol as thermometric liquid. The thermometer is made up of a glass tube with a narrow bore through it. At the bottom of the glass tube, a small bulb is blown, in which the liquid mercury or alcohol is kept. It is then put in a hot bath, as a result of which some of the liquid is expelled. The thermometer's range is decided by the temperature of the bath. Finally its upper end is sealed.

The sealed glass tube is now put in ice to mark the lower fixed point. This indicates

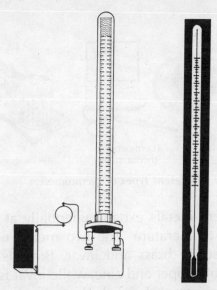

Resistance thermometer & clinical thermometer

the minimum temperature for the thermometer. Then it is put in another hot bath to ascertain the maximum temperature. The distance between the lower fixed point and the upper fixed point is divided into equal parts. When we wish to measure our body temperature, the thermometer is put into contact with the body. The thermometric liquid expands and stops when the temperature of the bulb becomes equal to the temperature of the body. The temperature is then read from the upper point of the liquid in the capillary.

Clinical thermometers also contain mercury. Meteorologists use 'maximum' and 'minimum' thermometers to record the highest and lowest temperatures of the day. They contain both mercury and alcohol.

Bimetallic strip thermometers : A bimetallic strip thermometer consists of a strip of two different metals having different co-efficients of expansion. This means that

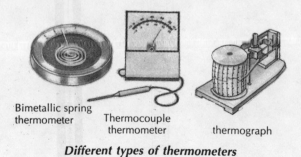

Bimetallic spring thermometer

Thermocouple thermometer

thermograph

Different types of thermometers

different metals expand unequally at the same temperature. The two metals used are usually brass and invar. Brass is an alloy of copper and zinc, while invar is an alloy of iron and nickel. The two strips are joined together. When the temperature changes, the two metals expand and contract at different rates. This causes the strip to bend. The strip is attached to a pointer which indicates the temperature. Bimetallic strip thermometers are used in refrigerators for temperature control. They are also used in thermographs. A thermograph records a graph of temperature. Instead of a pointer, a pen is attached to the bimetallic strip which records the temperature on a moving chart which is known as a thermogram.

Electrical thermometers : These are of two types: Resistance thermometers and Thermocouple thermometers.

A resistance thermometer works on the principle that the resistance of metals increase with the rise in temperature. The resistance thermometer consists of a sealed tube containing tightly-coiled platinum wire. As the temperature increases, the resistance of the platinum wire also

increases. By measuring the resistance, the temperature is determined.

A thermocouple thermometer consists of wires of two different metals. One of the ends of the wires is kept in ice, and the other with the source whose temperature is to be measured. The thermometer changes heat into electricity and produces a voltage known as thermo e.m.f. The voltage varies according to temperature. The voltage is applied to a galvanometer needle which then shows the current.

Gas thermometers : These are the most accurate thermometers, which also have the widest range (from -273°C to about 1500°C). In these thermometers, gases like Nitrogen, Hydrogen, Helium etc. are used. By recording the expansion of gas on heating, the temperature is measured. These thermometers are of two types (a) constant volume thermometers and (b) constant pressure thermometers.

There are four scales of temperature (I) Celsius scale (II) Fahrenheit scale (III) Reaumur scale and (IV) Absolute scale of temperature. The Celsius or Centigrade scale has 0° as the freezing point of water and 100° as the boiling point of it. Fahrenheit scale has 32° as the freezing point of water and 212° the boiling point. Reaumur scale has 0° as the freezing point of water and 80° as the boiling point. Absolute scale has 273° as the freezing point of water and 373° as the boiling point. -273° celsius is the lowest temperature which has not yet been achieved. This is also called absolute zero.

OOO

18

How can the temperature of stars be measured ?

We can measure our body temperature with a thermometer. Thermocouples and other devices are used to measure the temperature of furnaces. But how can we measure the temperature of stars ?

The surface temperature of stars is determined by various techniques. The most conventional and fairly accurate estimate can be made by colour alone. Red-coloured stars are cool while blue ones are extremely hot. On the basis of colour, stars have been classified in the table given below.

A more accurate determination of the temperature is made by the comparison of spectra of stars. Light, which comes from the sun and other stars, is made up of many different wavelengths. It can be separated into different wavelengths by a spectrograph (an instrument used to record spectrum). From the spectroscopic studies, it has been observed that stars are largely composed of hydrogen (about 75% on the average). Next in abundance is helium followed by various other metals. In the cooler stars, some compounds are present but at high temperatures, they disintegrate into atoms. In order to know the temperature, the spectra of stars are recorded. It will be different for different stars, depending upon their temperature.

Moreover, the intensity of spectral lines, bright or dark, vary with the temperature. It has been found that blue stars have O-type spectra, our sun has G-type spectra and so on. Blue stars emit 20 or more times the radiation per unit area than that of our sun does, whereas a red type may emit as little as 1/20 as much per unit area.

From this spectra, by measuring and comparing the intensity of different lines and using Wien's Displacement Law, the temperature may be determined. Intensity of emitted light is plotted against wavelength and the curve is drawn. The temperature of the star is directly proportional to the frequency at which most of its radiation is given off, i.e. to the highest point of the curve.

Colour	Star class	Approximate temperature in Fahrenheit	Example
Blue-White	O	Over 55,000	Lota Orionis
Blue-White	B	36,000	Rigel
White	A	20,000	Sirius, Vega
Yellowish-White	F	13,500	Canopus
Yellow	G	11,000	Sun
Orange	K	7,500	Arcturus
Red	M	5,500	Betegeuse

19

How are matches made ?

When a strip of wood, cardboard or waxed paper tipped with a chemical mixture is rubbed against a rough surface, the chemicals burst into a flame and produce fire. The first match was made in 1827 by an English pharmacist John Walker. It was a splint of wood tipped with antimony sulphide, potassium chlorate, gum arabic and starch. The match bursts into flames with a series of small explosions that showered the experimenter with sparks. The first safety match was invented in 1844 by a Swedish chemist Gustave E. Pasch. Let us discuss how matches are made?

Red phosphorous is the main substance used in the match industry. Matches are mainly of two types: Lucifer or friction matches and Safety matches.

Lucifer or friction matches light when rubbed against any rough surface. The match is basically a wood splint or shaft about 8 cm long and 0.3 cm in diameter. It may have a tip of two colours, red and white or blue and white. One-fourth of the wooden strip is first dipped in molten sulphur or paraffin wax. The small white tip is made from the paste of phosphorous trisulphide. Other substances are antimony trisulphide (kindling material), potassium chlorate (supporter of combustion), powder of glass or silica (friction producing substance) and gum or glue (to act as a binder). Red or blue part of the tip does not ignite by rubbing, but burns when the white tip has caught fire. It carries the flame to the rest of the match stick. These matches are made by machines which produce millions of matches per hour.

Nowadays only safety matches are used. Safety matches can only be ignited by striking them against a special surface. The surface is usually located on the sides of the match box. The tip of the safety match is made from the substances mentioned above except phosphorous trisulphide. Red phosphorous is used as the igniter in place of phosphorous trisulphide. When the head of the match stick moves over the rough surface, the molecules in the head and the surface collide with each other and the head of the match becomes hotter. The substances in the head become hot enough and make the head burst into a flame. These matches generally do not light when struck on any other surface. The chances of such a match stick catching fire accidentally are thus eliminated.

Rough surface   Heat generated   Match lights

20

How does a video-tape recorder work?

The unique feature of a video-tape recorder (VTR) is that it plays back both sound and picture. It is mainly used to record television programmes as magnetic patterns and play video cassettes. But how does the video-tape recorder work?

A video-tape is a band of plastic tape. On one side, it is coated with a film of magnetic iron oxide whose thickness is about one-five thousandth of a centimetre. The width of the tape is about 1.25 to 2.5 cm. For recording a programme, the tape is run by a magnetic video tape recorder.

A television camera changes an image into electrical signals. At the same time, a microphone changes sound into electrical signals. These signals are then fed into the recorder. The VTR contains recording heads that convert the signals into varying magnetic fields. As the magnetic tape passes these heads, they produce magnetic patterns on the tape. This tape can then be used to reproduce the original sound and picture. When the tape is played back, the changing magnetic fields of the pattern of iron oxide particles, create weak currents which exactly correspond to the recorded sound and picture.

The sound and picture signals are kept separated in the recorder, and are recorded on to different parts of the tape. Usually, the sound signal is recorded on to a narrow track at the top of the tape. The image signal is recorded on to a wider track in the middle of the tape. A control signal is recorded along the bottom of the tape. Television studios generally use 5 cm-wide tape. The tape moves at a speed of 37.5 cm a second.

The head that records the image signal rotates, as the tape passes by it. As a result, the recording is made in diagonal bands across the tape. This allows more information to be stored on a given length of tape.

Video tapes are used to record and reproduce various television programmes. They are also used for the reproduction of sport events during a live broadcast. Video tapes are also used in slow motion and stop-action techniques. Now a days video discs having pictures as well as sound recordings are also available to see a film on the disc, by playing it on a video disc player connected to a television set.

1. Guides 2. General erase head 3. Video recording and reading heads 4. Tape guide system 5. Audio erase head 6. Audio and control tracks recording head 7. Tape drive capstan 8. Rubber pinch wheel 9. Magnetic tape

A video tape recorder in operation

OOO

21

How are hard drinks made ?

Wine is probably the first type of hard drink to have come into existence. Archaeological evidence suggests that wine making began in the middle-east over 10,000 years ago, and gradually spread westward to the mediterranean countries and finally into Europe. The ancient Egyptian wall paintings reveal that the art of wine making was known to them long before the Westerners took to it.

Wine was common in everyday life of the early Greeks and Romans. It also played an important role in their religious ceremonies. The God of wine was called *Bacchus* by the Romans and *Dionysus* by the Greeks.

Wine can be made from a wide range of fruits and vegetables, but the real wine is made from grapes. Grape juice contains water, sugar, fruit acids and many trace elements. The outer grape skin has millions of tiny living organisms, primarily yeasts, including a number of moulds and bacteria, too.

The grapes are allowed to ripen until they attain suitable sugar content (18% or more) and acidity. When these grapes are crushed, yeasts come into contact with the juice. This brings about the process of fermentation by which grape juice changes into alcohol and carbon dioxide. During fermentation, grape juice loses its sugar and turns into wine. This wine has 10 to 14% alcohol content. The rest of wine consists of water containing traces of acids, sugar and other substances which give the wine its colour and flavour.

Another type of hard drink, beer, is known to have been made by the Egyptians and Babylonians at least 6000 years ago, and there is evidence that barley, from which it is made, was cultivated in Britain and northern Europe, some 5000 years ago. Europeans knew how to produce a fermented drink from barley. Beer is usually made from barley hops, yeast and sugar by the process of fermentation.

Pure brandy is made by the distillation of wine made from grape juice. The wine is heated and the alcohol that evaporates out of it is condensed and collected. Apart from alcohol, other substances are also given off during distillation. Some are poisonous substances and are removed.

Different types of whisky are made from grains such as barley, rye and corn. Rum is made from molasses, a syrup obtained from cane sugar. Gin is made from grain or molasses flavoured with juniper berries.

Major wine-producing areas of the world include France, Germany, Spain, Portugal, Italy and California in the USA.

OOO

22

What is a periscope ?

A periscope is a very useful and interesting optical instrument. It enables officers aboard a submerged submarine to observe whatever might be happening on the surface. A submarine's periscope can move up and down and turn to look in a complete circle. It allows tank commanders to view the battlefield from inside their armoured vehicles. It is therefore, useful in land and sea warfare. Now let us see what exactly is a periscope.

A periscope is an optical instrument with which a person can see around corners and other obstructions. This instrument is based upon the principle of reflection of light from two parallel mirrors. A simple periscope consists of a long tube bent twice at right angles. Two plane mirrors, parallel to each other, are fixed in such a way, that the reflecting surfaces of the two mirrors make an angle of 45° with the axis of the tube. Rays coming from an object in front of the periscope, after undergoing two successive reflections, reach the eye of the observer thus enabling him to see the object.

Some sophisticated periscopes also make use of reflecting prisms and magnifying optics, which make distant objects appear closer. They are also fitted with devices for

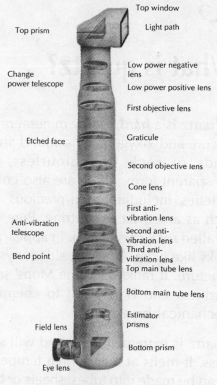

A periscope

estimating the range of the target. Objects can be photographed through a periscope.

Simple periscopes, made of cardboard, are also popular among spectators at parades and sporting events. With its help, they can see above people's heads!

Periscopes are also used in industry to observe nuclear reactions and the interiors of special furnaces and other dangerous devices.

The longest periscope in the world measures 27 m. It is located at the National Reactor Testing in Idaho Falls, Idaho. It is used to view nuclear reactor operations.

○○○

23

What is quartz?

Quartz is a common mineral. Some quartzs are used in jewellery

Quartz is a hard, glossy mineral made of silicon and oxygen. It is found in most kinds of rocks in colourless, often transparent form. There are also coloured varieties including semi-precious stones such as amethyst and citrine. Pure quartz is called rock crystal also. In appearance it looks like glass. It has six sided crystalline structure. It ranks 7 on the Mohs' scale of hardness and is resistant to chemical or mechanical breakdown.

Quartz is extremely hard and will scratch glass. It melts at a very high temperature. It can be made into tubes, sheets or blocks. It can also be blown into various shapes by using oxy-hydrogen flame.

Quartz has great economic importance. Sandstone, composed mainly of quartz, is an important building stone. Large amounts of quartz sand is used in the manufacture of glass and porcelain and in metal casting for foundry moulds. Quartz is used as an abrasive in sandpaper and grindstones. It is used to make prisms and lenses which can transmit ultra-violet light. Tubing and various vessels of fused quartz have important laboratory application. It is also used in ornamental work and industry where its reaction to electricity makes it valuable in electronic instruments. Quartz fibres are used in extremely sensitive weighing devices.

Quartz is a piezoelectric material, i.e. when pressure is applied across the two surfaces of a quartz crystal, an electric voltage develops across the crystal and when voltage is applied across the two faces of the crystal, it expands, or contracts. Due to this property, it can help to change electric signals into sound waves and vice versa. The piezoelectric property of quartz plays an important role in radios, television and radar. Quartz oscillators are used in Quartz crystal watches to give accurate time.

Natural quartz crystals of commercial grade are obtained from Brazil. Quartz can also be made synthetically.

○○○

24

How does an automobile engine work ?

An automobile such as a car, is an automatic self-propelled vehicle. It runs on a gasoline, diesel or electric engine. Petrol or diesel engines used in automobiles are internal combustion engines. In these engines, fuel burns in the cylinder. In an electric engine, there is a motor and a gear box. It is battery-powered and used for small cars on a limited and experimental basis.

Petrol engine is used in most automobiles. However, some automobiles even use diesel engines. Diesel engines are heavier and more expensive than gasoline engines, but they last longer and use less refined fuel.

Both the petrol and diesel engines are four stroke engines. Their construction and working can be understood as follows :

(I) Petrol Engine : It consists of a cylinder containing an air-tight piston. It is connected with the main shaft through a crank by means of a connecting rod. As the piston moves to and fro, its motion is converted into rotational motion of the crank shaft. The cylinder has two valves: one inlet valve and the other, exhaust or outlet valve. Inlet and outlet valves open and close automatically only once in every

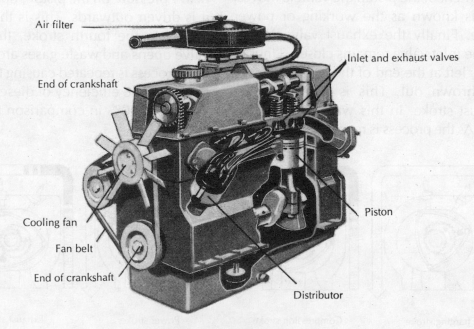

A petrol run automobile engine

cycle. Air is mixed with petrol vapour in a carburettor and is made to pass into the cylinder through the inlet valve. The mixture is burnt in the upper portion by means of an electric spark provided by the spark plug. The action of the engine may be explained in four strokes.

When the engine is made to work at the beginning by external force, the inlet valve opens and the mixture of petrol vapour and air is allowed into the cylinder. This is known as the charging stroke. Now both inlet and outlet valves close and the fuel mixture is compressed. This is known as compression stroke. The spark plug producess an electric spark and causes the mixture to burn. Due to combustion of the fuel, a large amount of heat is produced. This gives rise to heavy pressure and as a result the piston moves. With the movement of the piston the vehicle moves. This is known as the working or power stroke. Finally the exhaust valve opens, but the inlet valve remains closed. Unused gases, left at the end of the working stroke are thrown out. This is known as the exhaust stroke. In this way, one cycle is over. As the process is repeated, the vehicle goes on moving.

Most automobile engines have four, six or eight cylinders. Most of the engines are in the front and drive the rear wheels.

(II) Diesel Engine : This engine makes use of less expensive diesel as power fuel. It has three valves — one for the admission of air, other for the fuel and the third for the exhaust of gases. These valves open and close automatically.

A diesel engine is also a four stroke engine. In the first stroke, air is drawn into the cylinder and in the second, air is compressed and due to this compression, the temperature of air goes up to 600°C. In the third stroke, fuel admission valve opens and oil in the form of spray is injected into the cylinder. The oil begins to burn and the gases produced exert a heavy pressure on the piston, due to which it is driven outwards. This is the working stroke. In the fourth stroke, the exhaust valve opens and waste gases are expelled. This process is repeated causing the vehicle to move. The efficiency of diesel engine is as high as 40% in comparison to a petrol engine.

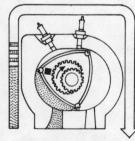 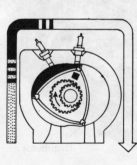 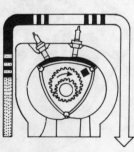 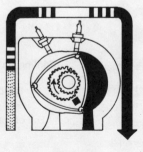

Charging stroke   Compression stroke   Power stroke   Exhaust stroke

The four different strokes of an engine

25

How is electricity conducted through wires?

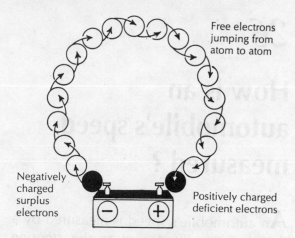

Free electrons jumping from atom to atom

Negatively charged surplus electrons

Positively charged deficient electrons

Current flows through the movement of free electrons from one terminal to the other

Electricity is supplied to our homes, schools, factories and stores through copper or aluminium wires from power stations. These power stations burn coal or oil, use nuclear reactions or the energy of falling water to produce energy to run the generators. The power thus generated is then transmitted to different cities and places where it is required. Electricity is then transmitted through transmission lines.

To avoid the loss of power, the output voltage from the generator is first stepped up to a high voltage by a step-up transformer. After being received at the city power station, it is again reduced to low voltage, before it reaches our homes or factories. Now question arises how is electricity conducted through wires ?

We know that all substances are made up of atoms. Materials which allow the passage of electricity are called conductors. Metals, such as copper, aluminium, silver and gold are good conductors of electricity. The atoms of these metals have loosely bonded electrons. These electrons are free to move within the metal. These are called free electrons and are responsible for the conduction of current. More the number of free electrons in the metal, better it conducts the electricity.

When electric battery is connected across the ends of the metal wire, the negatively charged free electrons move away from the end connected to the negative terminals and flow toward the positive terminal. This flow of electrons is nothing but the electric current. Hence the drifting electrons cause electricity to flow. Greater the number of free electrons in a metal, easier it is for electricity to flow through it.

Some materials are poor conductors of electricity because they have less number of free electrons. Poor conductors resist the flow of electricity. The resistance of a wire depends upon its material length and area of its cross-section.

Some substances do not allow electricity to flow through them and are called insulators. These substances contain tightly-bonded electrons that cannot move away from atoms. Hence they do not conduct electricity. Glass, mica, wood, plastic and rubber are common insulators. Some substances like silicon and germanium are neither good conductors nor insulators. They are called semi-conductors. OOO

93

26

How is an automobile's speed measured ?

An automobile's speed is measured by a speedometer fitted next to the steering wheel of a car. It indicates the vehicle's speed in kilometers per hour or miles per hour. The speed is read on the dial which is numbered from 0 to 160, by means of a pointer. Most speedometers also incorporate an odometer — a device that records the distance travelled by the vehicle.

A speedometer is driven by a flexible cable that is connected to a set of gears in the vehicle's transmission. When the vehicle moves, the gears turn a core or flexible metal shaft inside the cable. The core turns a magnet inside a metal drum called a speed cup. This is located inside the speedometer housing. The revolving magnet exerts a turning force on the speed cup. In turn the speed cup is held back from revolving freely with the magnet, by the opposing action of a hairspring. The movement of the speed cup is transferred to the pointer on the dial. The hairspring brings the pointer back to 'zero' when the vehicle stops moving. Most of the speedometers register 36 km/hr when the core inside the cable revolves at 1000 revolutions per minute.

The odometer registers total kilometers travelled by the vehicle. Some automobiles also have Trip odometers that can be reset to 'zero' at the beginning of a particular trip. An odometer consists of a chain of gears (with a gear ratio of 1000 : 1) that causes a drum, graduated in 10th of a mile or kilometer, to make one turn per mile or kilometer. A series, commonly of six such drums, is arranged in such a way that one of the numerals on each drum is visible in a rectangular window. The drums are coupled so that 10 revolutions of the first cause one revolution of the second and so forth, the numbers appearing in the window represent the accumulated mileage.

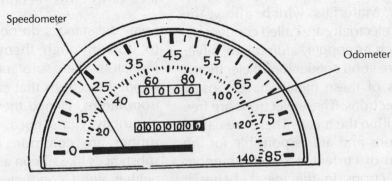

A speedometer

27

How does a crane work ?

A large electromagnet is used in a crane for moving scrap iron in factories or industrial units

You must have seen a crane lifting and moving heavy loads at construction sites and other places. The machine got its name from its resemblance to the crane bird which has a long neck!

Although cranes have been in use since ancient times, their widespread use only began in the 19th century with the development of steam engines, internal combustion engines and electric motors.

Basically, cranes are of two types : fixed and mobile. The mobile cranes are more common. Some have a jib or boom that can move up and down and can swing around in a circle. Some others form a bridge and can lift a load up and down, move it along a track and move it from side to side above the construction site.

A common mobile crane is the crawler. It is mounted on a vehicle with wheels. These cranes are mainly used for civil engineering and construction work. They can lift heavy loads upto around 72 tons and can have a boom length of 30 m (100 ft) or more.

Another type of crane is the hammer head or cantilever crane. It is used in the construction and erection of tall buildings. It has a long horizontal jib that is cantilevered and mounted on a tower. The tower can be raised by jacking it up, floor by floor, as the building becomes taller. The load is suspended from a trolley that moves along the jib.

Bridge cranes comprise another important class of cranes in which the hoisting apparatus moves on tracks along a horizontal beam. In most cases, the ends of the beam move along a pair of parallel rails, so that the crane can serve as a large rectangular area.

The forklift truck, widely used for moving goods between warehouse storage shipping vehicles, is a highly manoeuverable crane adapted to handling drums, crates or loaded skids or pallets. Gantry cranes, with long booms, are used for unloading ships while overhead cranes are used in factories.

The world's most powerful crane is owned by Heerema Engineering Service of Netherlands. It weighs 53,000 tons and is 178 m long. It can lift upto 3000 tons.

ooo

28

How is nylon made ?

Nylon is one of the most important chemical discoveries of the 20th century. It is one of the toughest, strongest and most elastic substances we have today. It is a synthetic plastic material which is made from chemicals derived from coal, water, air, petroleum, agricultural by-products and natural gas.

It was first developed by a research team headed by a U.S. chemist Wallace H. Corothers working in E.I. Dupant de Nemours & Co. He began experimenting with it in the 1920s. In 1935, he produced the first piece of nylon. It was converted into cloth in 1937.

Nylon is made from two chemical compounds : Hexamethylenediamine and Adipic acid. Hexamethylenediamine consists of carbon, nitrogen and hydrogen. Adipic acid contains carbon, hydrogen and oxygen. Each of these substances contains six carbon atoms and the nylon produced by them has been named as Nylon-6, 6. Manufacturers combine the two compounds to form a substance called nylon salt. A solution of nylon salt is placed in an autoclave (a heating device). The autoclave heats the solution under pressure. Water is removed and the small molecules in the compound, combine to form large molecules. This process is called polymerisation.

When caprolactam is used as the starting material, Nylon -6, 6 is obtained. It has been so named because it has six carbon atoms in the basic unit. It is comparatively a recent development.

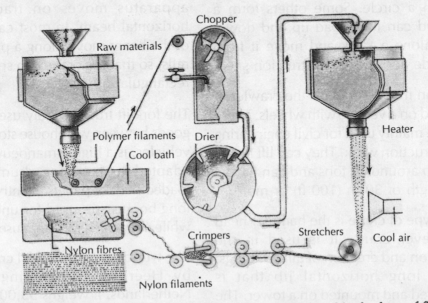

The making of nylon in a factory. It is a type of plastic widely used in the form of fibre

In some factories, the newly made nylon comes out of the machines as a plastic ribbon. This is then cooled, and cut into small pieces. Nylon fibres are made by forcing molten nylon through tiny holes in a device called spinneret. The thin streams of nylon that come out of the spinneret harden into filaments when they come in contact with air. Then they are wound into bobbins. From a single bobbin, as many as 2520 filaments are united into a textile nylon yarn. The fibres are drawn or stretched after they cool. The stretching action causes molecules in the fibre to fall into straight lines and make the fibres stronger and more elastic.

Nylon can be formed into fibres, bristles, sheets, rods, tubes and coatings. It can also he rendered into powdered form for making moulds.

Nylon fibres resist mildew and not harmed by most kinds of oil, grease and household cleaning fluids. It absorbs little water.

Nylon is used to make many articles of clothing, parachutes, carpets, ropes, fishing lines and upholstery. It is also used in tyres and bristles in many types of brushes. Solid pieces of nylon are used to make bearings, gears and small machine parts. Unlike metal parts nylon bearings and machine parts need little lubrication.

Recently a nylon derivative known as Qiana has been developed. It is a silk-like fibre used in clothing. Thus nylon has proved to be useful in many ways.

○○○

29

What is the Theory of Relativity ?

In the early nineteenth century people believed that light travelled through an imaginary stationary medium called ether. It was believed that ether filled all space, and all movements could be measured absolutely with respect to it. It was also thought that the speed of light relative to a moving observer, could be calculated in the same way as the relative speeds of any two moving objects. For example, just imagine two cars in the same direction :

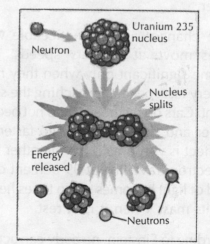

When an uranium nucleus splits, it releases great energy because a little mass is 'lost' in the process and this 'lost' mass reappears as energy

one going at a speed of 110 km/hr and the other at 80 km/hr. Passengers in the slower car would observe that the faster car is travelling at 30 km/hr.

Two American scientists, Michaelson and Morley, experimentally tried to measure the speed of earth through ether in 1887. But their result did not conform the existence of the hypothetical medium ether. Later the explanation of negative results was offered by Albert Einstein. According to him, nothing like ether exists in the universe and the concept of absolute motion is meaningless. He also said that the speed of light is constant, no matter how fast the observer is moving. No material body can travel faster than light.

On the basis of his conclusions, Einstein formulated the Special Theory of Relativity in 1905. He showed that physical quantities like mass, length and time are also not absolute. They change as the bodies move. If a body moves with a large velocity, its mass increases and it becomes shorter.

These changes are not noticeable when bodies move at ordinary speeds. They become significant only when they move at a very fast speed approaching the speed of light. Cars on the freeway do not become heavier and shorter as they go faster, but the effect is very small. On the other hand an electron travelling at 99 percent of the speed of light becomes seven times heavier than its mass when it is at rest.

According to Einstein, no body can actually attain the speed of light. If an object did, it would be infinitely heavy and have zero length. The increase in mass and decrease in length of a body as its speed increases, led Einstein to conclude that mass and energy are different aspects of the same thing, but are related to each other. This led him to the famous mass energy equation $E = mc^2$ where c is the velocity of light and m is the mass of the body. Nuclear energy is a direct consequence of this equation.

The second part of Einstein's theory is called General Theory of Relativity and was published in 1915. This theory applies only to bodies moving with constant speeds. It deals with the accelerated motion of bodies. It deals mainly with the way the force of gravity works. He suggested that the force of gravity is a property of space and time. He showed that space becomes 'curved' by the presence of mass. The motion of stars and planets is controlled by this curvature of space. Light rays, too, are bent by the curvature of space around a body that has mass. Strong fields of gravity such as that of the sun or a star would bend light rays. The bending of light rays has been observed in an eclipse of the sun.

Einstein's Theory of Relativity is one of the greatest achievements of the human mind. This theory gave birth to the production of nuclear power. Atom bomb and hydrogen bombs could be made only due to the conclusions based on Theory of Relativity.

Albert Einstein, one of the greatest scientists of the present century was born in Germany in 1879, and lived there and in Switzerland and the USA, where he died in 1955.

ooo

30

How do we see distant objects with binoculars ?

If you look through binoculars, you will find distant objects appear nearer and larger. Why does this happen ?

Binoculars are a pair of small telescopes built into a frame or casting. The two telescopes in binoculars are exactly similar in structure and meant for each eye. Each telescope is built into a funnel-shaped tube or cylinder. It consists of one objective lens and one eyepiece. The objective lens is kept towards the object and the eyepiece near the eye. The lenses are anti-reflection coated. Two prisms are also mounted between the objective lens and the eye piece to make the image of the object erect.

The light from the object falls on the objective lens and an inverted image is produced by it. This image is further inverted by the two prisms, thus the image becomes erect. The eyepiece further magnifies this image. This is how we see the erect and magnified image of the object.

Most of the binoculars have a single adjustable wheel or thumb screw for controlling the focus of both telescopes simultaneously. Some binoculars have separate focus wheels for each telescope for varying characteristics of the two eyes.

Binoculars usually have two numbers printed or engraved somewhere on the outer covering. The first number is the power of magnification and the second number shows the diameter of the objective lens in millimeters. If the binoculars are marked 6 x 35, then it will magnify an object six times through an objective lens which is 35 mm in diameter.

Binoculars provide stereoscopic vision, i.e. depth perception at great distances by using both eyes at the same time. People often use them to see matches in playgrounds. Many modern microscopes also use binoculars. This is to get a clearer and three dimensional image of the object.

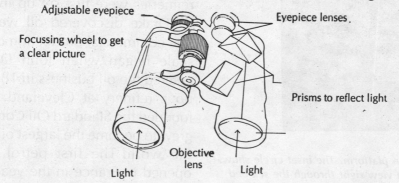

Adjustable eyepiece

Focussing wheel to get a clear picture

Eyepiece lenses

Prisms to reflect light

Objective lens

Light   Light

Binocular is an optical instrument for viewing an object in magnified size with both eyes

31

When was petrol first produced?

In the recent past petrol has become one of the most valuable commodities all over the world due to its wide use as a great source of energy. But what is petrol and how is it produced?

Petroleum is the complex mixture of hydrocarbons that occur in the Earth's crust, usually in liquid or gaseous form. It is believed to be formed from buried organic debris, chiefly from planktons and simple plants under marine conditions unfavourable to oxidation. Crude petroleum oil is procured from some depth within the Earth through boreholes. But do you know when was refined petroleum first produced?

The development of the production of refined petroleum went through various stages. When industries were developing at the outset of the Industrial Revolution, they required a convenient source of lubricants for this newly invented machines as well as an illuminating oil. Thus the stage was set for drilling of oil from oil wells. The first well was drilled by E.L. Drake in Western Pensylvania which was completed in August 1859 at a depth of 21 metres. This was the beginning of petroleum industry of modern times.

The advent of automobiles at the beginning of the 20th century necessitated a convenient source of fuel energy. Crude petroleum is the raw material which is processed and refined in an oil refinery to obtain the usable finished product.

In a refinery the crude oil undergoes several heating and chemical treatments. In the process some alkenes are formed which improve the quality of the petrol. Many by-products are also produced during the refining process such as paraffin, coal tar, kerosene and some lubricating oils. Oil refineries were first set up in 1860s after E.L.Drake discovered oil wells in 1859. The commercial production of oil in large scale began when John D. Rockfeller entered the oil business in 1862 by setting up a refinery at Cleveland. In 1870 he founded the Standard Oil Company which grew to become the largest oil company in the world. The first petrol station was opened in France in the year 1895.

Flare stack
Drilling tower
Helicopter pad
Power station
Impervious cap rock
Drill pipes
Gas
Oil
Pipeline

An oil-production platform. The inset circle shows a cross-section view right through the sea-bed

OOO

3
Plants & Animals

• Does any animal wash its food ? • Which sea animals emit light ? • How do birds hear ? • How do aquatic animals survive in frozen lakes ? • Do insects have organs and blood ? • Which plants feed on other plants? • Which are the roots we eat ? • Why do insects get attracted towards light ? • Why does a peacock display its feathers ? • Which insects have the longest lifespan ? • Which are the different oils extracted from seeds? • Why don't leaves get heated in sunlight? • How do insects reproduce and develop ? • What are the different types of rhinoceros? • Which is the most dangerous bird in the world ? • Why do woodpeckers peck the trees? • Which is the world's deadliest animal ? • Why do flies rub their legs together ? • Which are the large-sized flying birds ? • How can dogs be dangerous to us ? • Where do penguins live?

1

Does any animal wash its food ?

Racoons wash their food not for cleaning but may be to make their food tastier

Do you know any animal that washes its food before eating it ?

Racoon is such an interesting animal. Most racoons wash their food, and there have been instances when not finding water to wash their food, they refused to eat. However, they have also been known to eat food even when they could find water nearby. Some racoons have been observed to eat without ever washing their food.

Nobody really knows why racoons wash their food. They do not seem to wash it in an attempt to clean it, since they even wash it in muddy water. Besides they would even wash food caught in the water which certainly does not need washing. So the reason is probably that water makes food tastier for them.

The name 'racoon' comes from the American Indian word *arakhuman*. They are furry mammals and belong to the family *Procyonidae*. They are found in the stretch from Southern Canada to Panama, except in the high rockies.

Racoon is usually gray in colour, sometimes tinged with yellow or brown. It has a bushy, ringed tail which is about 25 cm long, dark brown in colour with four to six yellowish rings. The eyes are covered with black marks. They have pointed snouts and strong, sharp claws. They use their paws to find food.

Racoons live in places where there is water and trees for dens. Their food, which they hunt at night, is mainly crayfish, clams, fish and frogs. They find their prey in muddy water. They also feed on nuts, berries, fruits and particularly young corn.

There are two main species of racoons. The northern racoon (*Procyon lotor*) lives in Canada, the United States and Central America. It measures from 76 cm to 97 cm in length including the tail. They may weigh upto 10 kg. Males are generally larger than females. The crab eating racoon (*Procyon carnivorous*) lives in South America. This type of racoon has shorter hair and longer legs than its northern counterpart.

Northern racoons mate once a year between January and June. About nine weeks after mating, the female gives birth to one to seven young ones. Racoons are hunted for their fur and meat. ○○○

2

Which sea animals emit light ?

There are about 600 marine organisms which produce light from their bodies. The main groups of marine luminescent organisms include protozoans, coelentrates, polychactes, molluscs, crustaceans and fishes. Many sea bacteria are also luminescent. Sponges, jellyfish, beetles, flies and earthworms also produce light. This type of luminescene is called bio-luminescence.

Careful studies on fishes and other organisms have revealed that this light is the result of a series of chemical reactions taking place in the organisms. In this contest luminescence is basically of two types: Intracellular and Extracellular. Animals which produce luminescence by intracellular mechanism have luminescent glands. The others which produce luminescence by extracellular mechanism have unicellular or multicellular organs in some particular regions of their body. There are two substances (luciferin and luciferase) whose interaction produces luminescence. Intracellular light flashes range in duration from a fraction of a second to several minutes. Light producing organs in different sea animals are located in the skin on the ventral musculature and within the abdomen. Light is emitted only from the parts where they have these organs.

Lantern fish and angler fish are two well-known luminescent sea animals. The angler fish has its lighted baits placed in the mouth. Lantern fish produces definite patterns of light.

Luminescence produced by sea animals is helpful in locating fish shoals because the movement of a large number of fishes produces light which can be detected by light sensors. In the last two decades, significant progress has been made in the detection of fish shoals.

Simple water animals like sponges also produce light from their bodies

ooo

3

How do birds hear ?

According to ornithologists, the hearing abilities of birds are similar to those of man. Birds have ears for hearing which are in many respects similar to those of reptiles. The outer ear consists of a short external passage or meatus, ordinarily hidden under the feathers at the side of the head. Most birds have a muscle in the skin around the meatus that can partially or completely close the opening. The tympanic membrane bulges out. From the inner surface of the tympanic membrane, an ocular chain transmits vibrations of cochlea. The chain consists of an osseous inner element, the columella and a cartilaginous extracolumella that extends the columella peripherally and connects with the tympanic membrane.

It has been observed experimentally that most of the birds respond over a frequency range from 100 to 12,800 Hz. The frequency range of human ear is from 20 Hz to 20,000 Hz. Birds can separate sounds which appear as continuous to the human ear.

Birds use their hearing power to guard themselves against enemies and other kinds of danger. Some birds also use vocalizations to identify their mates or group member. Owls locate and catch their prey by auditory cues.

Birds are warm-blooded animals of the class 'Aves'. Like mammals they are vertebrates. They do not bear their young but lay eggs from which they are hatched.

Birds have feathers, wings and beaks that make them different from other animals. They don't have any teeth. They mainly feed on insects, seeds and animal flesh. Their sight is well-developed and highly efficient, but their sense of smell is rather poor.

There are about 9000 species of birds. They range in size from the tiny humming bird of about 5 cm in length, to the ostrich, which can grow 2.5 metres in height and can weigh as much as 136 kg!

Owls have keen ears. Some owls can catch mice in pitch darkness by listening to the sound they make

4

How do aquatic animals survive in frozen lakes ?

In cold countries, when the temperature falls below the freezing point, water, lakes and rivers get frozen. Under such conditions, how do aquatic plants and animals survive?

Generally all liquids expand on heating, but water is an exception. At 0°C, if water is heated gradually, its volume decreases and this contraction continues till the temperature rises to 4°C. Above 4°C water starts expanding and keeps on expanding with further rise in temperature. This shows that at 4°C, the volume occupied by a given mass of water is minimum. In other words, the density of water at 4°C is maximum. This irregular expansion of water is known as anomalous expansion.

This anomalous expansion of water plays an important role in nature. Due to this only the upper layers of water in the ponds and lakes in cold countries get freezed. Lower layers remain as water, and as a result aquatic animals survive.

In cold countries, during winter when the atmospheric temperature is very low, the upper layers of water in the lakes and ponds start cooling. When the temperature of the surface layer falls to 4°C, the water acquires maximum density and sinks down. The lower layers of water then rise up. This water also gets cooled to 4°C and again sinks down. The process continues till the temperature of the whole water falls to 4°C. As the temperature falls below 4°C, the density of water decreases and as a result water at the surface becomes lighter and does not sink down. The surface water finally freezes while the lower layers remain at 4°C. As ice is a bad conductor of heat, freezing in the lower layers is a very slow process. Thus underneath the frozen layer, fish and other aquatic animals and plants survive. Had the expansion of water been uniform, the lakes or ponds would have been completely frozen, along with the aquatic plants and animals. In this situation no plant and animal would have survived.

When the upper layers of water in the lakes or ponds get freezed, the lower layers still remain as water and hence the animals survive underneath

○○○

5

Do insects have organs and blood ?

Insect is such a tiny creature that it is difficult to believe that it has a circulatory system and has blood in its body. But interestingly insects have a heart, blood and other organs.

Insects are found everywhere in the world, except in the deep seas. Fossils indicate that they have existed on earth for more than 400 million years. They have been able to adapt quickly and efficiently, to environmental and climatic changes.

The body of an insect is divided into three sections : head, thorax and abdomen. The head has one pair of antennae which serve to convey the senses of touch, taste and smell. There are usually two compound eyes which provide proper vision and two or three simple eyes (ocelli) which detect light or darkness. The mouth may have biting or chewing jaws or piercing and sucking structures. The head also contains a brain which connects with nerve cords in all parts of the body.

The thorax or middle part of the body has three pairs of jointed legs. These legs are equipped with sticky pads or claws at the end. Insects are the only invertebrates with wings. Although most insects have two pairs of wings, some have only one pair or no wings at all.

The abdomen or end-part of the body contains organs for digestion, excretion, respiration and reproduction. There are tiny openings along the length of the abdomen called spiracles. These spiracles open to the tracheae through which an insect breathes. The oxygen diffuses into the blood from the tracheae at a fairly slow rate. This is probably a major reason behind insects staying small throughout their evolution.

In the circulatory system, blood passes into the heart through holes equipped with valves. When the heart contracts, these holes close and blood is driven out through arteries. Insects do not have a system of capillaries and veins as we do.

The abdomen also contains malphigian tubules. These tubules remove wastes from the blood while recycling most of the water to the body and for this reason, insects can live for long without water. A female insect often has an egg-laying tube called ovipositor.

An insects body is covered with a tough exo-skeleton which provides protection from injury and controls loss of moisture. Further, the entire body is usually covered with tiny bristles. These bristles are connected to nerves and are very sensitive to contact. This is the reason that an insect can detect even the faintest breeze or movement.

Many insects have special hearing organs located on the abdomen, thorax or legs. Some of these organs are just spaces covered by a thin membrane which responds to vibrations in the air.

OOO

6

Which plants feed on other plants ?

Saprophytic orchids obtain their food from dead organic matters

Do you know that there are certain plants which cannot produce their own food because of the absence of chlorophyll? Such plants, therefore, depend on other plants or dead animals for their food.

Plants which feed on dead organic matter are called 'saprophytes' and those which feed on plants are called 'parasites'. Saprophytes play an important role in the decay process. They clear the land of dead animals by digesting and absorbing nutrients from the dead material. For instance, all fungi and bacteria which do not contain chlorophyll fall in this group.

Parasitic plants feed on other plants. They obtain water and food from the host through specially developed organs called 'haustoria' which secure the parasite to the host and grow into the host's tissue. Parasitic plants do not give any benefit to their hosts in anyway. In some cases, they cause harm to their hosts.

The extent to which a parasite is dependent on its host largely determines its vegetative form. True parasites such as dodders, cuscuta and cassytha are entirely devoid of chlorophyll and rely entirely on the host as a food source. The dodder, which is a well-known parasitic plant, looks like a tiny slender snake. Its colour varies from

bright yellow to red. When a dodder seed germinates, the young plant begins to grow in a circular fashion, searching for the mother plant. Once it gets a host, the thin stem of this plant twines around the host's stem and starts taking food from the host.

Other parasites such as the toothwort and the broom are parasitic on the roots of other plants, rather than their stems. Correspondingly, these plants are less conspicuous than dodders because their vegetative parts are underground.

A well-known example of a partial parasite is mistletoe which grows as a cluster of branches hanging from trees. It produces a haustorium which connects with the host's stem and extracts water and mineral nutrients. It can produce food by photosynthesis but needs water and minerals from trees.

Mosses and lichen are also parasitic in nature. They cover the bark of the trees and take food from them. *Rafflesia Arnoldi* of Sumatra is also a famous parasitic plant.
ooo

7

Which are the roots we eat ?

The roots of certain plants get swollen with stored food. They can be eaten as vegetables. The plants that produce such roots are called root crops.

Root crops have long been cultivated as a food source all over the world. Since they extract different chemicals from the soil, as against grain crops, they have proved useful in crop-rotation systems.

The roots of beet are consumed mainly in cooked form and are usually served with a main course or in soups. Beet powder is used as a red colouring agent in sauces.

Carrots are bright orange-coloured roots. They contain high percentage of carotene. They are consumed in fresh or cooked form and are sometimes dehydrated.

Radishes are roots with strong flavour. White or red roots are usually eaten as appetizers and are also used in salads.

Rutabaga and turnip are more or less alike. But Rutabaga is more rounded or elongated as compared to turnip which is rather flat. Both are yellow in colour.

Sweet potatoes have orange flesh and are preferred for their sweetness. They are served cooked, and are often canned and dehydrated as flakes.

Some underground stems called tubers are also used as vegetables. Girasole, potato, taro and yam are among the important ones. They are used both in cooked and dehydrated form.

Some underground bulbs, such as garlic, leek and onion are also used as food materials. Garlic is used for flavouring soups, sauces and salads. Leek is used as a flavouring material. Onion is used in salads and cooked with other vegetables.

Roots are very useful for us as they give us many minerals and vitamins.

Some commonly used edible roots

108

8

Why do insects get attracted towards light ?

You must have seen insects buzzing around a glowing lamp or bulb in your homes. The surprising aspect is that it is only the male insects who get attracted towards light. Moreover, insects are not attracted equally to all sources of light. Do you know why this happens?

The attraction of insects to light has been a subject of interest to researchers since Aristotle's time. In the late nineteenth century, this phenomenon was studied in great detail by S.W. Frost of Pennsylvania University, U.S.A. Later, from an extensive study of this subject, a French entomologist, J.H. Fabre was able to provide a proper explanation.

Fabre put forth the theory that certain radiations coming out from the light source are responsible for the attraction of insects. This has now been confirmed by some experiments that a series of narrow bands of infrared radiations, emitted by the source of light, produce the attraction for insects. This study was conducted on moths.

There is a gland at the tip of the female's abdomen from which it releases some acetate molecules. These are called pheromone or sex scent. This chemical emits some infrared radiations which spread through air. The male moth, flying at some distance from the female, picks up these radiations and gets attracted towards the female.

The most acute sense of smell exhibited in nature is that of the male emperor moth (*Eudia pavonia*) which according to German experiments in 1961, can detect the sex attachment of the female at a distance of almost 11 km. Some moths get attracted towards light under the impression that some female moths are there. Thus the search for the female leads it to the light.

Candle lights emit sufficient amount of such radiations, thus attracting a lot of male insects. Insects are also attracted to street lights for the same reason.

It has been found from different studies that the pheromones of different insects are not alike. That is why all insects are not equally attracted towards light. Similar is the case with different light sources. If a light source does not produce these infra-red radiations, insects will not be attracted towards it. This process of insect communication is very complicated and needs sophisticated equipment for study.

OOO

Why does a peacock display its feathers ?

The male peacock displays its beautiful feathers like a fan to attract the female species

A peacock displaying its feathers provides one of the most spectacular sights. Do you know the reason behind it?

Peacock has a beautiful train of feathers which he displays during the breeding season. It usually attracts several females by such display, but as soon as any of them approaches, it turns its back. The reason for this peculiar behaviour is not clear. But it is certain that this is done to woo the female. In Greek mythology the pattern of the peacock's tail feathers represents the eyes of Argus — a giant with 100 eyes.

Peacock is the national bird of India. It belongs to the family *phasianidae*. Strictly speaking, the male is a peacock and the female is a peahen. Both are together known as peafowl. There are two species of peafowl. One is found in India and Sri Lanka and is blue in colour. The other species is found in South-East Asia which is green in colour. In fact, peacock is a native of Asia and the East Indies, from where it has been brought to other parts of the world.

The male of both species has a 75 cm long body and 150 cm long tail. The female is smaller than the male. The tail is made up of beautiful feathers. In display, the peacock lifts its tail, brings it forward, enveloping his body as he struts and quivers, audibly rattling the quills and uttering loud screams. Generally, a peacock has a train of upto 150 tail feathers, which are erected by it in display to form a showy fan.

The blue peacock's body is metallic blue green. The green peacock has a green and bronze body. The hens of both species are green and brown. They do not have the train of feathers or 'crown' on them.

In the wild, they live in open lowland forests, flocking by day and roosting high in trees. The male usually has a *harem* of one to five hens each of which lays four to eight buffy or white eggs. Peafowls are omnivorous, i.e. they eat both plants and animals. They can eat young snakes.

OOO

10

Which insects have the longest lifespan ?

Most insects live only for a short span of time compared to other living creatures on earth. Do you know which insects have the longest lifespan ?

The longest living insects are the Splendour Beetles (*Buprestidae*), some of which remain in the larva stage for more than 30 years. They pass through a complete metamorphosis. In the young larval forms they are very varied and include some of the largest and smallest of all insects. The largest is 'Hercules Beetle' of South Africa which is 15 cm long. The smallest is only 0.05 cm. Queen termites (*Isoptera*) previously thought to live 50 years or more, are now known to have a maximum lifespan of 15 years.

Apart from these two insects, there is one insect called cicada, that actually lives for 17 years. Its lifecycle is very interesting. The female cicada lays eggs on the twigs of trees. When the young one (nymph) hatches, it drops down to the ground. Then it burrows itself into the ground and attaches itself to the roots of plants and trees. Here it remains motionless for about 17 years, sucking at the sap of the roots. After this long *burial*, it is driven by some mysterious instinct towards light. It climbs the tree trunks and its skin splits open and the mature cicada emerges.

For about five weeks, it leads an active life in the sunlight. After this it just dies. So it takes 17 years to develop for just five weeks of active life.

The male cicada makes a shrill sound which can be heard in the countryside. It is well known for the monotonous, whining songs of males. This sound is probably a mating call. According to scientists, the noise-producing organ of the cicada is probably the most complicated musical organ to be found in nature. The male cicada has little drum-like plates which constantly vibrate by muscles that never seem to get tired.

There are more than 800 species of cicada and 100 of these are found in North America. But the 17-year cicada is found only in the United States. Most of the other species live only for two years.

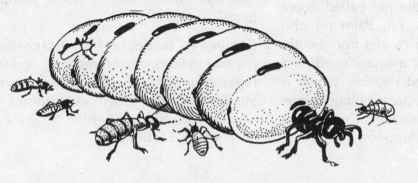

Queen termites have a lifespan of 15 years

OOO

11

Which are the different oils extracted from seeds ?

The oil, that we use in our kitchen or for the manufacture of margarine and other goods, is obtained from the seeds of many plants. The world production of major oilseed crops (in millions of metric tons) is Soyabeans 46.5, Peanuts 18.1, Cottonseed 22.1 and Copra 3.4. The other sources of vegetable oils are mustard, rapeseed, sunflower etc.

The basic process for extracting oil is essentially the same for all oilseeds. It involves either pressing or solvent extraction or a combination of both. The material that remains after removal of the oil contains primarily fibres, carbohydrates and proteins. This may contain protein upto 50%. This material is discarded and used as fertiliser or animal feed.

Most of the world's supply of coconut oil comes from West Africa. It is taken from the dried kernel of the nut called copra which contains 70% oil. Palm oil also comes from West Africa and from South-East Asia. These oils are produced in a hard fatty form called stearine, which is used in the manufacture of chocolate, cooking fats and medicines. Crude oil is used in soaps and shampoos.

Cottonseed provides about 37% oil. The cotton plant is grown commercially in the United States, India and Egypt. The fruit of the plant splits open to reveal fluffy white fibres and a number of seeds — each about six millimeters long. Cottonseed oil is used in margarine, cooking fat, and salad oil. It is also used in soaps, resins, grease and lubricants.

Linseed is the seed of the flax plant which is grown primarily in the United States, Russia, Argentina, India and Canada. Flax fibres are woven into linen cloth and the seeds are used for extracting oil. Linseed oil is used in paints, varnishes, printing and lithographic inks, linoleum, oil cloth and as a water-proofing agent. The residue is a valuable cattle food.

Groundnut or peanut is the seed of the plant *Arachis Lypogea*. The seeds of this plant yield oil and are cultivated mainly in China, West Africa, the United States and South-East Asia. It is mainly used as a cooking medium.

Soyabean is the most important of all the oil seeds. It is extensively grown in China and the Far East. Soyabean oil is used for cooking and as a base for paints, plastics, adhesives, etc. It is a rich source of protein. The seeds can be ground into a protein-rich flour which can be used in many foods.

Sunflower is becoming increasingly popular in European oil markets, and so is rapeseed in Canada and Northern Europe. Sunflower is now grown in countries like Mexico, Russia, erstwhile Yugoslavia, Turkey and South Africa.

OOO

12

Why don't leaves get heated in sunlight?

Anything exposed to the sunlight for some time becomes very hot, especially during the summer months. A scrap of paper or a piece of metal kept in the sunlight may even become too hot to touch after a while. But have you ever wondered why the leaves of trees and plants, which are exposed to the sun the whole day, don't get so hot?

This fact may be understood as follows : a plant leaf is made up of several layers of cells. The upper epidermis covers the top surface of the leaf and the lower epidermis

covers the underside. The lower epidermis has many openings called stomata, which act as valves. They regulate the exchange of gases between the leaf and air. When they are open, they allow carbon dioxide to go into the leaf. They also release oxygen and water vapour. When the stomata are closed, inhaling or exhaling cannot take place.

Each stomata is surrounded by two sausage-shaped guard cells, which control the size of openings. The stomata are usually open during the day and closed at night. The water vapour that is lost by the leaf through the stomata, is replaced by water from the roots. This process is called transpiration.

So when water evaporates, it cools the leaf. Hence this enables the plant to keep cool in the sunlight. ooo

13

How do insects reproduce and develop ?

Scientists have studied more than 800,000 species of insects. Do you know how they reproduce and develop?

Reproduction in insects is usually sexual, the male inserting sperm into the female's

body. The fertilized eggs are usually not tended by the insects, but they develop near or in a source of nourishment and protection. In some cases, fertilisation is external. This means that the female lays the eggs and then the male fertilizes them. Some insects produce eggs which develop into adults without being fertilized. This is a type of asexual reproduction and is known as parthenogenesis.

As an egg develops, it goes through several stages before becoming an adult. Some primitive insects develop directly from the eggs. Most of them, however, go through several stages of development called metamorphosis. In complete metamorphosis, there are four stages of development : egg, larva, pupa and adult. In incomplete metamorphosis there are three stages : egg, nymph, adult. The nymph is like a small adult. As the insect goes through its development, it moults several times. The entire process of metamorphosis may take a few days or several years depending on species and environmental conditions. Many insects lay eggs which can survive the winter or other unfavourable conditions.

Insects are both harmful and useful for us. Some of the harmful insects damage the crops and plants. Some others are germ-carriers. They spread diseases by causing infection through micro-organisms such as bacteria, fungi, viruses and worm like parasites.

As far as their usefulness goes, they are responsible for most of the pollination of plants. They serve as food for birds. In some countries insects are also used as food by human beings. Insects also provide us with some useful materials such as silk, honey and wax. They are also used in dyes, shellacs, medicines and many other products. You will be surprised to know that the eyes of some insects are made up of upto 30,000 tiny lenses called facets.

OOO

14

What are the different types of rhinoceros?

The name 'rhinoceros' has Greek origin. In Greek *rhino* means 'nose' and *keros* means 'horned'. The animal has one or two curved horns on its long nose. The horns grow throughout its life. Rhinoceros belong to the 'odd-toed' group of ungulates. Rhinoceros are found in Africa and South-East Asia.

The animal carries its large body on its four stout, short legs. It has three toes on each foot, each toe ending in separate hoof. Each front foot actually has a fourth toe, too, that is no longer used.

The skin of the rhinoceros is very thick and has little hair. They look as if they are wearing heavy armour plating held together with rivets. The horns are composed entirely of hair like growths set above thickenings of the nasal bones and frontal bones. They are not attached to the skull and may even be torn off in fighting. When this happens, they quickly grow again. The horn may be upto 107 cm in length.

There are five different kinds of rhinoceros existing today — two from Africa and three from Asia. The Sumatran rhinoceros have two horns whereas the other two Asian species — Indian and Javan — have only one. They are all in danger of extinction but the most endangered is the Javan rhinoceros, which survives only in one small reserve.

The largest of all these is the white rhinoceros from Africa. It stands 1.8 m (6 ft) high at the shoulder and can weigh over 3 tons. An interesting difference between the white and the black rhinoceros lies in the shape of their lips. The white rhinoceros has a wider, square-mouth which is very suitable for cropping grass. The black rhinoceros is more of a browser and has a pointed upper lip for grazing and plucking leaves and shoots from shrubs and bushes. The other two-horned species, the Sumatran rhinoceros, is the smallest of all, standing only about 4.5 ft at the shoulder and weighing less than a ton.

Rhinoceros feeds on grass, twigs and shrubs. They do not hunt other animals for food. During the afternoon heat, the rhinoceros usually buries itself in muddy water. And from here it emerges with a layer of mud on its skin. This dries and forms a protective coating against insect bites.

This huge animal is usually quiet and retiring. But if it is cornered, it can become very fierce and dangerous. A rhinoceros can charge at a speed of 30 miles an hour, and use its strong, pointed horns to attack its enemy. In captivity the rhinoceros may live upto fifty years.

A female bears only one young at a time. The calf is born about eighteen months after the mating season and remains with the mother for several years.

Now unfortunately the rhinoceros is a rare species. Over the centuries they have been hunted by man for their horns. This is because according to an ancient belief, its horn imparted magical properties to its owner. However, now this second largest land mammal is being protected by law to prevent it from becoming extinct.

The great Indian rhinoceros which looks as if wearing a heavy armour plate

The two-horned Sumatran black rhinoceros is the smallest of all varieties

OOO

15

Which is the most dangerous bird in the world ?

The flightless Australian Cassowary. It has its protective heavy, bony, crest like a helmet

The cassowary is the most dangerous bird in the world. Its inner toe has a long dagger-like claw that acts as a weapon and can slash open a man's stomach!

The cassowary is found in New Guinea and Northern Australia. It is a secretive forest dweller and is seldom seen, but often heard croaking and bellowing. It cannot fly, but runs at a great speed on its powerful legs. On each foot it has three toes, the inner one having a long straight claw. It can often be seen giving furious kicks at the trunk of trees without any apparent reason. Because of this strange habit the cassowary is regarded as having a very bad temper. In dense forests it can even speed upto 50 km an hour. It can grow upto a height of 6 ft and weigh as much as 180 pounds. When it gets annoyed, it jumps in the air and delivers a vicious kick.

It is a bony-headed bird. Its naked blue head is protected by a bony helmet. Its body is covered with coarse hair-like feathers. It is the only member of the family casuariidae. Unlike other birds, the male incubates eggs. At a time three to six eggs are laid. The eggs are green in colour and 13 centimetres long. They are incubated for 50 days in a leafy nest and on the ground. The adult provides parental care for the young ones.

Cassowaries live in family groups or in pairs. They like to be near water, for they swim readily. They are also good fishers.

According to zoologists, the cassowary's ancestors were able to fly. But in the process of evolution, it became flightless. It has adapted itself to make the most efficient use of its environment. Emu, kiwi, weka and takahe are also flightless birds. Most of the flightless birds are found in Australia and New Zealand.

ooo

16

Why do woodpeckers peck the trees ?

A woodpecker is a bird which gets its name as it pecks the wood of trees, looking for insects to eat. The woodpecker is a great help to the trees because quite often, the insects and worms are harmful for the trees. These grubs and insects remain hidden deep in the crevices of the bark of trees. The woodpecker can find them instinctively even when they cannot be seen outside. Then he drills a deep hole and straight gets down to them. Sometimes woodpeckers make two openings, like a front and back door. This is to enable them to get away if an enemy shows up.

The woodpecker has a chisel-like beak which can drill holes into dead or unhealthy trees. The structure of the head and neck of a woodpecker is adapted for driving its beak powerfully forward into the tree bark and absorbing the shock of the blow. It then uses its long tongue to capture and eat worms and insects. They can bore holes in the trees. Most woodpeckers nest in large holes that they dig in the branches or tree trunks.

A woodpecker is a member of the family *picidae*. There are 24 species of wood-

Woodpeckers have sharp powerful beaks with which they drill holes through the bark of trees

peckers found in North America. These include the flickers and sapsuckers. The downy woodpecker can grow upto a length of 14 cm. The pileated woodpecker, found in the Eastern and North-Western United States and in parts of Canada, often reaches a length of 34 cm. The pileated woodpecker chisels large, deep, oblong holes into tree trunks.

The European green woodpecker is green with red crown and yellow rump. The greater and lesser spotted woodpeckers are the British species. They have black, red and white plumage. There are about 210 species of woodpeckers worldwide except in Australia.

OOO

17

Which is the world's deadliest animal?

The world's deadliest animal is the sea wasp. It is a kind of jellyfish known as *chironex fleckeri*. Its tentacles are loaded with hundreds of thousands of microscopic stinging cells which inject a cobra-like venom with poisonous barbed threads into any unfortunate creature that happens to brush against them closely. This venom is highly toxic and kills anybody in a few minutes. Pain and burning sensation caused by its venom are insufferable.

The sea wasp is a colourless creature and has a bell-shaped body which consists of 95% water. It is so elusive that only careful eyes can spot it drifting in shallow tropical waters of seashores and beaches.

The size of a sea wasp varies from 4 cm to 20 cm across and 10 cm long. It has purple or blue tentacles which can be seen coming out of the bell. These may reach up to a length of 120 cm. One wasp may have upto 50 tentacles and one such tentacle may have 750,000 individual stinging cells, capable of injecting venom. They are mainly meant for securing food, and also to serve as a defence mechanism.

The deadly sea wasp have long tentacles which contain powerful toxic poisons

Chironex fleckeri is found in great numbers in waters of Northern Australia. They are also found in the United States, waters off the Atlantic coast from North Carolina to the south of Florida Keys. They have also been discovered in West Africa and Indian Ocean.

Scientists have not yet been able to devise any effective remedy for its venom. So one must be very careful while swimming in tropical waters !

There are also some very poisonous sea-snakes that live permanently in the sea and are fully adapted to an aquatic existence. They swim with a sculling action of the paddle-shaped tail. They feed on fishes after immobilizing them with a potent, fast-acting venom.

OOO

18

Why do flies rub their legs together ?

Fly is a two-winged insect that has some 90,000 different species of it. The housefly (*musca domestica*) is one of the most common of all flies. You must have seen flies rubbing their legs together. Do you know why they do so?

The housefly has a dull gray, bristled body that is about 7 mm in length. It has large reddish compound eyes. Its mouth cannot bite but consists of a spongy pad. It has a peculiar system of feeding itself. At first it releases saliva and digestive juices over food and then sponges up the resulting solution. In this way, flies contaminate large amounts of food with germs, and cause millions of deaths every year. Hence it is widely considered as a major health hazard.

The whole body of the housefly, including claws and padded feet, is covered with bristles. Even its tongue is coated with a sticky glue. A fly rubs its legs together just to clean itself. In the process of rubbing the legs, it scraps some of the material that has gathered on the bristles and thus drops germs of dangerous diseases on the food. When we eat this food, we may get infected. Some of the most common diseases spread by the housefly are typhoid, tuberculosis and dysentery. Flies gather such germs from garbage and sewage.

Houseflies usually live and breed in or near garbage or organic wastes. The female lays about 100 eggs at a time and as many as 1000 during her life. The eggs hatch into larvae in 12 to 30 hours. The larvae moult several times before becoming pupae. Within a few days, the pupae become adult and the cycle begins again. Most houseflies have a lifespan of about 30 days during summer and longer when the weather is cooler. Cold weather usually kills the adults, but larvae and pupae are able to survive the winter.

Houseflies rub their legs to clean the dirt gathered on their legs. This dirt might contain germs of dangerous diseases

19

Which are the large-sized flying birds ?

The largest of all living birds is the African Ostrich which cannot fly at all. It measures upto 2.4 m in height and may weigh more than 133 kg. On account of its weight, it finds it impossible to lift its body in the air.

The two groups of flying birds that have the largest wingspread are the albatross and the condors. Both of them weigh about 13.5 kg.

The wandering albatross leads among the largest flying birds with a wing-spread of 3.3 to 3.6 m. The albatross has a long, heavy beak and long, narrow wings. It is mainly found in places south of the equator. It is a sea bird. It needs some wind and a run before taking off. So it either runs along the ground or paddles with its webbed feet across the water for a long time before being able to fly.

Next comes the condor which has a wingspread of 3 to 3.3 m. It is a carnivorous bird. There are two species of condors in the world. The Andean condor lives in the Andes mountains in South America. The other one is the Californian condor which is found in the mountains of Southern California. They feed on carcasses of animals. While searching for food, the condor uses its broad wings to glide high in the air.

The third bird in this line is the king vulture which is found in South America, Mexico and Central America. It has a wingspread of 2.7 to 3 m. The white pelican comes after the king vulture. It has a wingspread of 2.4 to 2.7 m. It is found in Canada. One of its distinguishing features is a bag-like pouch under its bill. Functioning like the radiator in a car, it helps the pelican to keep cool.

The great bustard, a large goose-like bird related to the cranes comes next. It is found in parts of Europe, Asia and Africa and has a wingspread of 2.4 to 3.7 m. The American bald eagle is the next largest flying bird having a wingspread of 2.1 to 2.4 m. Then comes the sandhill crane, with a wingspread of 1.8 to 2.1 m.

Albatross — the largest flying bird is a seabird — mainly found in places south of equator

Condor — the second largest flying bird found in the mountains of South America and South California

◯◯◯

20

How can dogs be dangerous to us ?

The bite of a mad dog can cause fatal diseases like rabies

It has often been said that a dog is a man's best friend. In fact, the dog was the first animal to be domesticated by man. But dogs can also be a source of danger under certain conditions.

A dog can harm people by biting or transmitting several bacterial, viral, parasitic, fungal and rickettsial diseases.

Bacterial diseases transmitted by dogs are mainly tuberculosis brucellosis, splenic fever, scarlet fever, diphtheria etc. Dogs carry *Salmonella enteriditis* and *S. typhinurium* pathogens which cause gastroenteritis and typhoid in man.

Dogs along with other animals can transmit fungal diseases such as ringworm.

Rabies is the most dangerous viral disease caused by a dog-bite. Rabies virus is found in the saliva of rabid dogs. Sometimes even pet dogs can be the cause of this disease. Therefore it is essential that they should be vaccinated against rabies every three years.

Dogs occasionally get measles and mumps and can cause this infection to spread to human beings.

Dog is the host of rickettsia which causes tick-borne fever. It is also the main source of several parasitic infections. It can transmit protozoan, helminthic and arthropoid parasites to man.

Infections are passed from dog to man mainly by contact or food contamination. As children are fond of playing with pet dogs, chances of their catching infections are greater.

To check the spread of several diseases caused by dogs, it is essential to give them anti-rabies injection and oral anti-microbial therapy. Pet dogs should be kept away from patients afflicted with tuberculosis, scarlet fever, measles or mumps. Dogs may catch infection even from their rooms and spread them to other men.

Louis Pasteur was the first scientist to produce an effective vaccine, and the Pasteur Institute was founded to treat this disease.

ooo

21

Where do penguins live?

Penguins are a peculiar category of sea birds which can stand up straight and flat-footed like us. Do you know where these birds are found?

Penguins are found in Southern hemisphere. They live along the Antarctic continent and islands as well as on the cool Southern hemisphere coast of Africa, Australia, New Zealand and South America.

The wings of penguins have evolved into flippers. As a result, they can not fly but they are excellent swimmers. They walk in a strange manner. In the earlier phases of evolution they could fly like other birds. But over a period of time, their wings became very short. The reason is that penguins lived in the remote areas of Antarctica, where they had practically no enemies to attack them. So they lived safely in land and water without ever using their wings and in course of time their wings became very small.

Penguins live in flocks. A single rookery may contain more than a million penguins. They feed on fish, squids and crustaceans.

Penguins withstand extremely cold conditions on account of a very dense plumage all over their bodies. These feathers are waterproof and have tiny air spaces that help them keep warm. Underneath this thick coat of feathers, there is an insulating layer of blubber. This helps to keep the body warm and store food and water. They also have a thick coat of fat to protect them from the cold.

Female penguins lay one or two eggs, which are brooded by both parents. They do not take food during incubation. Young penguins are fed by regurgitation. There are 17 species of penguins. The species differ mainly in head pattern and in size. Their sizes vary from 40 cm (fairy penguin) to almost 120 cm (Emperor penguin). Both sexes are alike in size. Only two, the Emperor and Adelie penguins breed on the Antarctic coast. King, Macaroni, Chinstrap and Gentoo penguins breed on Sub-Antarctic islands. The remaining 11 species breed farther North.

Macaroni penguin   Chinstrap penguin   Gentoo   Emperor penguin   ○○○

4

Human Body

• Why do some people stammer ? • What are enzymes ? • Why do doctors examine the pulse? • Why do babies cry so much ? • What is typhoid ? • Why are head injuries dangerous ? • What is blood pressure? • Why do some people have a squint ? • When were anaesthetics first used in operations ? • What is the Iron-lung machine ? • What causes asthma ? • What is physiotherapy ? • Why are infants kept on milk ? • What are the functions of arteries and veins in our body? • What is electrocardiography ? • Why don't people have identical voices ? • What causes leprosy ? • What is the function of liver in our body? • What is chicken pox? • What do we mean by right-eyed or left-eyed people ? • What is allergy ? • What is blood cancer or leukemia? • Which are the different joints in our body ? • What is albinism ? • How do urine tests help in diagnosis of diseases?• What happens in our brain? • What is immunity ?

1

Why do some people stammer ?

The biological process of speech requires the amazing co-ordination of larynx, cheeks, tongues and lips to produce sound. A person who stammers, lacks of such coordination.

Technically stuttering or stammering is known as dysphemia. In one form, the speaker cannot utter a word clearly — spasms occur in the speech muscles and he gets stuck with the first sound. So instead of saying mother, he would say 'm - m - mother.'

The speech development of children starts with associating sounds with persons and objects. It is closely related to the association of auditory and visual symbols. Speech involves coordination of many aspects of brain functions. These areas in the brain, particularly those concerned with aspects of speech, are located in the dominant hemisphere of right-handed persons and in either hemisphere of left-handed people. Disease of these parts of the brain leads to characteristic forms of stammering.

In another form, the muscles in the tongue, throat and face get spasms, and despite the fact that facial muscles work to make sound, no words come out. The face gets twisted.

Stammering rarely shows up before the age of four or five. It mostly occurs after puberty. It is more common in males than in females. According to studies, the ratio between males and females is 4 : 1.

Doctors and researchers are yet in dark about the definite cause of this disorder. However it is often connected with a physical disorder or some emotional disturbance. In either case it can be corrected to some extent by special training in reading and speaking. The person is taught to read and speak slowly and carefully, and breathe regularly while speaking. Hereditary predispositions of stammering have been noted in many studies. In one study about 40% stutterers were found to inherit this disorder.

The treatment is difficult and it demands much skill and sense of responsibility on the part of the therapist. No medicines have so far been discovered for it's treatment. However psychotherapy and speechotherapy have been found quite effective. In this, attempts are made to overcome speech difficulties, this is particularly important in children.

Prevention of stuttering may even be aided through parent counselling. Parents can take care of their children in such a way that they do not develop the habits of hesitation, or syllable repetition etc. Parental guidance has also been found quite effective in reducing the number of stutterers. A very controlled, guided and conscious approach on the part of the stutterer often helps to redress the problem.

OOO

2

What are enzymes ?

The human body is a machine that needs energy to work. This energy is obtained from food materials through metabolism. These metabolic processes are carried on by activating agents or catalysts called enzymes. Let us see what enzymes are and what they do in our body.

An enzyme is an organic catalyst produced by a living cell. All enzymes are proteins made up of long chains of amino acids. They combine with the substrate to form an intermediate compound. This intermediate compound is an unstable complex, and breaks down to yield the reaction product, plus the original enzyme.

Enzymes are themselves synthesized by other enzymes derived from nucleic acids. An average cell contains about 3000 different enzymes. In order to function correctly, many enzymes require the assistance of related substances known as co-enzymes which are produced from vitamins in the diet.

The human body literally contains hundreds of different enzymes. Many are contained within the cells, but some others, such as those used for digestive purposes, act outside cells in the gut itself. Enzymes are involved in almost every chemical reaction taking place in our body.

Many physiological activities such as digestion, building up and breaking down of tissues, cellular respiration and muscle contraction depend on their action. The activity of an enzyme depends on the temperature, the degree of acidity or alkalinity (pH) and the substance upon which the enzyme acts. A single enzyme molecule is capable of bringing about the required changes on hundreds of molecules of the substrate in a few seconds.

Enzyme action can be blocked by some poisonous substances such as mercury, lead or arsenic. The presence of such substances hinders the enzymes from forming intermediate complex with the substrate. Normal metabolism is thus prevented.

Enzymes are classified into six major groups: Oxidases which bring about oxidation, transferases which bring about group transfer ; hydrolases which speed up the process of hydrolysis ; lyases that bring about group removal. Isomerases enzymes are responsible for isomerization and ligases for joining of molecules.

Enzymes are not only important for our body, but are also very useful in industry, medicine and analytical chemistry. Although enzymes normally work inside living cells still they are capable of working outside the cell. They are used to convert starch into glucose and glucose into fructose. They are also used in cheese-making industry and for the production of semi-synthetic penicilline. Artificial sweeteners are also produced with their help.

OOO

3

Why do doctors examine the pulse?

When a person falls sick, the doctor often examines his pulse by placing his fingers on the wrist of the patient. What does this pulse indicate ?

By pulse we mean the regular throbbing of arteries caused by the successive contractions of the heart. During the action of the heart there is a pause. During this pause, the wall of the aorta contracts. This contraction forces the excess blood to

age	pulse rate (per min.)
0	135
1	120
5	95
10	85
>25	75

126

The table shows the normal pulse rate of different age groups

proceed along the arteries. This alternate expansion and contraction of the aorta produces a throbbing in the arteries. This throbbing which can be felt at many points in the body, through the skin, is called pulse.

The pulse can be felt by placing fingers on the wrist over the radical artery. It can also be felt at the temples where we have temporal artery or at other places where an artery is near the surface. This sensation cannot be felt in the veins because the blood reaches them from the arteries by passing through the narrow capillaries.

The nurse or a doctor asks the patient to put the arm in a relaxed position with the thumb turned upwards. Then the doctor feels the pulse. The beats are counted for one minute. Since the pulsations mean the heart contraction, the pulse tells us about the heart rate. The pulse rate depends on the blood requirement of the body. This rate indicates how fast the heart is beating and the state of pressure in the circulatory system. An irregular pulse may indicate some abnormality in the functioning of the heart.

The number of pulsations per minute normally varies from 78 to 82 among women and from 70 to 72 among men. The pulse rate in children is much higher than the healthy adults. The normal rate for a seven-year old child is 90 beats per minute. A new born baby can have a pulse rate of 140. The old people can be in the 50-65 range of pulse rate.

OOO

4

Why do babies cry so much ?

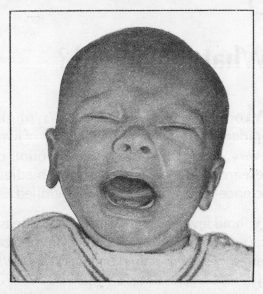

Since babies can't speak they cry to communicate a feeling of uneasiness or any other problem

In fact, crying is the baby's first sound message. It is the first attempt of the baby to communicate with the world around him. As the baby is unable to put its feelings and desires in words, it communicates by crying!

It is a matter of common experience that newborn babies cry a lot during the first few months. As the baby starts growing up, there is a marked decline in this practice. By the time the baby is two years old, this habit is almost gone.

It is interesting to note that this practice doesn't just express wants and discomforts like hunger or illness. Normally the tears do not appear unless the baby is really distressed.

Most mothers are able to distinguish between cries indicating hunger, anger or pain. They are able to tell, with some degree of accuracy what the baby wants. For example, if a baby is hungry, it will continue to cry even when fondled. But if it is crying from boredom, it will stop crying when picked up or when moved to other interesting surroundings.

Recent studies have shown that if a mother is sensitive in this regard, and responds accordingly, the baby will cry much less by the end of the first year as compared to one who is not. A knowledge of the basic food-stuffs essential to a growing child is necessary to become an ideal mother.

By the age of four or five months most babies start making certain special sounds. These sounds are called babblings. It has been observed that babies enjoy these sounds.

It is not always possible to know why a baby cries. There are occasions when the baby is neither hungry, tired, uncomfortable, bored nor frightened, but still keeps on crying. However, usually the baby's cries are meant to communicate some message.

ooo

5

What is typhoid ?

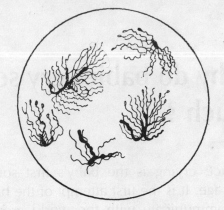

Typhoid is caused by Bacillus salmonella typhosa

More than 60 years back typhoid epidemics used to claim thousands of lives every year. But now, on account of research and advancement in medical science it has been largely controlled.

Typhoid fever is an acute infectious disease caused by the typhoid bacillus. In medical terminology it is called *bacillus salmonella typhosa*. It enters the body via contaminated food, water, or milk and finally reaches the blood stream. It infects the blood and poisons the system. Among its main symptoms are fever, cough, headache, skin eruption, enlargement of the spleen, and a fall in the number of white cells. There may also be a loss of appetite. Persistent fever develops which gradually rises, reaching up to 39.4°C or 40°C. After a spell of one or two weeks it starts falling. In about 30 days, the temperature becomes normal.

Formerly, the treatment was entirely symptomatic and supportive. After 1948 specific treatment with antibiotics was developed which proved to be very effective. Medicines like *Chloramphenicol* or *Tetracyclines* provide suitable antibiotic therapy. Cold sponge baths help to control the high fever. In some severe cases, the doctor may even go in for blood transfusion or infuse blood plasma.

There is a special blood test that becomes positive during the second week of the disease. This is called the widel test. Also the germ can be grown in the laboratory from the patient's blood, urine or stool, usually during the first week of the disease.

The present day treatment of typhoid is the bed rest, intravenous fluids to combat dehydration caused by diarrhoea and appropriate doses of *chloromycetin*.

Most of the major typhoid epidemics have been spread by pollution of public water or milk supplies. The uncooked food can also be contaminated by a typhoid carrier. Flies may also carry the bacilli to food. Some of the typhoid patients continue to carry its germs even after they are cured.

Public sanitation and personal hygienic care are vitally important to check the spread of this disease. Typhoid patient should not be allowed to handle food. Special vaccine made from dead typhoid germs can protect a person effectively for several years.

OOO

6

Why are head injuries dangerous ?

In times of war, soldiers use special helmets to protect their heads. While driving a scooter, the riders often wear helmets to protect their heads against any injury. In many cities the government have even made the helmets compulsory for riders. Do you know why the protection of head is necessary ?

The most important part of our body, the brain, is located in the cranium under the protection of bones. The human brain is divided into three main parts : the cerebrum, the cerebellum and medulla oblongata. It controls all the important functions of the body — sight, taste, smell, hearing, touch, movements, memory, speech etc. Any damage to brain can disturb the proper body functioning.

Our brain is protected by the thick bone of the skull. Further, a shock absorbing fluid cushions it against the blows of bumps. But if the blow is sharp or hard enough it can injure the skull. Thus to protect the brain from injuries it is essential to first protect the head.

Now the question arises what may be the consequences of head injuries ?

A severe head injury due to an accident may cause brain haemorrhage which eventually may lead to death. The injury may damage the memory unit of brain by which a man can loose memory temporarily or permanently. It has been often seen that after having a severe injury of head people remain in coma for long periods.

If the brain tissues are damaged it may give rise to multiple sclerosis. Parkinson's disease is caused by a disorder of brain chemistry which may result due to head injury. Brain injury may cause *aphasia*, a serious disorder of thought and communication. Apart from these effects many other disabling conditions can be generated by head injuries.

It is therefore essential to protect the head against injuries.

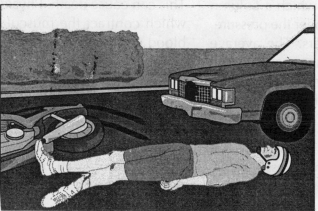

Helmet is a safety device against fatal head injuries like brain haemorrhage, etc.

OOO

7

What is blood pressure?

Blood pressure is measured by an instrument called sphygmomanometer

The heart is a vital organ that pumps blood to different parts of the body. The outflow of the blood takes place when the heart's left ventricle contracts. Then blood is forced into the arteries which expand to receive blood. These arteries have a muscular lining which resists this pressure. Thus blood is squeezed out of them into the smaller vessels of the body. By blood pressure we mean the amount of pressure that blood exerts on the walls of the arteries. The amount of pressure depends upon the strength of the heart muscle, the amount of blood in the circulatory system and the condition of the arteries.

There are two kinds of pressures — systolic and diastolic. Systolic is the maximum pressure that occurs when the left ventricle contracts. Diastolic is the minimum pressure that occurs just before the heartbeat which follows.

When a doctor measures blood pressure, he uses an instrument in which a column of mercury rises or falls under the pressure. It is marked in millimeters. The average systolic pressure in a young man is about 120 mm of mercury and the diastolic pressure is about 80. These figures are usually stated as 120/80 or 120 over 80.

Blood pressure usually rises with age because the arteries become less flexible. Anxiety or exercise may also cause pressure to rise temporarily. It is also increased by a number of diseases. A person is said to have high blood pressure or hypertension if it exceeds the figure of 100 plus his age or if the diastolic pressure exceeds 100. High blood pressure can cause heart failure, apoplexy, or kidney diseases. It may also burst a blood vessel in the eye or the brain, thus causing blindness or a haemorrhage. Symptoms of high blood pressure are headaches, hot flashes and anger.

Abnormally low blood pressure occurs when a person has an heart attack or loses large amount of blood because of some injury etc. When the blood pressure falls considerably, the oxygen supply to the brain and other parts also gets reduced. This can cause death. Physicians use drugs which contract the muscular walls of the blood vessels to raise the blood pressure.

Abnormal high blood pressure may be due to the constriction of arteries or due to damage to one or both kidneys. Excessive weight and lack of exercise can also contribute to hypertension. Temporary high blood pressure can be due to excitement or emotional stresses.

○○○

8

Why do some people have a squint ?

Squint eyes do not move together but look in different directions simultaneously

A squint is a physical defect in which both eyes do not point in the same direction. This is also called strabismus or heterotropia — a disorder of the eye in which the alignment of the two ocular axes is not parallel.

A person with this defect may have an inward squint (one eye may be directed towards the other eye), an upward or a downward squint. The squint is called 'comitant' if the deviation remains constant no matter in what direction the gaze is directed. It is called 'noncomitant' if the degree of misalignment varies with the direction of the gaze.

Long-sightedness in children often causes an inward squint. On the other hand short-sightedness may produce an upward squint. If one or more of these muscles are paralysed, the noncomitant squint occurs.

A squint is most often the result of some abnormality in the nervous controls. Acquired squints are usually due to nerve or muscle disease and cause double vision. In fact, the movement of the eye balls depends upon the action of six muscles — four of which are straight and two slanting. If the nerves of these eye muscles have

developed some defect, the eye can develop a squint.

With the progress in medical sciences now it has become possible to treat this defect. But it must be done at an early stage by wearing special glasses. These have a dark glass to cover the good eye to stop it from being used. This prevents the bad eye from becoming worse.

Squint can also be treated by some orthoptic exercise which helps to strengthen the eye muscles. In some cases, an operation is necessary to strengthen a weak eye muscle or to weaken an extra strong one. The good eye is covered for some period before the correctional surgery. This is to enable the patient to use the previously unused eye and build up its vision.

An interesting observation about squint-eyed people is that it is often difficult to judge the direction in which they look.

OOO

9

When were anaesthetics first used in operations ?

Before the discovery of anaesthetics, an operation used to be an agonizing experience for the patient. Even though different agents like herbs, gases, oils and drugs were used for relieving pain, the patient sometimes died from pain and shock. It was only with the discovery of modern anaesthetics that a major breakthrough was achieved in the field of surgery.

An anaesthetic is a substance that causes a loss of sensation or feeling in the body. The history of its discovery is very interesting. In 1799, the British chemist, Sir Humphry Davy inhaled some 'laughing gas' (nitrous oxide) and found that it produced unconsciousness. Davy published this experience and in 1844 in the United States Horace Wells performed the first dental operation using nitrous oxide as an anaesthetic. Two years earlier, i.e. in 1842, the first painless operation had been carried out by Craw Ford W. Long, using ether as an anaesthetic. In 1847, chloroform was reported to have similar anaesthetic effect. At last surgeons had found a method of overcoming pain to carry out lengthy operations without undue haste.

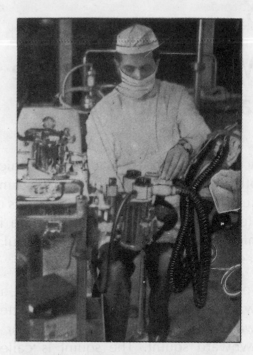

An anaesthetist plays an important role in any surgical operation where administering an anaesthetic drug is required to deprive sensitivity of the patient

Today, many new types of anaesthetics have been developed. Their application is of two types: local and general. Local anaesthetics are used to numb a particular part of the body. They act by blocking the transmission of electrical impulses along nerve cells, and are usually injected around the nerves that normally carry impulses from the area to be operated upon. The first of these anaesthetics was cocaine. This was superceded by another drug called procaine in 1905. Numerous drugs related to procaine such as lignocaine are nowadays used.

General anaesthetics render the entire body unconscious. Nitrous oxide, ether and chloroform are included in this category, together with a more recently developed drug, halothane. Once inhaled, they act within seconds but recovery starts immediately after the drug is withdrawn. Halothane has been found to have side effects on liver. Now it has been replaced by ethrane.

Under general anaesthesia, the patient's respiration may be controlled externally. There are two reasons for this. First, general anaesthesia depresses the area of the brain that controls respiration. Second, for many operations the patient's muscles need to be released which is achieved by giving a drug called curare.

A person called an anaesthetist is trained to give proper amounts of anaesthetic to patients being operated for different ailments. At least one anaesthetist is always present in the operation room during the surgery.

10

What is the Iron-lung machine ?

The iron-lung machine was one of the earliest life-saving machines. It was invented by Philip Drinker of Harvard, U.S.A in 1929. This device is meant to aid those who have difficulty in breathing, either due to a paralysis of chest muscles or due to some disease or an accident.

This machine has an air-tight chamber on wheels. The patient lies on a foam-rubber bed with an adjustable head and foot rests. It is operated by electricity, but has a safety device which gives a warning signal in the vent of power failure. The machine can then be operated by hand. It has a cover which can be opened to give access to the patient. The patient's head is usually enclosed in a plastic dome.

The machine helps in breathing by alternately reducing and increasing the air pressure around the patient's body. When the pressure is reduced, his chest expands and air comes into his lungs through the normal air passages, as his head remains outside the machine. When the pressure is increased, the chest contracts and air is automatically expelled from the lungs.

During a heart operation, a heart-lung machine is used. This takes over the function of the heart and lungs and the surgeon can perform the surgery safely. The technical name for this machine is the cardiopulmonary bypass machine, since it takes over the job of both heart and lungs. Blood returning along veins, from the body's organs to the heart, is led out of the body along a tube to a gas exchange unit. Here carbon dioxide is removed from the blood and oxygen is added — thus doing the lung's job. The blood then flows through a rotary pump which does the heart's job and back into the main arteries. This is a very important device during heart surgery. ○○○

11

What causes asthma ?

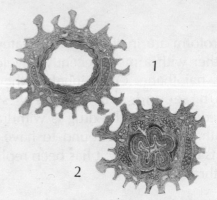

1. Normal bronchial tube wide open for easy breathing 2. During a severe attack of asthma the bronchial tube is greatly constricted owing to spasm and thick secretions

Asthma is a chronic disease of the lungs in which a person has sudden attacks of shortness of breath, wheezing and coughing. It is one of the most common diseases affecting respiration. It affects all races and both sexes equally. It usually begins in childhood or early adult life.

Asthma is caused by a blocking of the bronchial tubes in the lungs. This blocking is caused by shrinking of the bronchial muscles, swelling of membranes lining these muscles and the presence of thick mucus called phlegm.

Allergic bronchial asthma is the most common type of the disease. It is caused by adverse reaction to things like house dust, pollen, feathers, animal dandruff, drugs and certain foods. Strong odours or smoke may also cause its attacks. Asthma is often linked with hayfever, another type of allergy. Different kinds of asthma may even harm other parts of the body.

Asthma attacks often occur after heavy physical work or in case of emotional disturbance. An infection of the nose and throat can trigger off an attack. A drastic change in the weather may also prove troublesome in this regard. Exposure to sudden changes in temperature and humidity or both may also cause an attack. Common symptoms of asthma are wheezing, a sense of suffocation, dry cough

and an inability to expel air easily from the lungs.

Asthmatic attacks usually last for half an hour to several hours. Prolonged or frequent attacks may prove dangerous if the patient is weak or suffers from malnutrition. Some 35-40 percent of childhood asthma cases improve at puberty.

A physician identifies asthma by physical examination and allergy skin tests. From these tests, the substance to which the patient is allergic, can be detected. Most doctors usually prescribe drugs such as epinephrine or ephedrine to treat it in the initial stages. Patients with very serious cases of asthma however may need to take ACTH or cortisone. Some doctors prescribe small doses or injections of asthma-causing substances. And they slowly increase the strength of these injections until the patient's body develops a natural resistance to the allergic substances. Sometimes oxygen becomes essential for such a patient. To avoid asthma attacks one should avoid substances to which one is allergic and the situations that precipitate attacks.

○○○

12

What is physiotherapy ?

Physiotherapy is that branch of medicine which makes use of some physical agents or exercises to treat a disease or an injury. It is also called physical therapy. More strictly it is a branch of rehabilitation medicine. Doctors who specialise in this branch of medicine are called physiotherapists.

Physiotherapy is helpful in treating many kinds of disabilities and diseases. It is often used to treat paralysis and muscle weaknesses, such as caused by poliomyletis and multiple sclerosis. It is also used in treating heart and lung diseases. It can also be used as a treatment aid for amputations, fractures and other injuries. With the help of this treatment, the disabled person may lead a constructive and creative life.

Many kinds of devices and treatments are used in physiotherapy. Radiant heat lamps are used for warming up the body to remove the pains in the backbone. Electric heating pads, diathermy, hydrotherapy (water treatment) and special baths are used to apply heat to the diseases or damaged parts of the body.

Warming up of the body relieves the pain and improves the blood circulation in the body. Soon after certain injuries cooling methods are also used to reduce pain and swelling. Ultraviolet lamps are used to kill certain germs and to help healing because ultraviolet light has more energy and can destroy germs. Ultrasonic waves are used to treat inflammatory conditions of muscles and joints.

Exercise is the most important part of physiotherapy. In fact, a layman believes that physiotherapy is concerned only with different kinds of physical exercises. However, the physiotherapists make use of various equipments such as pulleys, weights, parallel bars, stationary bicycles and dumb bells. Splints, braces, crutches and wheel chairs are also used to help disabled persons. Physiotherapists help people learn how to use these devices and develop confidence in doing daily tasks.

Physiotherapists work in clinics, hospitals and schools for the handicapped. Nowadays the use of physiotherapy is constantly increasing.

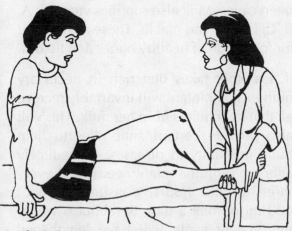

Physiotherapy cures many ailments which can not be cured through medicines or surgery

ooo

13

Why are infants kept on milk ?

The first kind of food a baby gets is mother's milk. Why is this so ?

Milk is a highly nutritious food substance with which the female mammals feed their young. It contains most of the nutrients needed for growth and is, for most mammals, the main source of nutrition for several months after birth. In fact the milk of each species of mammals, including human beings, is a complete, wholesome and easily digestible food for its own young ones after their birth.

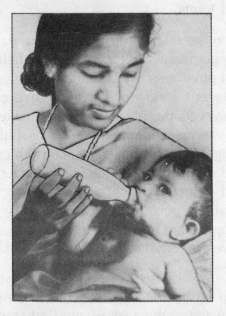

Milk is a complete, wholesome, nutritious and easily digestible food. It alone can fulfil a baby's food requirements and hence it is the most preferred diet

Milk is produced in special glands called mammary glands. Most of the female mammals have teats or nipples from which their young can suck milk. These teats are connected to the mammary glands by a series of tiny ducts.

Although the same ingredients are present in the milk of all mammals, their proportions vary. Milk is 80% to 90% water. It contains proteins, carbohydrates, fats, vitamins and minerals. These constituents are needed for growth and repair of bones and tissues and of the normal functioning of the endocrine glands which produce hormones for growth. Proteins (mostly casein and albumin) supply all the essential amino acids for growth and repair. The carbohydrates (mostly lactose or milk sugar) are a good energy source and help the body absorb calcium and phosphorus. The fats are in tiny droplets. Milk is converted into soft curd in the stomach of the young due to which digestion can proceed smoothly without the disturbance that fatty foods often cause. Milk also supplies vitamins A, B, C, D, E, K and niacin. These are needed for formation of healthy bones and tissues.

If a mother takes diet rich in necessary nutrients, her infant will invariably receive all that he requires from her milk. This will also provide certain antibodies to help build immunity to diseases. Immediately after the birth the infant needs food every three to four hours, consuming about 600 ml of milk a day. By about 6 weeks this hunger cycle will have lengthened and the infant may pass a night without needing to be fed.

If human babies are not fed by their mothers, they may be bottle-fed with pasteurized cow's milk, diluted and sweetened or mixing milk powder with water. These can be a valuable substitute for breast milk, but there are hazards involved. If not properly washed, the bottle may contain many bacteria which may cause harmful diseases to the baby.

Some mothers believe that a stronger milk helps the infant to sleep and grow better. But this is a faulty reasoning. A concentrated feed will contain too much sodium and the infant's kidneys would have to work furiously to eliminate it. This may cause dehydrations. Although the infant may appear to be growing quickly yet instead of building stronger bones and more muscles, the baby would just accumulate excess fat, which is not a healthy sign.

Babies have also been fed on milk of goat, buffalo, reindeer, caribou, sheep, camel, llama, and mare etc.

During the second part of the first year, the infant is gradually weaned from milk to solid food. It is important that a balanced diet is maintained for a proper healthy growth of the baby. ○○○

14

What are the functions of arteries and veins in our body?

Blood must reach every cell in the body to provide it with food and oxygen, and to remove waste products. The group of organs which circulate blood through the body is called the circulatory system.

In the human beings, the circulatory system has a muscular pump called heart. It pumps the blood through long, tube-like blood vessels. Blood vessels carry the blood throughout the body to the cells. In our circulatory system there are five types of blood vessels: arteries, arterioles, capillaries, venules and veins. An artery is a large vessel that carries blood away from the heart to the cells. It branches off into the smaller arterioles which further divide into very small capillaries. The capillaries carry blood to the cells. These reunite to form larger tubes called venules. These venules merge to form large tubes called veins. Veins carry impure blood back to the heart. According to a rough estimate if all the blood vessels are joined together in a single-line they would stretch to 60,000 miles.

Blood is pumped from the right ventricle of the heart into the pulmonary artery. The pulmonary artery carries it to the lungs where it absorbs oxygen and releases carbondioxide. The blood returns to the left auricle of the heart through the pulmonary vein. The left auricle pumps the oxygenated blood into the left ventricle of the heart which pumps it into aorta. The aorta is the largest artery in the body. It carries blood to other arteries and arterioles. The blood absorbs food when it passes near the small intestines. The wastes from the cells are removed from the blood when it passes through the kidneys. After the blood passes through the cells of the body, delivering food and oxygen and removing wastes, it returns to the heart through the vena cava. The vena cava is the largest vein in the body. The unoxygenated blood enters the right auricle which returns it to the right ventricle. It is then pumped to the lungs to receive more oxygen.

The muscular walls of the arteries are thick and elastic. They carry bright red, oxygen-rich blood. As the heart pumps, a wave of pressure travels along the walls of arteries and can be felt as pulse. Their walls can contract and release and can regulate the amount of blood flowing to the body tissues.

The walls of veins have three layers : elastic, muscular and lining. The veins are thinner and less muscular than the arteries. In the arms and legs the veins have valves that prevent the back flow and pooling of blood due to gravity. The veins that are swollen, stretched or coiled on themselves are called varicose veins. These can sometimes be found on the legs of older people as well as those whose jobs involve a lot of walking. Blood in the veins is under low pressure and flows slowly. Since it contains less oxygen, it turns purplish red in colour.

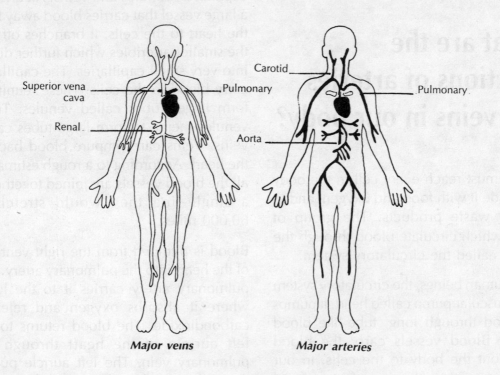

Superior vena cava   Pulmonary   Carotid   Pulmonary

Renal   Aorta

Major veins   **Major arteries**

15

What is electrocardiography ?

Electrocardiography is a system of tracing graphically, the electric impulses generated by the heart muscles during a heartbeat. The graphic record is called electro-cardiogram (ECG).

The working of the heart is regulated by electrical impulses. Its each part including the various valves from where the blood flows in and out, produces its own electric wave pattern. These electrical impulses are recorded by a machine called electrocardiograph.

Electrocardiogram provides extremely useful information regarding the condition and performance of the heart. It is very useful in the treatment of heart ailments.

Electrocardiograms are made by attaching electrodes to various parts of the body. These lead off the feeble heart current to the recording instrument. The four extremities and the chest become standard places for attaching the electrodes. When the electrocardiogram is switched on, an automatic pen recorder moves up and down on a chart paper and records each wave impulse.

The normal cardiogram shows typical upward and downward deflections that reflect the alternate contractions of the auricles (two upper chambers) and of the

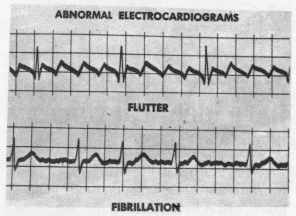

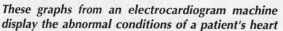

These graphs from an electrocardiogram machine display the abnormal conditions of a patient's heart

ventricles (two lower chambers) of the heart.

Variations in amplitude and direction of the current may give important information concerning the heart's function and state of health. It can tell whether the heart is enlarged and where the enlargement occurs, whether the heart action is irregular and where the irregularity originates, whether a coronary vessel is occulted and where the occlusion is located or whether a slow rate is physiological or caused by the heart block. High blood pressure, thyroid disease and certain types of malnutrition may also be revealed by an electrocardiogram.

During the late 1960s, computerised ECGs came into use in many leading hospitals. These instruments directly tell the abnormalities of the heart muscle. Much advanced tests such as Trad Mill Test, Holter, Thalium stress tests etc are now available for finding the abnormalities of heart. Echo cardiography is also considered as an important diagnostic technique for heart disorders. ○○○

16

Why don't people have identical voices ?

No two persons in the world have exactly the same voice! Do you know why it differs from person to person?

The act of speaking involves movements of hundreds of muscles in split-second co-ordination. The speech organ called larynx or voice-box is capable of producing an infinite number of sounds. It is part of the throat through which air passes. When we breathe, air passes through the larynx downwards, through mouth and nose into trachea (windpipe) and finally to the lungs.

The larynx is made up of a tough wall of cartilage. Its inside lining has two folds of tissue stretching on each side and leaving a gap between them. These are called vocal cords. In case of simple breathing, the gap between the cords remains wide open. The cords are slack. But talking, singing or shouting involves tightening of the cords. The exhaled air causes the cords to vibrate and produce sound. Our vocal cords can be found in any of about 170 different positions.

If the vocal cords are slack, they may vibrate about 80 times per second and the result is deep tones. If they are tensed, they vibrate rapidly, perhaps thousand times a second, and produce short soundwaves or high tones or high pitch sounds.

As a child has short vocal cords, they produce short air waves and consequently a high pitched voice. As a child grows, the vocal cords become longer and that causes the voice to become deeper. Thus the voices of adults are heavier and deeper than children's voices.

Similarly the voices of most adult men are deeper than those of women. This is because a man's larynx is larger than that of a woman with longer cords.

The pitch of a voice depends upon the length of the vocal cords. Each voice has a certain range of frequencies. It is this range that determines what kind of voice a person has. Voices can be divided into six groups: bass, baritone, and tenor for men; and alto, mezzosoprano and soprano for women.

The quality of human voice also depends on many other things, such as resonating spaces, lungs, nasal cavities etc. The nose, sinuses, pharynx and the oral cavity act as resonating chambers, and modify the vocal tone produced by the vocal cords. The movement of the tongue against palate, the shaping of the lips, and the arrangement of teeth also produce changes in the voice.

Since the structures and movements of all these organs are different in different persons the voices of no two persons in the world can be the same.

○○○

17

What causes leprosy ?

You must have heard of the great service, Mother Teresa of India, the Nobel Prize winner, is rendering to lepers. Even international organizations such as the World Health Organization, UNICEF, etc are engaged in a continuous worldwide fight against leprosy. What is leprosy and how is it caused ?

Leprosy is caused by certain bacteria called *Mycobacterium leprae bacillus*. They attack the skin and nervous system, causing lumps and patches of discolouration on the skin. These occur mainly on the ears, face, testes and the limbs. The inner surface of the mouth and nose also get affected. When the disease spreads to the eyes, it causes blindness. The affected nerves are destroyed. The fingers and the toes may lose all sensation and become paralysed.

Leprosy is mainly of two types : Lepromatous or Cutaneous ; and Tuberculoid. Lepromatous is marked by widespread infiltration of grainy masses of inflamed tissue under the skin, face, testes and mucosal membranes of the upper respiratory tract. But the tuberculoid is marked by stain-like lesions with raised, reddish borders and patches that become insensitive to physical stimulus as they spread. The symptoms of this disease are thickening of the skin, loss of hair, deformities of bones and joints and loss of sensation in various areas of the body.

Leprosy's treatment involves a long-range use of sulfone drugs to bring an immediate stop to the infection. Severe cases, however, might also need surgery. Other drugs used to treat it are sulfoxone and solapsone. An ointment named *ditophal* ointment is also used with some success by rubbing on the affected areas in the body. This is a volatile substance which is lethal to the leprosy bacteria. It is generally used with another therapy which is called dapsone therapy. These drugs are fairly inexpensive. According to rough estimates one in every five patients ever receives proper treatment.

Today the reported cases of leprosy throughout the world number at least 2,000,000 and the actual number of infected-people may be as large as 10,000,000. It is still not clear how its germs spread the infection. It appears that prolonged, close physical contact with an infected person usually precedes active infection in susceptible persons. According to the experts the disease is mildly contagious. Infants born of infected parents do not develop the disease if separated from them at an early stage.

Leprosy occurs mainly under humid, tropical and subtropical climates. The majority of lepers are found in different parts of Asia that include Japan, Korea, the Pacific Islands.

OOO

18

What is the function of liver in our body?

The liver is a large and vitally important organ in the abdomen. It can be thought of as a living laboratory and a chemical plant. More than hundred different processes are known to take place in it. It is reddish brown in colour and located in the upper abdominal cavity beneath the diaphragm and ribs.

The liver is basically concerned with the digestion of food, excretion, storage and conversion of food materials, the regulation of the composition of blood and the destruction of poisonous substances. If it stops working, death is imminent within a few hours.

In an adult person, the liver weighs about 1.5 kg. The liver is divided into two lobes — right and left. The right lobe is about three times the size of the left lobe. Pressed tightly against it is the gall-bladder.

The liver has a rich blood supply. The blood that supplies oxygen to the liver cells comes from the aorta, the main artery leaving the heart. It reaches the liver through a branch called the hepatic artery. The liver also receives blood from the intestines. This blood carries food materials that have been absorbed through the intestine wall. It reaches the liver through the hepatic portal vein. Blood leaves the liver through the hepatic vein to return to the heart. The main food materials that the liver deals with are sugar, glucose and amino acids. The amino acids come from the digestion of proteins. Sugar is stored in the liver as glycogen. It can be released to provide fuel for the body's cells as and when necessary.

Amino acids are converted by the liver into proteins for the plasma of the blood. Some amino acids are used to make more glucose. Amino acids cannot be stored in the liver like glucose. They must be used immediately.

Liver produces a digestive enzyme called bile. It is produced inside the cells and secreted into bile ducts. It helps in digestion. Bile is stored in the gall bladder before being poured into the intestine. The liver also acts as a storehouse for vitamins, iron and copper.

A vitally important function of the liver is the destruction of harmful chemicals in the blood. Alcohol, drugs and many poisonous substances are destroyed or changed into harmless substances. They are then passed from the body through the

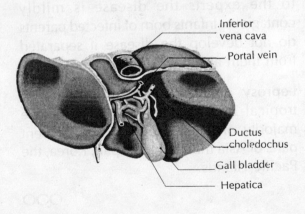

Inferior vena cava
Portal vein
Ductus choledochus
Gall bladder
Hepatica

A human liver

urine. Prolonged and excessive intake of alcohol can damage the liver. This condition is known as cirrhosis of the liver. If not treated well it causes jaundice and may eventually lead to death.

The liver carries out the following functions in the body : (a) the production and storage of proteins ; (b) the storage and regulation of sugar; (c) the neutralization of tonic and harmful substances; (d) the utilization and storage of fats; (e) the manufacture of bile; (f) the breakdown of drugs. It is the most vital organ of the body. ○○○

19

What is chicken pox ?

Chicken Pox is a contagious disease that mostly affects children generally in the age group of two to six years. Adults rarely get affected by it. This disease usually occurs in epidemics.

Chicken pox is caused by a virus, an organism too small to be seen under an ordinary microscope. It spreads easily as the virus can be carried by moisture in the air. It is transmitted by direct contact.

When a child gets infected with chicken pox small red spots appear on his skin. These red eruptions look like blisters and are filled with a clear fluid. There are practically no premonitory symptoms, though slight fevers for about 24 hours may precede the eruptions. Blisters keep on appearing for the first three days. However after 36 hours of the first ones having appeared, they start becoming opalescent. So by the end of three days, they can be seen in various stages of growth and decay. The blisters are more marked on the covered areas of the body, but also

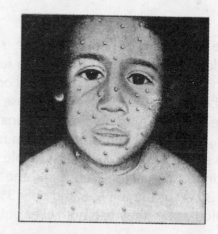

Chicken pox is caused by a virus **Varicella zoster**

occur on face, limbs and on the mucus membrane of the mouth.

When the blisters are filled with fluid, the disease can be spread most easily because the virus particles are in the fluid. If the blister is scratched, it releases the virus and can infect other children.

During this disease, the patient does not feel too sick. The temperature rarely goes above 39°C (102°F). However, sometimes he may feel tired and lose his appetite.

Chicken pox does not last for very long. After four or five days, the blisters dry up and small scabs are formed. These scabs should not be scratched as they may become ulcerated. ○○○

143

20

What do we mean by right-eyed or left-eyed people ?

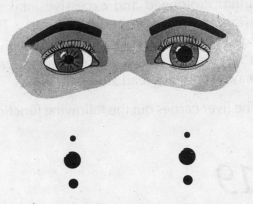

Only 3% people use both eyes equally. In fact, in most people the right eye is dominant and stronger than the left

We all know whether we are right-handed or left-handed. But only a few of us know whether we are right-eyed or left-eyed. This means that we do not use both our eyes equally. One eye is dominant or stronger than the other. It has been found from several studies that 65% people have an unconscious preference for the right eye, 32% for the left eye and only 3% are ambicular i.e. they use both eyes equally.

By the following experiment, you can know whether you are a right-eyed person or left-eyed.

Hold a pencil in your hand and stretch the arm in front of you at eye level. Keep both your eyes open and line the pencil up with a picture or shelf or some object on the wall. First close one eye and see the object. Then close the second eye and see the object with first. If the object remains lined up with your right eye opened, and seemed to move to the left when your left eye was opened, then your right eye is dominant and if it happens the other way, then you are left-eyed.

There are some other methods too by which the eye dominance can be determined. In this respect, one Stanley Coren conducted some experiments at the University of British Columbia. He concluded that when we see objects with the dominant eye, they appear somewhat bigger. He selected 45 people and tested them for eye dominance. It was found that 25 people were right-eyed and 20 people were left-eyed. It was interesting to note that 17 of the right-eyed subjects viewed the object bigger with their right eyes whereas 13 of the left-eyed persons felt the same difference in size with their left eyes.

According to scientists all individuals have equal refraction for both eyes, the difference in size felt by the right-eyed and left eyed persons was only psychological. It is just a matter of unconscious individual preference practiced from the beginning that leads to the dominance of one particular eye and makes people right-eyed or left-eyed.

○○○

21

What is allergy ?

Hay fever, rashes on the skin, reactions to certain injections (anaplylactic shock) and some types of asthma are the more common forms of allergy in man. What is an allergy ?

An allergy is an abnormal sensitivity of the body to certain substances especially proteins. In our environment different substances causing allergic reaction are present in countless forms. They may be in pollen or dust that enter the nose or eyes, in the serum of a vaccine or an antibiotic (such as penicillin), or in some food article. Some people are also allergic to feathers and bee stings. There are literally hundreds of allergens.

In an allergic reaction the substance causing the reaction is called allergen or antigen, and substances formed within the body during the processes of sensitization are known as antibodies. Though antibodies are one of our main defences against infection but in the event of an allergy they produce unpleasant reactions. The abnormal antibodies on coming in contact with an allergen such as a pollen or fungus, release chemical agents such as histamine, serotonin and other slow reacting substances. The release of these substances produce symptoms of allergy characterized by a running nose, rash and breathing difficulty. Some allergic reactions take several hours to develop while there are others which occur promptly and may cause unconsciousness or even death. They produce fall in blood pressure, difficulty in breathing and a bluish tinge in the skin.

It is believed that an allergic substance combines with its antibody and releases a substance called 'histamine' in the body. It is this histamine which acts on the blood or other parts and causes allergic symptoms such as sneezing, wheezing, shortness of breath, itching, swelling and redness of the skin. On the basis of this theory antihistamine drugs have been developed for the treatment of several types of allergic reactions. The first antihistamine drug was phyrilamine maleate and today there are wide range of similarly acting drugs. They block the action of histamines through their chemical structure.

Antihistamines can be used to combat hay-fever, asthma, drug rashes, reactions to stings and vaccines. So far, scientists have not succeeded in developing medicines for acute allergic reactions. Development of specific antagonists of chemical media-tors of the allergic reactions is required for rational therapy of these diseases. It is important to note that allergic diseases attributable to antigens in the environment are best controlled by avoiding or elimi-nating the offending substance.

Medical sciences have yet not been able to explain why certain people are allergic to certain agents, and not others. According to many doctors and scientists heredity has a role in deciding who would be allergic and to what.

OOO

What is blood cancer or leukemia ?

Leukemia or blood cancer is a fatal disease of the blood-forming tissues wherein abnormal white blood cells are found in the blood stream. It can occur at any age and in either sex. It is even more dangerous because its cause is still unknown. Do you know what happens in this disease ?

Blood is a vital body fluid and all its constituents have a specific function. Blood has a large number of red blood cells and a comparatively smaller number of white blood cells. The red blood cells carry oxygen to all the tissues of the body. The white cells defend the body. White blood cells are produced mainly in the bone marrow and lymph glands. In the case of leukemia, something goes wrong with the tissues that produce white cells. So these cells start multiplying at an abnormal rate. A person afflicted with leukemia may have 30 to 60 times the normal number of white

blood cells, that a healthy person has. Simultaneously, the rate of production of red blood cells becomes extremely slow, and this causes anaemia.

Even the behaviour of the sex cells becomes abnormal. The afflicted person is liable to infection and there can be haemorrhage in nose, gums or internal organs. The lymph glands and spleen get swollen. The patient might get fever and develop pain in the legs. In the initial stage one loses weight and appetite and feels weak and fatigue. Slight fever also persists.

There are two main varieties of leukemia — myetogenous and lymphatic. Both may be acute or chronic. Acute forms may be fatal within weeks or a few months, while chronic forms may not lead to death for 3 to 10 or more years. The cause of this disease is not known but it occurs more to the people who are exposed to radiations and chemicals.

Medical sciences have progressed in the treatment of leukemia. Drugs are given to destroy the abnormal cells, and patients may be treated with X-rays and radioactive isotopes. Sometimes doctors also go in for blood transfusion. Chemotherapy is also effective in leukemia.

Red blood cells

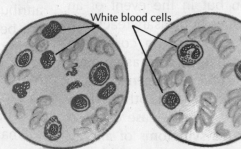
White blood cells

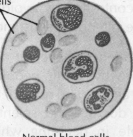

Normal blood cells   Excessive white blood cells   Less white blood cells

In a state of lymphatic leukemia excessive white blood cells are produced whereas in myetogenous, output of white cells is less

23

Which are the different joints in our body ?

The place where two or more bones meet in the body is called a joint. Depending on their structure, joints permit different degrees of movement of bones. Do you know the different types of joints in our body ?

Basically, there are three kinds of joints in our body. They have been grouped on the basis of the degree of movement they allow. They are : (I) Immovable or fixed joints, (II) Partially movable or cartilaginous joints, (III) Freely movable or synovial joints.

Immovable joints : In an immovable joint, the bones are held tightly together. Because dense bundles of tough and strong fibres hold the bones, they cannot change the position relative to each other. The elasticity essential for joint movements is almost absent. Joints in the tooth sockets and between the skull bones are of this type. Immovable joints are also known as fibrous joints.

Partially movable joints: In a partially movable joint, the bones are linked by a cartilage. A cartilage is a very tough, spiny material. These joints have very little movement. The different vertebra of the spinal column are joined together by a cartilage. The joints of the spine are partially movable so that the spine can bend. Between the vertebrae there are disks of cartilage. They are called intervertebral disks. In addition to allowing the vertebrae to move against each other, they also act as shock absorbers. At the front of the chest where the ribs meet the breastbone are also partially movable joints.

Freely movable joints : These are the main joints of the body. These are found in the bones of the ankle, hip, wrist, elbow and knee. The ends of the bones that are the part of the movable joints are covered with caps of tough cartilage. A cartilage does not wear out easily. Its surfaces are very smooth and reduce friction between the moving bones.

In a freely movable joint, the space

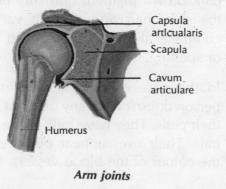

Capsula articualaris
Scapula
Cavum articulare
Humerus

Arm joints

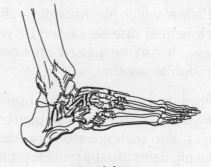

Foot joints

between the bones is filled with a special oily fluid called synovial fluid. It helps the parts to move easily. It is produced by a thin membrane that lies around the joint and is kept within the joint by this synovial membrane. Outside the membrane are tough, flexible ligaments (connecting tissues). The ligaments in addition to joining one bone to another also allow movement. The membrane and the ligaments together form what is called the joint capsule. Synovial (freely movable) joints may be of different types depending upon the nature of articulation and degree of freedom. They are explained below:

Ball and Socket joints : In this the ball of one bone fits into the socket of another. So it makes movement possible in all directions — bending and stretching from side to side and rotation. The shoulder and hip joints are of this type.

24

What is albinism ?

Albinism has been derived from the latin word 'albus' which means 'white'. Albinism is an inherited disease caused by genetic changes. It can be passed on from one generation to another.

Albinism is caused by the absence of yellow, red, brown or black pigments in the eyes, skin scales, feathers or hair. The natural pigments usually provide protective

Hinge joints : These are found in the elbow, knee and fingers. The ends of the bones fit into each other in such a way that the movement is possible in one direction only.

Angular joints : In joints like the wrist, movement is possible around two axes. Such joints are called angular joints.

Pivot joints : In these joints, turning or rotatory movement is possible around one axis only. Skull joint to the spine is a pivot joint.

Gliding joints : In joints between tarsal bones in the ankle, carpal bones in the wrist and between sternum and clavicle, the end of one bone glides across a certain portion of the surface of the other bone.

Injuries and diseases may affect joints. Arthritis is a painful disease that attacks cartilage in joints.   OOO

colouration and act as a screen against the light rays. Since albino animals lack them, they rarely survive in the wild.

Albinos are found in plants, animals and human beings. In human beings, it is caused by the absence of melanin, the dark brown pigment normally present in the skin, hair and eyes. It varies from complete albinism to localized albinism or spotting.

In the case of complete albinism, the person doesn't have any pigment in any of their cells. They have milk-white skin and hair. Their eyes appear pink because of the colour of the blood vessels. Since the light-absorbing pigments are absent, an albino is extremely sensitive to bright light like that of the sun.

In partial albinism, only some tissues and organs lack in pigment. Some animals are also partial albinos. One case of complete albinism is found in every 20,000 people.

However some plants too, with white flowers, are partial albinos. A complete albino plant lacks even the green pigment - chlorophyll. As a result, it is unable to make its food by photosynthesis, and dies shortly after its food supply in the seed is exhausted.

OOO

25

How do urine tests help in diagnosis of diseases?

Diagnosis of different diseases by urine examination has been a common practice since a long time. But the traditional methods were not very scientific as the modern methods. Although special urine tests in laboratory can reveal many diseases, even a casual examination can indicate certain diseases. Let us see how different urine tests help in diagnosing some diseases.

Normal urine is straw yellow in colour due to the presence of the pigment 'urochrome'. If a person has fever, it becomes deep yellow. In case of jaundice, it becomes still deeper in colour. Consumption of vitamin B-complex also makes the urine deep yellow. This is because of the presence of riboflavin in the tablets. If the colour of urine changes to brown or black due to atmospheric pressure, it indicates a congenital disease

called alcaptonuria. If its colour is brown or black, it suggests derangement of haemoglobin metabolism.

If the urine of a diabetic patient is left in the open for some time, it would attract ants. This is due to the presence of glucose in it. Its taste is also sweetish. To test the presence of sugar in urine, it is boiled with Benadict solution. If a red precipitate is formed, it indicates the presence of glucose.

To test albumin in the urine, dilute acetic acid is added to it and heated. If a white precipitate is formed, it indicates the presence of albumin. Normal urine should not contain albumin.

Another test is performed to detect the derangement of fat metabolism in the body. In this test, urine is treated with ammonium sulphate, sodium nitroprusside and alkali. If red colour develops it indicates abnormality. Normal urine should have no such colour.

Urine culture test also provides valuable information regarding the bacterial infections in the body. It is done only when the doctor advises it. Nowadays many more complicated urine tests like urine culture are done to detect the diseases and sensitivity to antibiotics. OOO

26

What happens in our brain?

Normally mammals have bigger brains in relation to their size when compared with other living creatures and the human brain is the biggest and most developed among all the mammals. It controls all the activities of the body throughout our life. It remains active every moment directing and guiding all other organs of the body. That is why it is called the control centre of the body? But what is our brain made of and how does it carry out its different functions?

The human brain is largely made up of grey and white matter. The grey matter contains nerve cells and the white matter contains the nerve fibres. The nerve fibres carry messages from the nerve cells to different parts of the body. Thousands of electrical impulses are constantly passing through these nerve cells. All messages are first sent to the brain through different nerves from the sense organs in all parts of our body. Consequently it sends signals to different muscles and glands in the body to carry out necessary actions. The most important human activity 'thinking' takes place in our brain. All the energy produced in the body is used by the brain.

The central nervous system consists of the brain and the spinal cord. Different parts of the brain are interconnected and they

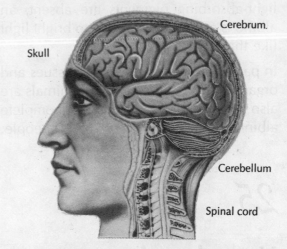

Brain contains nerve cells which constantly carry thousands of electrical impulses

Skull

Cerebrum

Cerebellum

Spinal cord

control different activities of the body. The medulla and hypothalamus control the involuntary activities such as breathing and heart-beat. The cerebellum controls muscles and organs of balance in activities like walking or riding a bicycle, that is, carrying out work automatically once we have learnt them. The cortex controls conscious feeling and voluntary movements such as writing and running. The front part is called cerebrum which has two cerebral hemispheres – the left hemisphere and the right hemisphere. This part (cerebrum) does most of the thinking and is responsible for our memory and emotions. The left hemisphere is associated with the right side of our body and the right hemisphere, with the left side. People with a more developed right hemisphere are left-handed and vice-versa.

Our brain works even when we are asleep. An adult's brain weighs about 1.4 kg and has 14 billion nerve cells in it. The fastest messages pass along the nerves at a speed of 400 km/hr. OOO

27

What is immunity ?

Immunity is described as the ability of the body to resist or to recover from the invasion of disease-causing microbes (bacteria, viruses, protozoas) and larger parasites (helminths). Thus a person said to be immune to a particular disease would not contact it although others might do so.

Microbes and parasites cause several diseases in man. The disease-causing germs often release toxins (poisonous substances). Normally our body is able to defend itself against most disease-causing microbes. First the skin acts as a barrier to the entry of many microbes. And secondly the white blood cells destroy many microbes. But if the number of microbes exceeds the capacity of white blood cells they fail to protect the body against them.

Many persons are able to resist diseases to certain extent due to immunity mechanisms in their systems. The blood of a person produces substances called antibodies which fight the invading organisms. Each kind of antibody acts against only one type of microbe. Different antibodies have different characteristics. Some antibodies neutralise the toxins released by microbes. Certain others clump them together which can then be easily attacked by white blood cells. Some other antibodies dissolve the bacteria. Sometimes a certain amount of antibodies is permanently left in the blood plasma and this serves to protect the

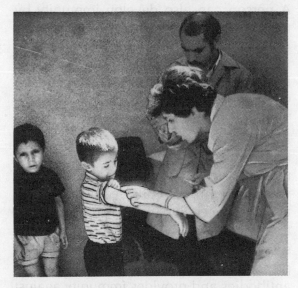

individual from future attacks. Such persons are said to be immune to that particular disease.

Immunological mechanisms are either specific or non-specific. Specific immunity, also called acquired immunity, which refers to mechanisms that are activated individually after a microbe or some other foreign material invades the body. Non-specific immunity refers to general protective mechanism that either kill or prevent the multiplication of microbes and other parasites.

Some persons are immune to certain diseases right from the birth. These people are said to have natural immunity or inborn immunity. In an epidemic of a particular disease, say cholera, people with natural immunity do not suffer from cholera. If someone gets smallpox or chickenpox once, he will not get it again during his whole lifetime. The body in such a case retains adequate levels of antibodies as a protection against future infection.

A person can also develop immunity by treatment with appropriate antigens. This is called artificial immunity. For instance, in the case of epidemics of smallpox, the health authorities vaccinate the people by which immunity is produced artificially. This vaccine was invented by Edward Jenner. It is produced by infecting a calf or horse with the smallpox virus. The virus in the calf or horse gets weakened. This weakened virus is collected as a vaccine and introduced into the human body. Since the virus is weak, it is not able to cause a severe attack of smallpox in man. But its presence induces the body, to produce antibodies and provides immunity against smallpox for several years. The introduction of weakened microbes in the body is called active immunity, the effect of which may last for even a lifetime. Immunity may also be passive. In this readymade antibodies are injected into the human body. An animal like a horse is infected with disease-producing microbes. The antibody is produced in the blood of the horse. The serum of the horse containing the antibody is extracted and introduced into the human body. The human body makes use of antibodies against the disease thus producing passive immunity. Passive immunity is produced almost instantly when the serum has been injected, but the effect lasts only for a short period.

Vaccines are now produced to provide immunity against diseases like whooping cough, diphtheria, measles, tetanus, typhoid, polio, rabies tuberculosis, mumps, scarlet fever, German measles, and chickenpox. All infants should be provided immunity by vaccination for different diseases.

In our country Haffkine Institute at Bombay and the Virus Institute at Poona produce several kinds of vaccines.

IMMUNIZATION TABLE

A suggested scheme for children is given below:

Age	Vaccine	Visit No.	Interval
3 Months (pref. 6 months)	Triple vaccine (Dip/Tet/Pert) and oral Polio vacc.	1	—
		2	6 to 8 weeks
		3	6 months
Early in 2nd year	Smallpox	4	
Early in 2nd year	Measles	5	1 month
5 years or school entry	Dip/Tet oral Polio	6	
	Smallpox revaccination	7	1 month
12 to 13 years	B.C.G. (for tuberculin neg. cases only)	8	
15 to 19 years	Polio booster	9	
	Tet booster		
	Smallpox revaccination	10	

ooo

5
Scientists & Inventions

• Where was Zero invented ? • When were the early hospitals established? • When was the elevator invented?
• Who is known as the Father of Medicine ? • Who was C.V. Raman? • Who made the first milking machine?
• Who was Michael Faraday? • Which discovery made Dr. Hargobind Khorana famous ? • Who made the first artificial limbs ?

1

Where was Zero invented ?

The inconsequential number zero was a major invention which has had a tremendous impact on the history of mankind because it made the development of higher mathematics possible. Without the invention of zero higher mathematics would not have been developed to its present status.

Although it is not known with certainty who invented it, yet there is no controversy about the claim that it was invented in India around 2nd-3rd century A.D. Right from the beginning of civilization, man has tried many different methods to write numbers. For this purpose, Greeks used letters of their alphabet and Egyptians, appropriate pictures. Romans used a complicated system. They used 'X' to represent 10, 'C' to mark 100 and 'M' for 1000. For 1 they used 'I', for 5 'V', for 50 'L' and for 500 'D'. They represented 4 by 'IV'. If they had to write 1648, they wrote 'MDCXLVIII'. This was indeed a complicated method.

However long before the birth of Christ, the Hindus in India had invented a far better number system but without zero.

Later zero was invented. Unlike many ancient systems, today we have a zero to represent nothing. It was introduced in the modern role by Hindu mathematicians. It was brought to Europe about the year 900 A.D. by the Arab traders, and is called the Hindu-Arabic System. In this system, all numbers are written within the nine digits — 1, 2, 3, 4, 5, 6, 7, 8, 9 and the zero (*sunya*). Here each figure has a value according to the place in which it is written. The Romans didn't have a zero in their system.

Zero has some peculiar properties. When it is added or subtracted from any number, the result remains the same. When any number is multiplied by zero, it becomes zero. It is the only number which can be divided by any other number, but it cannot divide any other number. The expression $0/0$ is neither meaningless nor meaningful. In fact, it is indeterminate. Zero is similar to all other natural numbers.

In a nutshell, zero is a number smaller than any finite positive number, but larger than any finite negative number. Division by zero is an undefined operation. It may be regarded as the identity element for addition in the field of real numbers.

The invention of zero became the turning point in the development of culture and civilization — without which progress of modern science, industry and commerce was inconceivable.

OOO

2

When were the early hospitals established ?

A hospital is an institution devoted to the care and treatment of sick people. Do you know when and how did hospitals come into being ?

The history of hospitals began in Babylonia, Greece and India. These early hospitals were temples. Very little medicine were given to patients. Hospitals existed in Ceylon (Sri Lanka) in 437 B.C. and were established in India somewhat earlier during the time of Buddha. Eighteen hospitals built by Emperor Ashoka in 3rd century B.C. are said to have some characteristics similar to modern hospitals.

The advent of Christianity gave impetus to the establishment of hospitals. Their growth accelerated during the crusades which began by the end of the 11th century.

Three persons — Florence Nightingale, Louis Pasteur, and Lord Lister contributed most to the growth of hospitals in modern times. Florence Nightingale known as the 'Lady with the Lamp' was a great reformer of hospital conditions and re-organiser of nurses training programmes.

Louis Pasteur contributed a lot in germ theory and Lord Lister put his research in practice. Developments in anaesthesia made it possible to perform major and

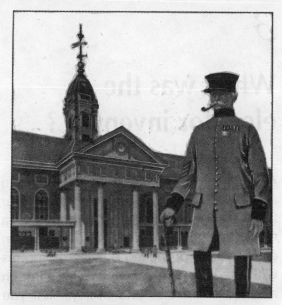

Chelsea Royal Hospital in London is one of the oldest hospital in the world — founded by Charle's II in 1632

more difficult operations.

The first hospital in North America was built in Mexico City in 1524 by Cortez. The French established a hospital in Canada in 1639 at Quebec City.

During the 20th century, outstanding contributions have been made by scientists in the field of medicine and surgery. As a result, the number of hospitals has greatly increased. Today we have private hospitals, military hospitals, general hospitals and also specialised hospitals for mental diseases, tuberculosis, heart diseases, cancer and eye disorders etc.

The largest hospital in the world is the District Medical Centre in Chicago, Illinois, U.S.A. It covers 478 acres and includes five hospitals, with a total of 5600 beds. At present China has the greatest number of hospitals — 61929 in 1989. ooo

3

When was the elevator invented ?

The first passenger elevator was introduced by Elisha Graves Otis of USA in 1853

An elevator or a lift is a car that moves in a vertical shaft carrying passengers or freight from one floor to another in a multistoreyed building. Most modern elevators are propelled by electric motors with the help of a counterweight through a system of cables and pulleys. Do you know who invented the elevator ?

Elevator was not invented by one man or in a single day. Its development is a result of combined efforts made by several people.

The practice of lifting loads by mechanical means during building construction goes back to Roman times. The Roman architect-engineer Vitruvius Pollio in the Ist century B.C. had described lifting platforms that used pulleys and capstans, operated by humans, animals or water power. In 1800 A.D. steam power came to be used to operate such devices in England. In the early 19th century, a hydraulic lift was introduced. These lifts were used only to hoist freights because they were most unreliable.

In 1853, Elisha Graves Otis introduced a safety device and gave birth to the first passenger elevator. This was put into service in the Haughwout Department Store in New York city in 1857. It was powered by steam. It climbed five floors in less than a minute. Improved versions of the steam - driven elevators came into use in the next three decades, but the most significant progress was made after 1889. In 1894, push button operations were introduced. After that many design improvements were made.

Once the problems of safety, speed and height were overcome, attention was turned to convenience and economy. Soon more sophisticated elevators came to cater to the need of tall buildings. Their speeds were increased to 365 m per minute. Automatic operations were also introduced by the 1950s, eliminating the need of operators.

Modern elevators are made in a variety of types for many purposes. In addition to freight and passenger operations, they are used in ships, dams and rocket launchings. They are also used in construction operations. All elevators are electrically propelled — either by cables, pulleys and counterweight, by a winding drum mechanism (low height elevators) or by an electro-hydraulic combination. The drive motor is usually an AC motor for slower speeds and DC motor for higher speeds. Modern elevators are automatic ones using various control systems. They have the safety devices also.

In most modern elevators even automatic loading and unloading devices have been incorporated. A cell button activates the automatic pick-up, the elevator arrives, the load is pulled into the car, the car goes to the proper floor and the load is discharged.

See-through elevators, rising on the outside of buildings and towers, have recently become popular. First it was the Eiffel Tower of Paris which had this kind of elevator. These elevators have glass enclosed cabs affording the passengers a bird's eye view.   OOO

4

Who is known as the Father of Medicine ?

Hippocrates, a Greek physician, is known as 'the father of medicine'. He was born on the island of Cos where he later founded the first school of medicine. He lived between 460 BC to 377 BC. Modern medical students make a promise to be ethical in their work which is known as the Hippocratic Oath.

Doctors at the Hippocratic school of medicine were taught that diseases were the result of improper functioning of parts of the body, rather than of possession by demons as was believed superstitiously in those days. But Hippocrates and his followers didnot know about the structure of the human body. They believed that diseases were caused by the imbalance of four vital fluids — blood, bile, phlegm and black bile. Hippocrates also pointed out that malaria and certain other diseases were associated with particular localities or climate conditions.

Hippocrates and other members of the school have written more than 50 books on medicine. Some of the descriptions of diseases in these books are very clear and accurate. In his writings, some of which may in fact be by other members of his circle, is found the important theory which tells that every disease is related to the natural law just like everything else and therefore should be carefully observed and treated accordingly. But this theory is not wholly accepted in modern medical science. However, no other medical books as scientific as these were written until modern times.   OOO

5

Who was C.V. Raman?

Sir C.V. Raman was one of the greatest scientists of India who was awarded the Nobel Prize in 1930 for his outstanding discovery in Physics. It was named after him and is known as 'The Raman Effect'.

Chandrasekhara Venkata Raman was born on 7th November, 1888 at Tiruchirappally in Tamil Nadu. Raman was a very brilliant student right from his childhood. After passing his matriculation at the age of 12, he was admitted to the Presidency College, Madras. From there he passed his B.Sc. in 1904 and M.Sc. in Physics in 1907 with the first position in the University. While he was a student in the Presidency College, he modified Melde's theory on sound.

In 1907 after passing a civil service competitive examination, he became the Deputy Accountant General in Calcutta. In 1915, he met Sir Ashutosh Mukherjee, the Secretary of the Indian Science Association. Raman joined this Association as a member, and started his research work. In the year 1917, he resigned from his post and became the Professor of Physics at Calcutta University.

During a sea voyage to Europe in 1921, he observed with wonder, the brilliant blue colour of the Mediterranean, and later the blue colour of glaciers. After returning to India, he experimented on the diffusion of sunlight during its passage through water, transparent blocks of ice and other

Sir C.V. Raman (1888–1970)

materials. He then explained the reason for the blue colour of the ocean. His studies on scattering of light led him to the discovery of 'Raman Effect' in 1928. 'Raman Effect' describes the change in the frequency of light passing through transparent mediums. He used monochromatic light from a mercury arc and the spectroscope to study the nature of diffused radiations emerging from the material under examination. For this discovery, he was awarded the Nobel Prize in 1930.

In 1933, he became the Director of the Indian Institute of Science, Bangalore. He held this post for 10 years. In 1934, he sponsored the foundation of the Indian Academy of Sciences, of which he became President. In 1943, the Raman Research Institute was set up by him. Then he conducted research work for the rest of his life. He died on 21st November, 1970 at Bangalore.   ⭕⭕⭕

6

Who made the first milking machine ?

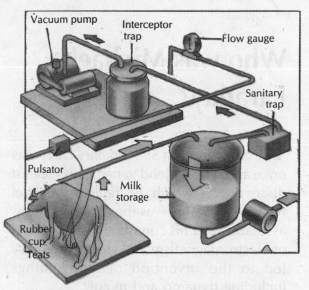

Milking machine is a device used for milking the cows. The first milking machine was patented by an American engineer I.O. Colvin in 1860. It had four rubber teat cups which were connected to a vacuum chamber attached to the side of a pail. The chamber was similar in appearance to a bellows and a vacuum was created by pumping the handle after the cow's teats had been placed in the rubber cups. It was gradually realised that continuous suction caused pain to the cow and often caused internal bleeding which contaminated the milk.

Tubes with rubber cups are placed on the teats of the cow and a device alternatively squeezes the tube and releases air into it — this movement enables sucking of the milk into the tube through which milk passes to the containers

In 1889 William Murchland of Kilmarnock, Scotland patented an elaborate suction milking machine. It also had some problems. Its improved version was produced by Dr. Alexander Shields of Glasgow in 1895. This model was very costly for the farmers. This was further improved in the early 20th century by several firms in Scotland.

The modern carousel milking machine consists of a large slow-moving platform, powered by an electric motor, with places for several cows. As the cows approach the platform, they are placed at their own feeders and a milking machine is attached to each cow. The milk produced is collected in glass containers.

Since the late 1960s the animal feeding methods in milking parlours have advanced dramatically. Many of the parlours are computerised and some include electronic sensors which pickup signals from small transmitters fixed around each cow's neck and which reveal the animal's feeding requirements. Automatic dispensers then provide the requisite ration.

○○○

7

Who was Michael Faraday?

Michael Faraday (1791-1867)

The great scientist Sir Humphry Davy was once asked by a friend to name his greatest discovery to which he replied 'Michael Faraday'. Faraday was then working as his assistant. Later his contributions in the field of electromagnetism and electrochemistry led to the invention of many things including dynamo and motor.

Born in 1791 in a poor blacksmith family, Faraday began his career at the age of thirteen as an errand boy in a bookshop and moved along the pavements of London carrying and delivering newspapers. But his curious and inquisitive mind accompanied by hard work enabled him to reach great heights. His considerate employer in the bookshop taught him the art of book production. Thus Faraday found an access to books and devoted his spare time to reading. He had always the inherent desire to achieve something great.

One day Faraday got the opportunity to attend a lecture by Sir Humphry Davy. Faraday noted down his lectures and sent them to Sir Humphry along with suitable diagrams. In return Sir Humphry offered him the post of a laboratory assistant and Faraday served him for a long time.

When Faraday got the opportunity to work on his own, his genius flourished. Chemistry was his first love and he invented stainless steel, liquid chlorine, new kinds of optical glasses, benzene etc. He also propounded the laws of electrolysis. He got instant fame when he ventured into the field of electricity. Oersted had earlier discovered that electricity could produce magnetic effects but Faraday started thinking of the reverse phenomenon. He thought if electricity could produce magnetic effects then there must be a way for magnetism to produce electricity. Later he invented the 'magneto electric machine' that had a spinning disk between the poles of a magnet which became the forerunner of a dynamo. A dynamo converts mechanical energy into electrical energy. It consists of a powerful magnet and in between the poles of it a suitable conductor (a coil) is rotated. The mechanical energy generated by rotation is thus converted into an electric current in the coil.

Faraday could not make money out of his inventions as he never bothered for money. Though at some stage of his life he earned a lot of money, he remained poor in his later days. He was generous, charitable and deeply religious. He died in 1867.

ooo

8

Which discovery made Dr. Hargobind Khorana famous?

Dr Hargobind Khorana — the third Indian to win a Nobel Prize

Dr. Hargobind Khorana is one of the renowned biochemists of the world. He developed a method for the synthesis of deoxyribonucleic acid (DNA) and ribonucleic acid (RNA). For his independent contributions, he was awarded the 1968 Nobel Prize in physiology and medicine, along with M.W. Norenberg and R.W. Holley.

Dr. Hargobind Khorana was born on 9th January 1922 at Rajpur in Punjab (now in Pakistan). He studied in a village school, and distinguished himself right from the beginning by winning many scholarships.

He passed his B.Sc. examination from D.A.V. College, Lahore and obtained his M.Sc. degree in chemistry in 1945 from Punjab University, Lahore. His main interest was biochemistry. He went to Manchester University, in England for higher studies. There he worked under Prof. A. Robertson and got his Ph.D. in 1948. In the same year he came back to India, but could not get a suitable job. He remained without a job for several months, and finally a disappointed man, he went back to England for further research. There he worked with Nobel laureate, Sir Alexander Todd at Cambridge University. And in 1952

he went to Canada and got married to the daughter of a Swiss M.P.

In 1953, Dr. Khorana was elected as the head of Organic Chemistry Group of Commonwealth Research Organization. He remained in this position upto 1960. In 1960 he went to the United States of America and started working with Norenberg on the creation of artificial life. In the Institute for Enzyme Research at the University of Wisconsin, he developed methods to synthesize RNA and DNA. Due to his research it has now become possible to treat some hereditary diseases.

In 1970, he joined the Massachusset Institute of Technology as Professor of Biology. In addition to the 1968 Nobel Prize, he has been honoured with many prestigious international awards.

He was awarded the Padma Bhushan by the Government of India and was conferred with the honorary degree of D.Sc. by Punjab University, Chandigarh.

○○○

9

Who made the first artificial limbs ?

Today, medical sciences have become so advanced that many limbs of the body are made artificially and replaced by the competent surgeons. This advancement has come to this stage after a long process. The first person who made the artificial limbs was a French surgeon named Ambroise Pare (1510 - 1590).

In the 1500s, surgery was not practised by physicians but it was one of the specialities of the hair cutting profession. As a young boy Pare had the barber's training. In 1541 he became a barber surgeon in Army. Eventually he became surgeon to the French king Henry II and to the king's three sons who later succeeded him.

Ambroise Pare was a very popular surgeon largely because he introduced many improvements in the existing methods. For example, he gave up the practice of cauterizing wounds with boiling oil, instead he tied off the exposed arteries and covered the wounds with simple dressings.

Pare developed several artificial limbs such as arms and hands. He made an arm that could be bent at the elbow and a hand with movable fingers. Even today Pare is considered as the first person to devise artificial limbs.

Today we have modern artificial legs and muscle activated electric arms driven by electric motors. They have become very useful for the patients who have lost their natural limbs.

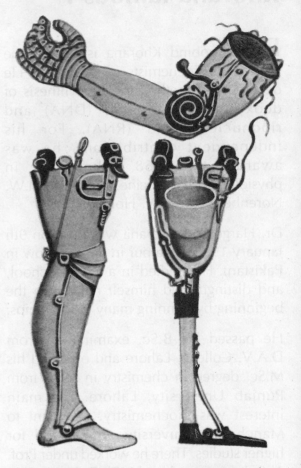

Modern artificial limbs look very natural and are quite comfortable to wear. The latest electronically operated limbs work by minute electrical impulses from the body muscles. Apart from limbs, the other parts of the body that can have artificial replacements include heart (pace maker), heart valves, teeth and eyes, etc.

○○○

6
Sports &
Entertainment

• What are walking races ? • What is Surfing ? • How old is the game of Billiards ? • What is Pelota game?
• What is Pentathlon ? • Where did the game of Badminton originate ? • What is Impressionism? • Who was
Elvis Presley? • What is bull fighting? • What are Oscar Awards? • What are the different types of musical
instruments ? • Why is Hollywood famous ?

1

What are walking races ?

Most of the race competitions involve running but now walking races are also found as Olympic events. Another name for the walking race is heel and toe racing.

The rules for walking races are more strict than usual races. No contestant is allowed to break into a run to beat his rivals. The runner should never break the contact with the ground. One foot must always be in touch. The legs must also be held straight as if walking and not be bent as when running. A competitor is entitled to one warning signalled by a white flag. A red flag is a signal of final disqualification for an erring competitor. Action is taken against a competitor after the independent recommendation of three judges, or two judges if one is the chief judge.

Walking races are different than marathon races. In marathon races running is allowed but not in walking races.

The methods for race walking is nothing like normal walking. The hips are rolled rhythmically, the legs are pulled or jerked up and down very rapidly and the shoulders and arms are swung in very exaggerated pumping movements. The overall effect is very comical to watch. It is something like a penguin's waddley yet it enables racers to move upto 16 kilometres per hour.

The walkers are entitled to take refreshments at official refreshment stations if the race exceeds 20 km. Stations are sited at 10 km apart and after 20 km, every 5 km apart. No other unofficial refreshments are allowed for the walkers. Additional sponging points, supplying water only are provided at points after 20 kms.

Events of walking races are very long. In the Olympics the events cover 20 kilometres and 50 kilometre distances. Walk-races present an interesting and entertaining scene to the spectators.

In walking races at least one foot must always touch the ground. Any sort of running disqualifies a contestant. Walking distance in some games covers upto 50 km

○○○

2

What is Surfing ?

Surfing is an exciting water sport in which the sportsmen ride ocean waves on a long, narrow surfboard. When Captain James Cook discovered Hawaii in 1788, he found that it was already a very popular sport among the Hawaiians.

The Hawaiians held surfing contests and the winners were given prizes. These people used 4-5m long boards which were about 67.5 kg in weight. In 1957 lightweight boards were developed which brought a radical change in this sport. These boards, which are about 3m long and 30cm wide weighing around 10kg, have made it possible for women and even children to take up surfing. The new boards are generally made of foam plastic and coated with fibre glass and resin. A surfboard is the only special equipment required for this sport.

When riding a wave, the rider first swims out beyond the breaking crests of waves to the point where the larger rollers peak up. As a wave approaches him, he paddles his board towards shore to attain sufficient speed to coast down the face of the wave. Once the rider has caught up with the wave, he may rise to a standing position and ride it until it dies out near the beach. To increase the speed and distance, experts usually ride diagonally towards the shore. Riders usually surf 500m or more. Surfboards skim the surface at speeds much faster than the speed of water.

Development of cheap plastic foam, fibre glass coated boards, the increased media publicity all have contributed to the rapid growth in the popularity of surfing.

National and International competitions are being held on both coasts of North America and in Peru, Hawaii, South Africa and Eastern Australia. Groups of 5 to 12 surfers take part in this sport. They are judged on a point system for their credit in take off, turns, length of ride and difficulty extent of waves selected.

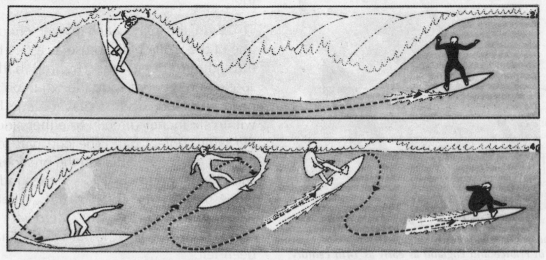

3

How old is the game of Billiards ?

The game of billiards is so old that no one can say when it began. There are some authorities who claim that it was played in ancient Egypt. The Greeks knew the game as long ago as 400 B.C.

The earliest recorded mention of billiards goes back to 1429 A.D in France. Louis XI, the King of France from 1461 to 1483 A.D, is reported to have had a billiards table. The first recorded public billiards room in England was the Piazza Covent Garden, London, in the early part of the

12 ft
3.66 m

2 ft 5 in
73.7 cm

2 ft 10½ in
87.7 cm

6 ft ½ in
1.86 cm

The origin of billiards is not known but it was popular in France and England as early as 14th century

19th century. The first description of billiards in English is to be found in a book called *Compleat Gamester* by Charles Cotton, published in 1674.

About the year 1800, the game had largely assumed the modern form. In 1807, the first English book written on this subject was published in England. The billiards it describes is very much like the billiards we know today. The world professional championship for this game was instituted in 1870, and organized on challenge basis. This was restored as an annual tournament since 1980.

How is this game played? The game of billiards is played with three balls (two white and one red) on a table. The player's object is to score caroms by driving one of the white balls through the other two balls. One carom gets him one point.

The standard table used for this game is 10 ft (305 cm) long, 5 ft (152 cm) wide and 2 ft 7 in (78.8 cm) high. The table is marked with three spots — one near its head, other at its centre and one near its foot.

To begin the play, each player chooses one of the white balls to use as a cue ball throughout the game. The red ball is spotted on the foot spot, the white on the head spot and the first player's cue ball within six inches directly to either side of the white object ball. The cue ball must contact the red ball first on the break (first) shot. On subsequent shots either red or white may be the first ball hit. When a player fails to score, he yields to his opponent, who plays the balls as they have been left.

If the cue ball is knocked off the table, the striker loses a point. The ball is respotted and his opponent takes over the play. If an object ball leaves the table, it is respotted with no penalty other than loss of turn if no score was made. If a score was made before the ball left the table, the ball is respotted and the striker continues to play.

If all balls are knocked off the table, it is a foul and this results in loss of one point and turn at play. The balls are respotted as at the beginning of the game and the opponent makes the break shot.

A game is usually continued until one player scores an agreed number of points, which is often 50.

OOO

4

What is Pelota game?

This is one of several games played with a small hard ball known as a pelota. This is the fastest ball game. The fastest pelota game is known in Spanish as *Pelota vasca* meaning Basque pelota. The Basque name is *Jai Alai* or 'merry festival'. *Jai Alai* may have begun in 13th century Italy. In fact pelota is a Spanish game and pelota means ball.

The players in this game wear a long basket-like *Cesta* strapped to one arm. They use the Cesta's curved hollow end to catch and throw the small, hard rubber ball called a pelota. There are two rival teams. Each team may have one, two or three players.

The team plays the game on a *cancha* or court with high walls on three sides. A server hits the ball on the front wall. The opponent must catch it and throw it back before it hits the floor twice. The game is very fast and interesting.

Pelota game is similar to squash and is played in a three-walled court. Each player has a wicker-racket (cesta) with which he tries to bounce a small hard rubber ball off a wall, beyond his opponent's reach

The ball moves with a tremendously high speed. One pelota reached a measured speed of over 300 kilometers an hour.

OOO

5

What is Pentathlon ?

Pentathlon is a five part competition for athletes involving five different events. The name pentathlon has come from two Greek words: *pente* meaning five and *athlon* meaning contest. In pentathlon each participant must take part in all the five different events. The one who has the highest aggregate score is selected as the winner.

In ancient Greece and Rome the chosen events were ones thought to test all the strength and skills of an athlete. The five events in those days were wrestling, footracing, jumping, javelin throw and discus throw. Javelin was a light spear and discus was a flat plate made of stone or metal. The player had to compete in all the five events as above in one day.

In 1912 when Olympic games were modified to modern style, wrestling was replaced by a 1500 metre race. At the same time the military pentathlon was introduced in the Olympics. The five events for military pentathlon were riding, fencing, swimming, shooting and 4000 meters race. These events were made to test the abilities of a messenger which might have been needed for cavalry warfare.

The Olympic games dropped the Greek-style pentathlon for men in 1924 but retained the military style. In 1964 the games introduced the women's pentathlon. The five events for women athletes were high jump, long jump, 200 metre race, 80 metre race over hurdles and shotput (throwing a heavy metal ball).

Later the racing distance for women was made 800 metres instead of 200 m and over 100 metres for hurdles.

Fencing   Shooting   Swimming   Running

Riding

The modern pentathlon is an event comprising fencing, shooting, swimming, running and riding

○○○

168

6

Where did the game of Badminton originate ?

The Duke of Beaufort started the game of badminton on his estate in Gloucestershire. On one wet day in 1873, when the Duke wanted to entertain his guests, he improvised the game by placing a string in between to hit shuttle cocks over it. The guests were very delighted with this game, and they began to circulate it. In the beginning it was known as the 'game from Badminton' and later on Badminton became it's official name.

As per the Royal Court records of U.K., badminton was first played in the 12th century. Some say that it was first played in England in the 17th century. But most sport historians are unanimous in the view that badminton originated in India centuries ago from where it was exported to England and then spread to other parts of the world. In India it was first played in Poona and was called Poone. Around 1870 some British army officers who were stationed in India, introduced the game to some friends in England.

In 1893 the first Badminton Association was formed in England. It formed laws based on Poona rules of 1876. National Badminton Championship was first organised in England in 1899. This championship included men's doubles, women's doubles and mixed doubles. The first International Championship was played in 1902 between England and Ireland. The International Badminton Federation, the world-governing body of the sport, was formed in 1934. Sir George Thomas was elected as its first president. He continued as the chairman for 21 years.

How is this game played ? Badminton is a game played in court with lightweight rackets and a shuttlecock which is a small cork hemisphere with 14 to 16 feathers attached and weighing about 5 gms. Badminton competitions are usually played indoors because even light wind can affect the shuttle's course. The court is 13.4 m (44 ft) long and 5.2 m (17 ft) wide for singles, 6.1 m (20 ft) wide for doubles. A 1.5 m (15 ft) high net stretches across the width of the court at its centre. Play involves hitting the shuttle back and forth across the net without letting it touch the ground, within the boundaries of the court. The doubles and men's singles game consists of 15 or 21 points. The women's singles game consists of 11 points.

International supremacy is determined by the Thomas Cup instituted in 1948. The Uber Cup championship is for women only and decides the women's International Championship. ,

ooo

7

What is Impressionism?

The art of painting is as old as the human civilization. It is considered as one of the most creative form of all arts. During different periods of history, different styles of painting were evolved and each type had its own breed of great painters. Impressionism is one such style of painting which was first used by some French artists in the 1870s'. All paintings of this type give an impression of something, not an exact picture of it.

The name impressionism came from Claude Monet's painting *Impression*:

Monet's painting Impression: Sunrise *was the trend-setter in the art of Impressionism*

Sunrise, which was exhibited in 1874 at the first impressionist exhibition. The painters used dabs of pure colours to show objects as they appear in natural lights. They also made use of blobs (drops of liquid colour) and strokes (single movement of a brush). They didn't paint details as exactly as most other artists did. Another important feature of the impressionists was that they didn't like painting in a studio, rather they preferred to paint outdoors in natural light. Light was of primary importance to them. Sometimes they painted the same scene several times as the light on it changed throughout the day.

The impressionists hold the view that the principal element in a picture is the light. They followed the principle of simultaneous vision. This means that the human eye will focus only on one small part of any scene at any time and the details within that part will be sharp. Over the rest of the scene details will be less clear. Among the prominent impressionists the foremost are Camille Pissaro and Alfred Sisley, apart from Monet.

Another important form of painting that began in the 1920s, by the French writer Andre Breton was called Surrealism. This art represented the things in people's psychological state — hidden deep in people's mind, or just strange, disturbing ideas and objects, bizarre and sometimes abstract things. Surrealist paintings portrayed the curious distorted world of dreams which Freud thought so important in his psychological studies.

ooo

8

Who was Elvis Presley?

Pop songs have been a craze with the youngsters over the past few decades. Its ever increasing mass popularity has produced a breed of pop stars at different times who have entertained the music lovers in their own distinct styles. Elvis Presley was one of the first 'pop' stars — a rock 'n' roll singer whose appearance on stage could create a rage among the audience. Rock 'n' Roll was a form of dancing and the singers danced to the rhythmic beat of their music. Presley's popularity was at the peak in the 1950s and 1960s with hits like 'Blue Suede Shoes', 'Heartbreak Hotel' and 'His latest Flame'.

Born in 1935, Elvis came from a poor white family of East Tupelo, Mississippi in the south of America. He spent much of his childhood in Memphis, Tennessee. As a teenager, he spent a great deal of his time with black musicians. In 1953, on his mother's birthday, he himself paid money to record his songs at Sun records in Memphis. The owner of the recording studio liked his unusual mixture of country, blues and gospel styles and offered him professional recording work.

In 1955, he was signed on by a big recording company. He achieved instant international fame though his popularity was limited to only the younger generations. His first local hit was, 'That's All Right', in 1954 and he created a

Elvis Presley — one of the first pop musicians who generated hilarious excitements among youngsters during mid-50s and 60s

sensation by swivelling his hips while singing. Many people were shocked to see his wiggling hips. It outraged the adults but entertained the teenagers. He sang loudly with a strong rhythm.

His mega hits like 'Hound Dog' and 'Jailhouse Rock' had made him a national hero by the year 1956. He was popularly recognized as the King of Rock 'n' Roll.

Elvis's music had tremendously influenced the later day pop singers such as the Beatles. By the mid-1960s the Beatles had started reigning the world of rock music. But Presley continued his recording spree along with live performances. He had eventually recorded 94 gold singles and over 40 gold albums. He also starred in 27 films, earning over one million US dollars for every role.

He was always abnormally anxious about his health and took large number of pills. These resulted in death due to heart failure in 1977.   ○○○

9

What is bull fighting?

The bullfighter provokes the bull by showing a red cloth and the bull starts attacking the fighter. This begins the thrilling and daring duel

As old as Roman times, Spanish wild bulls were hunted by men with axes and lances who played with the beasts before killing them. The concept of bull fighting thus originated from those ancient ages.

Bull fighting is a popular sport in Spain, Portugal, Southern France and Latin America. This sport was first introduced by the Moors in the 11th century and it was taken over by the aristocratic professionals, particularly in Spain and Latin American countries, in the 18th century.

It is a very exciting sport and is highly enjoyed by people. In this 'sport', a bull, specially bred for the purpose, fights a man in the arena. In modern bull fighting, the fighter is called a 'Matador'. He makes use of a red cloth to make the bull angry. When he waves the cloth, the bull is excited and attacks the fighter. Since the bulls are colour blind they can't distinguish between colours; the popular belief that only red colour can excite a bull is not correct. Simply waving of a cloth of any colour can excite the bull. In Spain the sport is called "Corrida de Torros".

The greatest Matadors of the 20th century have been Rodolfa Gaona, Armillita Chico and Carlos Arruza from Mexico. Belmonte, Joselito, Dominga Orgata and Manlete from Spain are also recognized as daring and graceful bull fighters.

The modern bull-fighting descends from the earlier customs that originated during the 18th century. Today it has more to do with the skill of the Matador than with the killing of a bull. He must be graceful and daring in his movements and able to thrill the crowd by playing as near to the bull's horns as possible.

The best Matadors are often gored by bulls and perhaps as many as a third of the greatest of them have been killed in the ring.

10

What are Oscar Awards?

Oscar awards are annual awards given by the United States Academy of Motion Pictures Arts and Sciences for excellent and outstanding achievement in various branches of film-making. The major awards are for best leading and supporting actor and actress, best direction, best screen play and best film. Another special Oscar award is given for the best life-time achievement. These awards are considered the most prestigious international awards in the field of world cinema.

The award was instituted by the Academy on 16 May 1929 and named after Oscar Pierce of Texas who was a wheat and fruit grower. The Academy was founded by Louis B. Mayer in 1927 with an objective to prevent the creation of an union of actors and artisans. Another aim was to improve the image of film industry by issuing awards for merit and distinction. Originally the award was intended to be a modest one with citations within the Hollywood film industry. But the importance of the award kept on increasing as broad media coverage generated widespread popular interest. Oscar award winning movies assured box-office success as was noticed from the increasing revenue of winning movies. Labelling of an Oscar worked like a trademark for the commercial success of a film.

Norma Shearer receives the Oscar for best actress category in 1930

The US Academy of Motion Pictures has an elected membership of some 3,000 film-workers who are considered to have reached the top in the industry or in their own field of specialisation. Out of these members, specialists in 13 sections select the winning nominations, normally five in each category. A gold statuette known as Oscar is given to the winners in an annual ceremony in Los Angeles. The gold statuette is 13.5 inch long designed by Cedric Gibbons. It is a gold-plated naked male figure that clutches a sword and stands on a reel of film with five holes — each representing a branch of the Academy.

The publicity value of the award was realised immediately after the first ceremony in 1929 and it is even more now. Today it is televised live. The Oscar ceremony traditionally draws the largest audience in USA. In the world film industry, it is considered to be the supreme award. This award opens the door of the

Emil Jannings in **The Last Command,** *winner of the first ever 'Best Actor' Oscar*

Disney of Disneyland fame, has won more Oscars than any other person. His medal count comprises 20 statuettes and 12 other plaques and certificates including posthumous awards. The youngest winner was Shirley Temple who received an honorary Oscar at the age of five and in competition section it is Tatum O'Neal who won it at the age of 10. The film with most awards was Ben Hur (1959) that won 11 awards in all. Actress Katharine Hepburn was nominated for a record 12 times for Oscar Awards.

Among the Indians to win a Oscar, the first was Bhanu Athaiya, who won one for the best costume designer in 1982 for the film 'Gandhi' and the other one was Satyajit Ray for his lifetime achievements in the year 1992. Ruth Jhabvala — a German woman but an Indian by marriage won it in 1993 for the best adapted screenplay for the film 'Howards End'.　　 ooo

golden hall of fame and hence all film personalities dream and strive to get an Oscar at least once in their lifetime. It is the ultimate thing that they can aspire for.

Among the record award winners, Walt

11

What are the different types of musical instruments ?

Music is an art that permeates every human society. We have all listened to the soothing music of a piano or the strumming of a guitar and experienced a sense of thrill. Music is mainly of two types: vocal

and instrumental. Vocal music involves harmonious combination of words and depends upon the sweetness of the singer's voice. Instrumental music is that part of music which is produced by musical instruments. In a larger context dance is also considered as a part of music.

Musical instruments are classified as follows: (a) Woodwinds (b) Brass (c) Percussion (d) Strings (e) Keyboard and (f) Electrical and electronic types. These classes are useful in grouping instruments in a general way for the kind of sounds they produce, even though woodwind instruments are not necessarily made of wood, nor are brass instruments of metal.

Woodwind instruments: The flute, clarinet, piccolo etc are examples of woodwind instruments. In these the vibrating length of the air column is shortened by opening lateral side holes in succession. Sound is generated by different means. In flute and piccolo, the player blows across a hole near one end in such a way as to cause periodic puffs of air to enter the tube. These puffs excite the air column longitudinally and sound is produced. Control of holes controls the tone of sound.

Brass instruments: The horn, cornet, saxhorn, euphonium etc fall in this category. A typical brass instrument consists of a cup shaped mouth piece, a slightly tapered mouthpipe, cylindrical tubing with valves and a bell. Puffs of air are introduced by the player, via vibrating lips stretched over the mouthpiece. Different tones are produced by tensioning the lips to incite different modes of vibration.

Percussion instruments: Instruments such as the timpani (kettle drums) and xylophone are called percussion instruments because the sound is produced by a blow or beating.

Some percussion instruments such as drums, cymbals and triangles are useful for rhythmic effects.

Stringed instruments: Guitar, harp, violin, viola etc are all stringed instruments. For guitar and harp, strings are set into vibration by plucking. For violin and viola the vibration is usually initiated by bowing:

Keyboard instruments: Instruments such as the celesta, pipe organ, accordion and piano are put in this category because the respective vibrating pipes, reeds and strings in these instruments are selected by use of keys in a keyboard.

Electrical and electronic instruments: Musical instruments described above become quasi-electrical instruments by the addition of a microphone, an amplifier and a loudspeaker. A vibration pick-up can be used to generate an electrical signal from the vibration of the string. This is the case with electric guitars and electric piano. Electronic circuits have been developed which produce musical sounds. During the last 30 years, tremendous progress has been made in developing electronic musical systems controlled by computers.

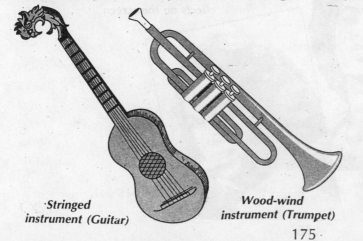

·Stringed instrument (Guitar)

Wood-wind instrument (Trumpet)

Keyboard instrument (Piano)

12

Why is Hollywood famous ?

Hollywood is situated in the north-west of Los Angeles, California. It has been the centre of the American film industry. It has an ideal sunny climate and a varied terrain — most suited for film industry.

Supposedly one of the richest and most glamourous places on earth, Hollywood's greatest days were in the 1930s and 1940s. In 1908 one of its first feature films 'The Count of Monte Cristo' was completed. It was shot in Chicago. By the end of 1911, more than 15 film producing companies had sprung upon the area. Some of the famous film personalities in Hollywood, before World War I, have been Charlie Chaplin, Samuel Goldwyn, Douglas Fairbanks and Cecil B. Mille. The 20th

Century-Fox, Metro-Goldwyn- Mayer, Paramount Pictures, Columbia, Warner Brothers etc. were among its greatest film producing companies.

However with the advent of 'talkies', many famous stars of the silent era were virtually forced to retire. But the greatest threat to Hollywood came with the introduction of television in the late 1940s. Many film companies had to pull down their shutters. This brought a great change in Hollywood. By the early 60s, Hollywood had been supplying about 80% of the programmes to US Television network.

Some of the other highlights of Hollywood are the Hollywood Bowl (a natural amphitheatre), the Pilgrimage Play Amphitheatre and Greek Theatre in Griffith Park, Grauman's Chinese Theatre and the California Art Club.

Hollywood has carved out its present place in the map of world cinema through allround cinematic activities. Its use of latest and advanced technology in film-making makes it the trade leader.

Hollywood, dubbed as 'dream factory', presented a few talented artists whose talent when combined with their glamour produced magical effects on the screen

Rita Havworth

Sophia Loren

Brooke Shields

○○○

176

100 Ways to Bring Out YOUR BEST
Never Underestimate Yourself
Roger Fritz
168 pp • Rs. 120/-

7 Mantras to Excel in EXAMS
Pranav B Bhalla
New
160 pp • Rs. 80/-
Also available in Hindi

20 Keys for SUCCESS in JOB & CAREER
144 pp • Rs. 80/-

ANALYTICAL WRITING & ESSAYS for admission to FOREIGN UNIVERSITIES GMAT, GRE & TOEFL
M.J. ASHOK
New
172 pp • Rs. 125/-

Become a Successful SPEAKER
A step-by-step guide to presenting powerful public speeches.
Don Aslett
136 pp • Rs. 96/-

BEGINNERS' GUIDE TO JOURNALISM
128 pp • Rs. 96/-

Bite-sized bits on Common-sense Management
Gerard Assey
100 pp • Rs. 150/-

Boost Your Brain-Power
Dr G Francis Xavier, PhD
The Great Motivator
144 pp • Rs. 96/-

Business Ideas you can turn into Cash
128 pp • Rs. 80/-

Create your own SUCCESS STORY & Live Life King-Size
120 pp • Rs. 80/-

Directory of Management Courses in India
392 pp • Rs. 60/-

Getting Rich with Contentment
Enjoy Earning Money with Right Attitude
New
144 pp • Rs. 96/-

GREAT SPEAKERS AREN'T BORN
The Complete Guide to Winning Presentations
GEORGE KOPS & RICHARD WORTH
200 pp • Rs. 88/-

GROUP DISCUSSION For Admissions & Jobs
200 pp • Rs. 88/-

How to be a favourite with your BOSS
DON ASLETT
Discover how Sincerity and hard-work always pay in your Career
106 pp • Rs. 80/-

How to be the Complete Professional Salesperson
Robert L. Shook
248 pp • Rs. 150/-

HOW TO GET A JOB IN THE USA TODAY!
SACHA DEVORETZ
336 pp • Rs. 175/-

HOW TO MAKE A GREAT PRESENTATION IN 2 HOURS
Frank Paolo
World's #1 Corporate trainer
192 pp • Rs. 150/-

How to Motivate Others
to turn them into super performers
128 pp • Rs. 80/-

It's time to live-up SMART Teens talk about ...A Youngster's GUIDE
New
120 pp • Rs. 75/-
Earlier printed as
Teens to Twenties

LET'S GET RESULTS NOT EXCUSES!
James M. Bleech & Dr. David G. Mutchler
New
240 pp • Rs. 195/-

MARKETING WITH SPEECHES AND SEMINARS
Your Key to More Clients and Referrals
Miriam Otte
176 pp • Rs. 150/-

Mastering Salary Negotiations
How to skilfully negotiate the best remuneration package
96 pp • Rs. 96/-

MEDICAL TRANSCRIPTION
BLANCHE ETTINGER ALICE G. ETTINGER
472 pp • Rs. 450/-

Multiple Career Choices For Graduate & Post-Graduate Courses
280 pp • Rs. 135/-

Rapidex Professional Secretary's Course
262 pp • Rs. 120/-

Rapidex Television Technician's Course
424 + Maps pp • Rs. 150/-

Rate Yourself As A Manager — A practical, workable action plan to guide you to the top! ROGER FRITZ *New*
240 pp • Rs. 195/- (H.B.)

Secrets of Leadership — Insights from the Panchatantra
136 pp • Rs. 80/-

Sharpen Your Competitive Edge — Re-examine Your Instincts and Habits for a practical change — Roger Fritz *New*
192 pp • Rs. 120/-

Skills for Excellence
184 pp • Rs. 88/-

Smart Memory — Techniques to Improve Memory
138 pp • Rs. 80/-

Solve Your Problems — The Birbal Way
200 pp • Rs. 80/-

Study & Immigration in U.S.A.
128 pp • Rs. 95/-

Success Secrets — A COMMON-SENSE GUIDE TO LIFELONG ACHIEVEMENT
256 pp • Rs. 120/-

Sure Success in Interviews
152 pp • Rs. 96/-

The Book of Etiquette and Manners
136 pp • Rs. 68/-

The Portrait of a Super Student *In Colour*
160/- pp • Rs. 80/-

The Street Smart Salesman — Making Opportunities Happen
208 pp • Rs. 88/-

The Voyage to Excellence
280 pp • Rs. 195/-

U.S. VISA MADE EASY — a practical guide
188 pp • Rs. 220/-

Winning Résumé
136 pp • Rs. 80/-

Youngsters' Guide for Personality Development
120 pp • Rs. 68/-

Making friends and doing business in Europe
288 pp • Rs. 96/-

10 Fundamental Rules of Success *New*
128 pp • Rs. 96/-

in press — 10 Sutras to Get Rank in Exam

Electronics Projects for Beginners — A. K. Maini
296 pp • Rs. 150/-

101 Science Games / **101 Science Experiments**
120 pp each Rs. 60/- each

Spice in Science — The best of Science Funnies
144 pp • Rs. 60/-

Bathroom Science / **Kitchen Science Tricks** — James Lewis
104 pp each Rs. 36/- each

104 pp • Rs. 60/-

376 pp • Rs. 120/-

New

— pp • Rs. 96/-

New

184 pp • Rs. 96/-

New

208 pp • Rs. 96/-

240 pp • Rs. 96/-

136 pp • Rs. 96/-

240 pp • Rs. 120/-

120 pp • Rs. 80/-
Also available in Hindi

155 pp • Rs. 80/-

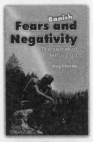

156 pp • Rs. 80/-

192 pp • Rs. 96/-

160 pp • Rs. 96/-

140 pp • Rs. 80/-

64 pp • Rs. 60/-
Also available in Hindi

136 pp • Rs. 80/-
Also available in Hindi

168 pp • Rs. 120/-

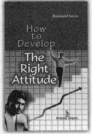

96 pp • Rs. 68/-

112 pp • Rs. 80/-

80 pp • Rs. 60/-
Also available in Hindi

160 pp • Rs. 68/-
Also in Hindi & Bangla

192 pp • Rs. 96/-

176 pp • Rs. 68/-

218 pp • Rs. 80/-

174 pp • Rs. 80/-

Self-improvement & Quotations

New

PLEASE, MOM! IT'S MY LIFE

A BOOK FOR TEENAGERS WHO THINK THEY KNOW EVERYTHING

112 pp • Rs. 80/-

WITH 8 BESTSELLERS TO HER CREDIT

SECRETS OF HAPPINESS

Tanushree Podder

India's Leading Author on Mind, Body and Soul

192 pp • Rs. 96/-

OVER 250,000 COPIES SOLD

SECRETS OF MIND POWER

Harry Lorayne

The World's Leading Expert on Mind and Memory Training

184 pp • Rs. 96/-

Self ANALYSIS

290 pp • Rs. 88/-

Kick out your **STRESS**

140 pp • Rs. 60/-

S.P. Sharma

SUCCESS THROUGH POSITIVE THINKING

It is half empty or half full ...is the way you look at it

180 pp • Rs. 80/-

The 4-Lane Expressway to **STRESS MANAGEMENT**

112 pp • Rs. 95/-

THE 12 UNIVERSAL LAWS OF SUCCESS

Herbert Harris

Time Magazine estimate

192 pp • Rs. 195/-

A common-sense approach to lasting happiness

The Art of **Happy Living**

168 pp • Rs. 96/-

The Complete Guide to **MEMORY MASTERY**

ORGANISING & DEVELOPING THE POWER OF YOUR MIND

HARRY LORAYNE

312 pp • Rs. 160/-

The Meaning is to **KNOW THYSELF**

How to Attain Happiness and Good Life

128 pp • Rs. 60/-

The Portrait of a **Complete Man**

176 pp • Rs. 60/-

The Portrait of a *Complete Woman*

A guide to woman's personality development

304 pp • Rs. 120/-

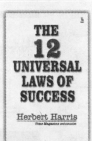

The Portrait of a **Perfect WOMAN**

128 pp • Rs. 80/-

Understanding Emotional IQ

176 pp • Rs. 80/-

Dr. Aparna Chattopadhyay

UNLEASH YOUR HIDDEN POTENTIAL

Over 40 self-analysis modules to help you achieve excellence in your career.

176 pp • Rs. 80/-

What's your Emotional **IQ**

176 pp • Rs. 68/-

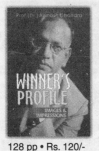

Prof (Dr.) Avinash Chandra

WINNER'S PROFILE

IMAGES & IMPRESSIONS

128 pp • Rs. 120/-

in press

4 Objectives of Human Life

in press

100 Pearls of Successful Surviver

A Treasury of **Inspirational Thoughts**

144 pp • Rs. 68/-

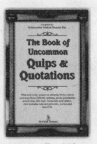

Notable Quotes & Noble Thoughts

96 pp • Rs. 68/-

The Book of Uncommon Quips & Quotations

128 pp • Rs. 80/-

The Book of COMMON & UNCOMMON PROVERBS

Over 1,000 fully annotated proverbs

128 pp • Rs. 96/-

& many more...

5

A guide to Happy Retirement for the salaried people
128 pp • Rs. 60/-

All you need to know about HEART ATTACK — 4th Revised & Updated Edition — Dr. G.D. Thapar, M.D.
152 pp • Rs. 96/-

A Treatise on Home REMEDIES
224 pp • Rs. 120/-

Ayurveda for All — Effective Ayurvedic self-cure of common and chronic ailments
224 pp • Rs. 150/-

Ayurvedic & Herbal Remedies for Arthritis
192 pp • Rs. 96/-

Bowel Care — The Natural Way
112 pp • Rs. 60/-

Cooking for Diabetics
115 pp • Rs. 80/-

Cholesterol Busters + A 15-Days' Detox Plan to Reduce Cholesterol
104 pp • Rs. 60/-

Dental Care & Oral Hygiene
136 pp • Rs. 68/-

DIABETES CONTROL In your Hands
120 pp • Rs. 88/-

Diet in Diseases
104 pp • Rs. 69/-

FIT & FINE IN BODY & MIND
232 pp • Rs. 90/-

FOODS that are Killing You Slowly but Steadily
144 pp • Rs. 80/-

FREEDOM FROM CERVICAL AND BACK PAIN — THE NATURAL WAY
128 pp • Rs. 68/-

GREEN REMEDIES — Healing Power of Herbs
243 pp • Rs. 135/-

HALE & Hearty Ever After fifty
168 pp • Rs. 88/-

HEALING POWER OF FOODS — Nature's Prescription for Common Diseases
136 pp • Rs. 80/-

HEALTH & WELLNESS
304 pp • Rs. 120/-

HEALTH CHARTS & TABLES FOR YOU
144 pp • Rs. 80/-

HEALTH REJUVENATING EXERCISES FROM HEAD TO TOES
52 pp • Rs. 24/-

HERBAL CURE — Discover the Curative Power of 100 HERBS
152 pp • Rs. 80/-

Hidden FOOD Allergies
126 pp • Rs. 80/-

HOMEOPATHIC SELF-CARE — THE QUICK & EASY GUIDE FOR THE WHOLE FAMILY
428 pp • Rs. 175/-

HOMEOPATHY CURES where Allopathy fails
312 pp • Rs. 120/-

YOGASANAS and SADHANA — New Revised & Updated Edition
176 pp • Rs. 60/-

You are What you Eat
180 pp • Rs. 80/-

YOUR DIET AFTER 50
150 pp • Rs. 68/-

YOUR KITCHEN A CLINIC AT HOME
128 pp • Rs. 68/-

Youthful Forever
242 pp • Rs. 80/-

Homoeopathy The Scientific Medicine
140 pp • Rs. 96/- (Vol.
224 pp • Rs. 135/- (Vo

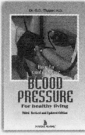

128 pp • Rs. 96/-

136 pp • Rs. 68/-

96 pp • Rs. 40/-

112 pp • Rs. 60/-
Also in Hindi & Bangla

128 pp • Rs. 48/-
Also in Hindi & Bangla

96 pp • Rs. 48/-

112 pp • Rs. 60/-
(Also available in Hindi)

120 pp • Rs. 60/-

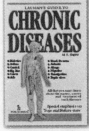

176 pp • Rs. 96/-

192 pp • Rs. 96/-

224 pp • Rs. 88/-

232 pp • Rs. 80/-
Also available in Hindi

168 pp • Rs. 80/-

272 pp • Rs. 195/-

224 pp • Rs. 80/-

96 pp • Rs. 80/-

132 pp • Rs. 96/-

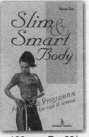

128 pp • Rs. 60/-

192 pp • Rs. 68/-

228 pp • Rs. 120/-

152 pp • Rs. 80/-

176 pp • Rs. 96/-

128 pp • Rs. 68/-

184 pp • Rs. 96/-

124 pp • Rs. 96/-

136 pp • Rs. 60/-

64 pp • Rs. 48/-

144 pp • Rs. 88/-

240 pp • Rs. 88/-

84 pp • Rs. 48/-

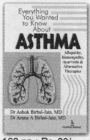

168 pp • Rs. 80/-

224 pp • Rs. 96/-

200 pp • Rs. 96/-

180 pp • Rs. 68/-

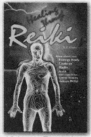

104 pp • Rs. 60/-

120 pp • Rs. 60/-

128 pp • Rs. 68/-

200 pp • Rs. 80/-

128 pp • Rs. 68/-

242 pp • Rs. 96/-

280 pp • Rs. 88/-

304 pp • Rs. 120/-

264 pp • Rs. 150/-

112 pp • Rs. 80/-

112 pp • Rs. 68/-

264 pp • Rs. 108/-

144 pp • Rs. 80/-

168 pp • Rs. 96/-

112 pp • Rs. 68/-

& many more...

Palmistry, Hypnotism, Astrology & Numerology

264 pp • Rs. 120/-

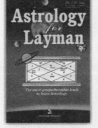
184 pp • Rs. 80/-

144 pp • Rs. 80/-

264 pp • Rs. 110/-

200 pp • Rs. 96/-

208 pp • Rs. 125/-

144 pp • Rs. 60/-

136 pp • Rs. 80/-

248 pp • Rs. 135/-

160 pp • Rs. 75/-

152 pp • Rs. 80/-

336 pp • Rs. 195/-
Hardbound

142 pp • Rs. 80/-

272 pp • Rs. 96/-

222 pp • Rs. 80/-

120 pp • Rs. 75/-

282 pp • Rs. 88/-

180 pp • Rs. 80/-

236 pp • Rs. 75/-
Also available in Hindi

365 pp • Rs. 80/-
Also available in Hindi

272 pp • Rs. 88/-

107 pp • Rs. 80/-

184 pp • Rs. 88/-

160 pp • Rs. 60/-
Also available in Hindi

92 pp • Rs. 60/-

304 pp • Rs. 75/-

Dictionaries, Encyclopedias, World Famous etc.

2000 English Phrases & Sentences
128 pp • Rs. 60/-

IMPROVE YOUR WORD POWER **New**
220 pp • Rs. 80/-

Many Faces of WORDS — An easy route to Word Power
152 pp • Rs. 24/-

Official Notings & Draftings
231 pp • Rs. 120/-

Rapidex Dictionary of Spoken Words with usages
196 pp • Rs. 60/-

THE HUTCHINSON CONCISE DICTIONARY of SCIENCE
--- pp • Rs. 108/-

Rapidex PICTURE DICTIONARY — In Colour
48 pp • Rs. 48/-

Sentence Correction for admission to Foreign Universities — A. P. Sharma **New**
168 pp • Rs. 60/-

WORDS & PHRASES that carry UNCOMMON MEANINGS **New**
136 pp • Rs. 50/-

लोकोक्तियां (PROVERBS) — हिन्दी तथा अंग्रेजी में
136 pp • Rs. 60/-

Bloomsbury Dictionaries

POCKET REFERENCE LIBRARY — DICTIONARY OF CALORIES

POCKET REFERENCE LIBRARY — DICTIONARY OF PHRASE & FABLE

Price: 30/- each

The Children's Picture Dictionary — In Colour **New**
58 pp • Rs. 72/-

CHILDREN'S SCIENCE ENCYCLOPEDIA
520 pp • Rs. 380/-

OVER 300 GREAT LIVES
344 pp • Rs. 120/-

The World's Greatest BLUNDERS — That dramatically changed the history of mankind
128 pp • Rs. 68/-

SPICY SIDE OF SPEECHES FOR WITY ENGLISH
128 pp • Rs. 60/-

The Funny side of ENGLISH — A read-n-laugh manual to the English language
232 pp • Rs. 80/-

World Famous

Rs.60/- each
Also in Hindi

101 Great Lives (3 vols.) • Adventures • Great Treasures • Discoveries • Ghosts • Anecdotes • Unsolved Mysteries • Prophesies & Predictions • Scientists • Strange Mysteries • Supernatural Mysteries • Mythologies

Famous Indians of 20th Century
224 pp • **Rs. 80/-**

Immortal Speeches **New**
136 pp • **Rs. 80/-**

J. Krishnamurty and Problems of Human Life
168 pp • **Rs. 80/-**

The World's Greatest Seers & Philosophers
224 pp • **Rs. 80/-**

Furniture Catalogue, Gates, Grills, Windows, Railings...

How best to Plan & Build YOUR HOME — A total guide for the owner
200 pp • Rs. 150/-

New STEEL FURNITURE CATALOGUE
120 pp • Rs. 195/-

NEW FURNITURE CATALOGUE
256 pp • Rs. 120/-

Top Designs of Window Grills & Rolling shutters
56 pp • Rs. 72/-

GATES GRILLS RAILING SETS
136 pp • Rs. 60/-

DESIGNS OF GATES
88 pp • Rs. 60/-

DESIGNS OF WINDOWS
88 pp • Rs. 60/-

DESIGNS OF RAILINGS
88 pp • Rs. 60/-

MORE AND MORE DESIGNS OF GATES, GRILLS, RAILINGS & STAIRCASES
136 pp • Rs. 90/-

Computer & Quiz Books

THE WAP BOOK — 144 pp • Rs. 95/-

How best to use the Internet and e-mail — 136 pp • Rs. 99/-

BASIC COMPUTER PROGRAMMING — 264 pp • Rs. 80/-

Dreamweaver 3 — 360/- pp • Rs. 195/-

Computer for Beginners — 192 pp • Rs. 80/-

The Java Book — 416 pp • Rs. 195/-

Low-cost Web Site — 444 pp • Rs. 225/-

Internet Marketing & Promotions — 392 pp • Rs. 225/-

Microsoft FrontPage 98 — 184 pp • Rs. 90/-

Microsoft Outlook 2000 — 252 pp • Rs. 125/-

How To Dotcom — 296 pp • Rs. 140/-

Strategy — 164 pp • Rs. 120/-

Rapidex Straight to the Point Series

Microsoft Excel 2000 — Price: 60/- each

Rapidex Condensed Users Guides

Core Java 2 — Price: 140/- each

Microsoft Word 2000 — 448 pp • Rs. 175/-

Microsoft Windows 98 — 520 pp • Rs. 195/-

QUIZ BOOKS

4000 Quizzes — 240 pp • Rs. 88/-

ASTRONOMY QUIZ BOOK — 208 pp • Rs. 60/-

BIRDS & ANIMALS QUIZ BOOK — 128 pp • Rs. 60/-

Electronics & Computer QUIZ BOOK (New) — 260 pp • Rs. 60/-

ENVIRONMENT QUIZ BOOK — 176 pp • Rs. 60/-

GLOBAL Quiz Bank — 256 pp • Rs. 96/-

HISTORY Quiz Book — 232 pp • Rs. 60/-

MATHEMATICS QUIZ BOOK — 216 pp • Rs. 60/-

MEDICAL QUIZ BOOK — 192 pp • Rs. 48/-

QUIZ TIME — 208 pp • Rs. 80/- Also in Hindi & Bangla

SCIENCE QUIZ BOOK — 192 pp • Rs. 60/-

& many more...

11

Religion, Parenting / Love, Sex & Romance

New

Hindu Rites, Rituals, Customs & Traditions
In Colour
328 pp • Rs. 160/- (H.B.)
Also available in Hindi

50 Themes from BHAGAVAT GITA
208 pp • Rs. 75/-

Essence of Maharishi Patanjali's Ashtang Yoga
96 pp • Rs. 60/-

DEHYPNOTIC MEDITATION
132 pp • Rs. 96/-

Glory of Spiritual India
224 pp • Rs. 80/-

New
Know the Puranas
328 pp • Rs. 96/-

New
KNOW THE UPANISHADS
120 pp • Rs. 80/-

Know the Vedas At a Glance
136 pp • Rs. 80/-

Pearls of Spiritual Wisdom
158 pp • Rs. 80/-

New
The Life after Death — Born, to be born again (TRANSMIGRATIONS)
144 pp • Rs. 80/-

New
The Wisdom of the Gita
112 pp • Rs. 50/-

The Yoga of GITA
156 pp • Rs. 80/-

VEDA
144 pp • Rs. 80/-

Vedantic Truth Revealed
104 pp • Rs. 48/-

Parenting

A Parent's Guide to CHILD Care
232 pp • Rs. 120/-

Baby and Child Home Medical Care
240 pp • Rs. 88/-

In Colour
BABY RECORD & PHOTO ALBUM
52 pp • Rs. 100/-
Also available in Hindi

Bringing up a Dream Child
118 pp • Rs. 75/-

DISCIPLINE YOUR CHILD Without SHOUTING Or SPANKING
193 pp • Rs. 80/-

How to shape your Kids Better
120 pp • Rs. 88/-

MOTHERHOOD with a smile
100 pp • Rs. 60/-

Mummy, I'm Hungry!
136 pp • Rs. 80/-

New
Parent's GIFT to a Child
84 pp • Rs. 50/-

PRACTICAL PARENTING TIPS
204 pp • Rs. 80/-

Raising a Daughter
136 pp • Rs. 60/-

The Art of Successful Parenting
150 pp • Rs. 68/-

The Joy of Parenting
144 pp • Rs. 80/-

All you want to know about
144 pp • Rs. 60/-

Better SEX the Herbal Way
128 pp • Rs. 80/-

Get Smart in Sex
64 pp • Rs. 30/-

Sex Education Dictionary (For Teenagers)
120 pp • Rs. 60/-

SEXUAL PLEASURE Through the Rhythm Verses
160 pp • Rs. 80/-

Strange Customs & Practices
116 pp • Rs. 60/-

THE ART OF LOVING
120 pp • Rs. 60/-

Taoist yoga for better Sex life
208 pp • Rs. 135/-

Other Books

● How to Stay Married 160 pp • Rs. 40/-

12

Cookery, Women Orientation, Beauty

101 All time Savoury Snacks
102 pp • Rs. 60/-

101 Ways to prepare Kababs
136 pp • Rs. 80/-

Bread Bonanza (New) (In Colour)
152 pp • Rs. 125/-

Cooking Made Easy
The ideal cookery book for beginners that goes beyond cooking
104 pp • Rs. 60/-

Wide range of delicious vegetarian and non-vegetarian Dishes and Desserts from four corners of India
86 pp • Rs. 80/-

Nutritious Mushroom Recipes (New) (In Colour)
96 pp • Rs. 96/-

Modern Cookery Book
144 pp • Rs. 68/-
Also in Hindi & Tamil

Over 100 Fat-Free Recipes
120 pp • Rs. 80/-

101 Chinese Recipes
112 pp • Rs. 60/-

101 Mix & Match recipes with Vegetables
144 pp • Rs. 80/-

Paneer Bonanza (New)
168+16 colour pp
Rs. 80/-

Rice Bonanza (New)
144 pp • Rs. 125/-

101 ways to prepare Curries
140 pp • Rs. 60/-

101 ways to prepare Soups & Salads
86 pp • Rs. 60/-

Home Hints — How to save time and money

First Aid for Every Home

Spot Check — How to cope with household stains

32 pp each • Rs. 40/- each

1000 plus Household Hints
192 pp • Rs. 96/-

Hello! Just married or about to marry?
144 pp • Rs. 80/-

Me & My Hubby — Made for each other
248 pp • Rs. 96/-

Smart Housekeeping for the Woman of Today
296 pp • Rs. 150/-

The Secrets of Marital Bliss
176 pp • Rs. 80/-

Beauty Solutions ...from top to toe
152 pp • Rs. 110/-

Body and Beauty Care
112 pp • Rs. 80/-

Home Beauty Clinic
128 pp • Rs. 80/-
Also available in Hindi

Home-made Herbal Cosmetics
128 pp • Rs. 68/-

Herbal Beauty & Body Care
144 pp • Rs. 75/-
Also available in Hindi

Reveal your Glow
124 pp • Rs. 60/-

Advanced Beauty (in press)

Humour, Fun, Facts, Magic & Hobbies

176 pp • Rs. 68/-

112 pp • Rs. 48/-

New
144 pp • Rs. 60/-

New

224 pp • Rs. 120/-

New

176 pp • Rs. 80/-

128 pp • Rs. 40/-

120 pp • Rs. 48/-

New
128 pp • Rs. 80/-

New

160 pp • Rs. 80/-

168 pp • Rs. 8/-

New

244 pp • Rs. 120/-

128 pp • Rs. 60/-

120 pp • Rs. 60/-

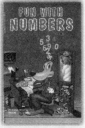
176 pp • Rs. 80/-

248 pp • Rs. 295/-
(Hardbound)

152 pp • Rs. 60/-
also available in Hindi

112 pp • Rs. 96/-

115 pp • Rs. 48/-
also available in Hindi

104 pp • Rs. 48/-
also available in Hindi,
Bangla, Kannada &
Assamese

115 pp • Rs. 48/-
also available in Hindi

112 pp • Rs. 48/-
also available in Hindi

104 pp • Rs. 60/-

112 pp • Rs.48/-
also available in Hindi,
Kannada and Marathi

124 pp • Rs. 48/-
also available in Hindi

124 pp • Rs. 48/-
also available in Hindi

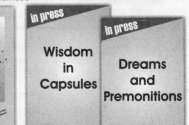

in press

Wisdom
in
Capsules

in press

Dreams
and
Premonitions

64 pp • Rs. 50/- each

124 pp • Rs. 68/-

180 pp • Rs. 60/-

184 pp • Rs. 80/-

120 pp • Rs. 60/-
Also available in Hindi

124 pp • Rs. 68/-
Also available in Hindi

Animal Folk Tales from Around the World Vol. 2

3 Vols. • pp: 24 each
Rs. 36/- each
Also available in Hindi

Witty Tales of Tenali Rama

2 Vols. • pp: 56 & 60 each
Rs. 60/- each
Also available in Hindi

Tales of Gopal the jester
Full of Wit, Wisdom & Humour

2 Vols. • pp: 56 each
Rs. 60/- each
Also available in Hindi

Ancient Tales of Wit, Wisdom & Humour

pp: 120
Rs. 48/-

JATAKA TALES

pp: 96
Rs. 48/-

Earth & Mars

pp: 144
Rs. 80/-

The Great Adventure of Lav Kush

24 pp • Rs. 36/- each
Also available in Hindi

Enchanting Fairy Tales

60 pp • Rs. 60/- each
Also available in Hindi

Folk Tales of India

48 pp • Rs. 50/- each
Also available in Hindi

71 Golden Tales of Panchatantra

5 Vols. • pp: 60 to 68 each
Rs. 60/- each
Also available in Hindi

71 Golden Tales of Panchatantra

Combined Edition
pp: 304 • Rs. 350/-
Also available in Hindi

50 Moral Tales ...from The Gurukul

160 pp • Rs. 68/-

50 WITTIEST TALES OF BIRBAL

120 pp
Rs. 48/-

The Funniest Tales of Mullah Nasruddin

144 pp • Rs. 48/-
Also available in Hindi

TALES OF WISDOM
Morale-building 57 Tales for Children

160 pp • Rs. 72/-

Stories from Panchatantra

115 pp • Rs. 60/-

Interesting Stories to Learn PROVERBS

98 pp • Rs. 72/-

in press

Jungle Lore

Natkhat the naughty Monkey

32 pp • Rs. 36/- each
Also available in Hindi

The Matchless Pearl

128 pp • Rs. 80/-

The Red Monster

104 pp • Rs. 68/-

The Witches of Waitiki

176 pp • Rs. 68/-

The Woman in White

144 pp • Rs. 80/-

The Khan's Talisman

164 pp • Rs. 80/-

PICTURE BOOK OF ALPHABETS

24 pp • Rs. 36/-

MY FIRST STEP OF ALPHABET

MY FIRST STEP OF BIRDS AND ANIMALS

MY FIRST STEP OF NUMBERS

MY FIRST STEP OF VEGETABLES AND FRUITS

MY FIRST STEP OF NURSERY RHYMES

Rs. 15/- each
Fully coloured & illustrated.
Can be wiped off.

15